"This is an excellent chronicling o.   .t of the Staby family history in Namibia. The author takes the reader on a vivid personal journey of the family's move from Germany to the beginning of their roots in Namibia as they struggled with political affiliation issues, and facing racial challenges besetting them in their new environment. Anyone reading this would have their appetite whetted to write their own family history. It is an easy and an exciting read."

— **Ngondi A. Kamatuka**
Former High School Student of Helge Staby,
Director of Educational Opportunity Programs in the U.S.A.

"Helge Deaton meditates on her identity as one who was born and grew up in Southwest Africa but whose parents and grandparents are Europeans, German nationals: "I am Africa, this Africa, I thought… I am the people I grew up with, the animals that shared our land. I am the space, the distant horizons, the barely blue of the sky, the violet of the mountains, the blinding brightness of the light, and the heat of the sun. I am the drought and the terror and the pain. I am the yearning for rain, always more rain, for the hesitant green and the everlasting, enduring hope of life." The depth of this passage reflects the depth of Deaton's complex insight as revealed in this memoir of who she is—of what her African experience has made her."

— **Donald B. Gibson,** Professor Emeritus, Rutgers University

"This is the gripping tale of a German born Namibian. With a distinct personal style she tells of her family's life there since 1867. The geography presented its own challenges for making a living, as did their encounter with the different cultural peoples, thus creating a heritage with which she tries to come to terms with until she left in 1970. It is certainly a most enlightening book about life in Africa during this century."

— **Gunter v. Schumann,** Librarian, Namibia Scientific Society.

A previous version of chapter 4 was published as "Alwine," Palo Alto Review 12, no. 2 (Fall 2003): 3–9. A previous version of chapter 1 was published as "Fences," Palo Alto Review 11, no. 1 (Spring 2002): 34–38. A previous version of chapter 15 was published as "The Visitors," Palo Alto Review 7, no. 2 (Fall 1998): 13–16. A previous version of chapter 14 was published as "The Oryx," Palo Alto Review 6, no. 2 (Fall 1997): 10–13.

ISBN-10: 1463727313
ISBN-13: 9781463727314
LCCN: 2011912559

Beyond Fences

A Memoir: 1937–1970

Helge Staby Deaton

Epigraph

"Grau, teurer Freund, ist alle Theorie,
und grün des Lebens goldener Baum."

"Gray, dear young fellow, is all theorizing,
and green life's golden tree."

Mephistopheles

Johann Wolfgang Goethe, *Faust*
(*Verlag Knaur,* 1957, part I, translation by Walter Arndt, Norton, 1976)

To Tony and Sue.
from
Inge Staby Doolitt

Dedication

To my daughter Rebecca, and my son Adam.
To my sister Karen, and my brothers Jürgen and Hans-Erik;
To my students of the Sekondêre Skool, and all those who
struggled growing up in South-West Africa.

Contents

PART THREE: FENCES IN THE WORLD AT LARGE

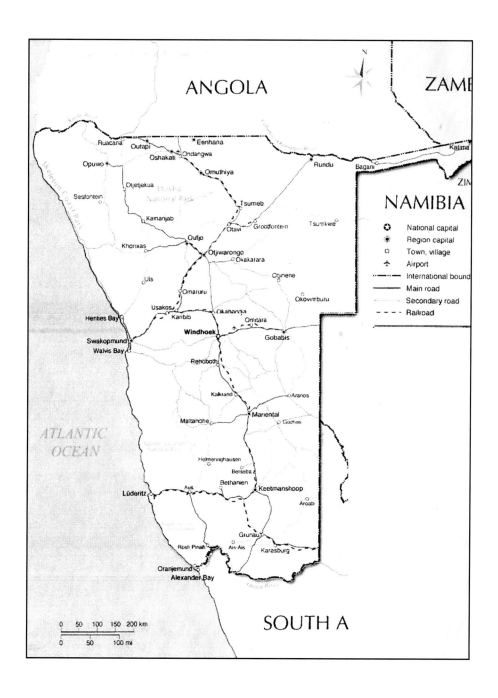

Where on Earth is This Country?

I N SEPTEMBER 1974, after having lived in London, U.K. for a year, I
stood at the counter of the post office on Finchley Road in Hampstead,
prepared to mail a package home. It was a whole three months till December, but so what! I wanted my mother and the rest of my family to receive my gifts in time for Christmas. I had already boxed them up to send
them on their way. I expected this post office visit to be yet another of many
frequently experienced challenges. No one there could ever tell me how long
a package would take by sea or by land to reach South-West Africa, if, indeed, they even knew where that was. I had learned from experience that
mail could take any length of time. Four weeks would be a veritable postal
miracle. But it could also take two, even three months.

I restrained myself to be patient, knowing that a hundred years ago a
letter from Europe took up to two years to reach our part of the world. In the
early nineteenth century the few hunters, traders, and explorers who occasionally traveled to the area carried mail and brought news. Later, missionaries
established a system of relay messengers. Mail could then be received twice
a year! The postal carriers had to face many dangers during their travels on
foot: lions, hunger, thirst, floods, and even human enemies. Their skeletons
were sometimes found along abandoned tracks, the carrion long since dealt
with by scavengers, the mail pouches and their contents devoured by termites.
Still later, when human traffic to this corner of the African continent increased

further, when the sea route to Walvis Bay was ploughed more often, a safer and more regular way of communication came about.

But I often wondered why mail took so long to reach its destination. Perhaps, I imagined, packages and letters were put in a bag, on a boat, where they remained, and were forgotten until the ship was halfway to India. Given that the mail was that slow, the business of this particular package was urgent.

On entering the building, I saw a long queue and quickly counted twelve people already ahead of me. I groaned. It would take ages. After a long time of waiting in line, it was finally my turn. The young man behind the counter at last addressed me.

"Yes, Miss?"

"I'd like to mail this package, please," I replied, pushing the parcel through the door in the brass railing that ran along the counter and that he had opened for me.

First he looked at the address, then said in a firm tone, "This address is not complete. Please complete it," and pushed the box back to me.

"What do you mean, it isn't complete?" I asked, puzzled, pushing it back to him through the railing.

"No, it's not complete. You've got the country missing. Which country are you sending this to?"

"I'm sending it to South-West Africa! Don't you see I put that down?" I asked him, my voice mildly irritated.

"Yes, I do see that. But South-West Africa is not a country," he replied peremptorily. My heart skipped a beat in disbelief.

"What do you mean it's not a country?"

"Not one I know of!" he argued back, his obstinacy my obstacle.

For a while I was at a loss for words. I felt invisible, my being erased. I was terrified of being unknown, so incognito. The image of my home under the palm trees appeared in my mind. I became teary-eyed. This place that was the center of my being was not supposed to exist because it was unknown in the wider scheme of things? Unthinkable! Oh, I absolutely agreed with him that "South-West Africa" was not much of a name, and quite an un-imaginative one at that. There was no doubt in my mind that the colonizers from Germany a century or so ago were more interested in gaining a share in the general scramble for a piece of Africa than in finding a more appropriate name for it. But it functioned.

I collected myself, took a deep breath, then countered emphatically, "But it is a country. I should know! I was born there! I grew up there! My family lives there!"

"Well," he said somewhat superciliously, "I work here. I have worked here for many years and no one has ever yet sent a parcel to a direction. There is East Africa, and West Africa, and South Africa. But South-West Africa? I've never heard of such a country in my life. It's not a country, it's a direction," he repeated with great assurance.

It struck me then, derisively, how Africa had been parceled out according to directions. In the minds of the powerful there was not much detail about this continent and its people. Europe had forgotten that Africa existed long before they actually attempted to discover it, that its diverse peoples – Berbers, Nubians, Bantu, and many others – lived and traded goods across the Mediterranean and the Indian Ocean for centuries, had established their own kingdoms just as they themselves had. Africa, although it unquestionably existed, was either mostly unknown, or, if it was known, this knowledge was not necessarily considered. It still happened, as it did to me just now in the post office. To early settlers from Europe, Africa was a dark place because home was uppermost in their mind. Their vision of the present was blurred not only by loss, but also by anxiety about the unknown. Having also set out with minds preoccupied with ideas of race, Africa became even blacker because of all the unknowns. But in the dark we cannot see. In the dark black becomes invisible. Under the circumstances boundaries were drawn quite arbitrarily, establishing ideas of countries, not sustainable societies of clans and tribes, like puzzles in which the pieces did not fit. Often places were named as reminders of home, names that had little to do with the actual geographic location. In addition, the minds of explorers and settlers alike, with an extraordinary effort of imagination and desire, created images of El Dorado, that mythic paradise with its abundance of gold, of ivory, and other desirable riches. New land sighted was called *terra nullis* (empty land) or "a wilderness," filled with mirages of "manifest destiny." With assumedly no one around, it was obviously there for the taking. As strangers they gave little, but desired all. They lived on islands of isolation, fenced in against people they deemed so dark, so savage, against all the unknowns of the continent they deemed so hostile because of their own hostility and ignorance.

3

Standing there at that precise moment in the Finchley Road post office, I remembered an experience I had had five or so years before, while I was teaching geography back at the Sekondêre Skool in *Karibib*, a small town in this little known country. I had told a class that, given the globe as a whole, South-West Africa was quite an unimportant country even though its territory was much, much larger than, for example, Texas. It was mostly desert and semi-desert. It had no agriculture to speak of, just some cattle and sheep farming. In the early days whalers had visited the cold waters of the *Benguela* current along the Atlantic coast from as far away as the island of Nantucket in the United States. While whaling died out, fishing of sardines, pilchards, and crayfish continued. Tons of guano, called black gold, were found on an island off shore and exported as fertilizer. Mining was the country's most important resource. The first ore to be found, near Otjimbingue, was copper. One of the world's richest fields existed in the north in Tsumeb. Our desert lands contained lead, zinc, tungsten, and dozens of other minerals, and numerous kinds of gems. In 1908 diamonds were discovered in the sands of *Kolmans Kop*, in the heart of the Namib Desert, just off the Skeleton Coast near Luderitz Bay, fulfilling those persistent dreams for riches. Through subsequent years, millions of diamonds were sifted from the alluvial desert sands and scraped from the Atlantic seabed, known as De Beer's diamonds. Eventually deposits of uranium became another valuable resource.

But apart from this, there were no other industries that were even worth mentioning. Perhaps beer, Windhoek Lager and Hansa Tafel – Germans knew how to brew good beer. But in general water was simply too scarce. Of course, there was also the land itself, the expansive, sunburned, ferociously unforgiving land, and the large numbers of wild animals, as untamed as the bleak earth on which they were accustomed to survive. Even in the 1960s the average of just half a person occupied a square mile. It was not an optimal number of people to establish a thriving country.

"So what does that amount to?" I asked the class, the students incensed, arguing against my statement of our country's apparent unimportance. "No control over resources, even sparse ones, no money, no status, no power!" I continued. They still refused to believe me in spite of this painful reality.

And now, here in London, I was trying to convince someone who had never heard of this place that it really existed. I looked at him. He was a young man with dark hair, light blue eyes, and a fair complexion. It was clear that he had not seen much sun apart from London's two-and-a-half hours of average shine a day. Perhaps he'd not traveled much either. Perhaps he knew only his London enclave of brick and concrete houses, of tar-surfaced streets and smog. Still, my country's unimportance and his persistent disbelief rankled. Surely I was proof, absolute proof in person, of its existence! But then, perhaps only a birth certificate might have proved what he refused to acknowledge. Of course, I thought, in this city of millions he had not met me before. To him I was just another body in the line of people he had to serve. The realization allowed a feeling of helpless isolation and loneliness wash through me, especially now with thoughts of Yuletide on my mind. I longed for the place where people knew each other or had at least heard of one another.

Despite these thoughts and feelings I attempted to remain positive in that post office, even though my irritation had escalated to dangerous heights. I kept the word "ignoramus" that had rushed to mind to myself, trying again to convince this young man behind the brass railing that I was right.

"Look," I said, "it is true. You can believe me. South-West Africa is definitely a country, not a direction. Could you perhaps look at your list of countries or maybe check it with a colleague?" I asked him, tensely courteous.

"Fine," he replied and vanished through a door at the back. I heard raised voices emanating from behind it, and when he reemerged he pulled a face. "I guess you're right," he said, shaking his head. "I've never heard of this country before, never!"

Still muttering to himself he proceeded to weigh my package. He charged me, I paid, and I assumed my parcel would go off on its timely long journey in the right direction.

I left the building and walked back to my flat in Hampstead. While trudging along the busy Finchley Road I drowned in the noise of the London trunk highway. Cars and trucks, vans and smoke-belching red buses roared by, the road a jarring techno river, a noisy smelly desert of cold steel and suffocating carbon dioxide. I shivered. The sidewalk was filled with rushing pedestrians running their endless and pressing errands. The small shops along the road brimmed with goods, too many of which you never really needed, while hideous neon-bright signs polluted my sight. I longed for the haunts of silence and solitude on the farm. I thought of my geography teacher in *Omaruru's* junior school. Mr. Peter had so loved the globe he kept in his classroom.

He taught us about the world and its many peoples, their countries, their different ways of life. Such a variety of people, their differences always intriguing me, just as Alwine's had, while at the same time I myself felt acutely strange. Right now, here on Finchley Road, this love of mine was stretched thin between variety and solitude, between the overwhelming world of man's creation and the enduring embrace of nature.

As the city's traffic and its people noisily milled around me, my heart yearned for home, my mind churning with thoughts and memories of *Omburo*, the farm, my home. Somehow this patch of land was important to me, part of my life, part of me. My thoughts turned to the morning star in the east with the sliver of the new moon close by, the old moon falling out of its arms. My thoughts became a song about the fragrant fresh smell of earth after a rain, about smiles shining in dark faces, the dark velvet eyes of an oryx, the timeless days in the bush. I could sing about all these wondrous things that tie me to the land's stony earth, wondrous things that erase the worry and the hardship through endless cycles of barely wet green followed by dry white seasons!

As I walked along, numerous occasions came back to me, when I had been introduced to strangers. "She's from South-West Africa," people were told. At least while it was still known by this name they'd then know I was from Africa. Yet once the name changed to *Namibia* it became more difficult to locate. The root of this name, *Namib*, is the evocative Nama word signifying the expansive coastal plains of the desert, those vast, seemingly empty spaces. Every time I heard the name, I saw those plains. But the changed name meant that most people I was introduced to would now furrow their brows.

"Namibia?" they'd say in puzzlement. "Where's that?"

"In Africa," I'd reply, patiently.

"Oh." And I could see them vainly searching their African map to locate this country. "Oh, I'm sorry. I don't think I know it. Tell me where it is!"

"In the southwestern corner of the continent," I'd continue, still feeling generous.

"You know South Africa?" I'd ask them. Nod.

"Know Angola?" Another nod followed.

"Well, it's wedged right in between." Eyes would light with sudden comprehension.

"Oh, there! Yes, of course. Really! I've never met anyone from there before. You're the first one. How interesting!"

I could then read in their eyes that somehow I was perceived differently, a strange creature from a strange land. Was it because, in their minds, I did not really belong there? After all, I was white. Black Africans also sometimes felt I did not belong there, even though I was born on the Skeleton Coast, even though I too had walked my country's hard, grainy soil and had sweated under its sun. Was I not an African because I happened to be white, because I spoke German, because I had been raised in a culture that was foreign to this soil? I did not feel at home in Germany. Instead, this was the place on earth that I knew, Omburo, South-West Africa. I knew it in the marrow of my bones, as unimportant as it may have been in the larger scheme of things on earth. Was the land where one grew up not part of one's identity?

I recalled a brief visit I once paid to Mombasa in Kenya. Together with many others traveling south by boat from Italy to Cape Town, I had stepped ashore for a few hours to explore the city. On a strip of palm-shaded street several local craftsmen were selling their goods. I stopped to take a look at the items the venders were offering for sale. One of them asked me, "So where are you from?" With a glint in my eye, waiting to see his surprise, I told the fellow nonchalantly and with pride, "I am an African!" He looked at me, amazement streaming from his eyes while grinning with disbelief, white teeth shining against his brown skin. "No!" he exclaimed. "No! Really!" I felt hurt and asked him what it was that made one an African. Indeed, what made you be this or that? What imbued you with the feeling of belonging?

Right then we began a long, traditional conversation about our families. We told each other where we lived, how we made a living, all about our families from grandparents to grandchildren, and shook hands on parting, the African way. I walked back to the boat in deep thought.

Another memory from later now comes to mind, a small yet significant comment a student of the Sekondêre Skool once made. We had been working on a one-act play and the actors were to have a last rehearsal before the final presentation, starting at six in the late afternoon. By six-thirty no one had yet showed up. I was pacing angrily at the door. *Could they not ever be on time?* Finally the first student arrived, saw me stewing, and calmly said: "Miss, one day you'll be an African too." I had to smile, but knew that this concept of time, that the idea that arrival itself was more important than the timing of it, this concept would never be mine. So maybe I would never truly be an African.

Where indeed was I from? What kind of culture was mine? Where indeed did I belong, which place, which country, which nation? How important was it to belong to a nation? What was a nation anyway? As I boarded the boat, I pushed the myriad questions aside, confidently tossing my head, allowing the sea breeze to ruffle my hair and caress my face. I belong to Africa, I told myself. I am an African!

I turned off Finchley into Bayswater Road. It was quieter here. Soon I stood on the steps of the large, solid building that had been built for just one family. Now it housed several parties. Two tall and solid pillars framed the door. For a moment I stood there looking back, taking in my surroundings. Well, I mailed my parcel, I thought with satisfaction, hoping that everyone would like the small gift I had wrapped for each one. Then I stepped inside, thinking of Christmases past, of my home on Omburo, of Africa.

I am Africa, this Africa, I thought. I do not know what is to come, or who I will be, but I know I am what had been for me. I am the people I grew up with, the animals that shared our land. I am the space, the distant horizons, the barely blue of the sky, the violet of the mountains, the blinding brightness of the light, and the heat of the sun. I am the drought and the terror and the pain. I am the yearning for rain, always more rain, for the hesitant green and the everlasting, daring hope of life.

Beginning the Search of Place and Self

PLATO SAID THAT writing is about forgetting rather than remembering. I think it is the other way around. I see writing as the act of recovering and integrating memories, imbuing them with a new life, living with them instead of banishing or erasing them. Memories are our timeless ocean of life. Some of them will forever remain hidden in the depth of our minds, some may surface unexpectedly, while others are always vividly present.

I began to write twenty-six years after leaving what is now called Namibia, where I was born and grew up, and thirteen years after moving to the United States. Until then all I had written were personal letters and required papers for my studies. That changed over Thanksgiving in 1995, when a dozen friends and family members gathered to celebrate the day. We were a happy company, sitting around the table, sated after the delicious meal, still sipping a great BV red, when the conversation moved to memories of previous celebrations of the holiday. From there the men took over, remembering their childhood, their interests then, their evolving love for woodworking and fishing, and how they came to be interested in their work as economists.

While the men recalled their pasts, we women were more or less silent. We made occasional comments and asked some question or other, but mostly we listened. Why was it, I wondered, that only the men were telling their stories? Why did we, the women, not tell ours? Did we not have any to tell? My heart beat faster as I chipped in spontaneously. I felt anxious at my sudden assertiveness, but I wanted to share my story also!

I took a deep breath. "I'm thinking of something that happened when I was on our farm, about thirty years ago," I began. "I had to shoot an oryx. It was early one winter's morning. Dogs had cornered the wounded animal. It was emaciated, a living skeleton in skin. It had been injured. It would die anyway, probably soon. So I shot it." I got it all out as fast as I could.

Silence spread through the room like a heavy fog. For a moment everyone's wordless attention was focused on me. They nodded, impressed, just a bit, and teased me. "Wow! You really shot an animal! You used a gun!" That "you" grated with its tone of "We can't imagine that." Surely none of them had ever used one! There had been no need. And in their youth theirs had been a different world.

As the conversation veered to other topics, my story suddenly became nothing. Had anyone really heard it? Few people I had met in life really knew much about this other world where I had grown up. I sat as if in a vacuum. I was disappointed for telling my precious story in merely eight sentences, for not capturing at all what I had wanted to convey. My words seemed to have disembodied the experience instead of shaping and imparting it. Why had I been at such a loss for words? Had I not known what I wanted to say? Why had I been so concerned about what the others might think of what I said or how I said it?

Back in my boarding school days in Omaruru I was able to tell stories. After the lights in the dormitory were switched off at bedtime, I told tales in the dark to the other girls until even I fell asleep. To me, storytelling was like singing a song, its tune striking a chord in the listener; like painting a picture with words for others to see and feel. Back then I told my stories in German. Was something getting lost in the translation when I told them in English? What words could I use now, so many years later, to write the song of my past?

On returning home from that Thanksgiving celebration, I sat down and wrote this first one of my stories, "The Oryx." It became much more than the story of that one animal. It indeed also defined a part of me that, until then, I had been unable to comprehend, that I could understand only in the telling of it, as if becoming a witness to myself. It revealed much that I had experienced, much that I had become.

For a long time I couldn't articulate why I felt the story implied "more", or say what this "more" was. That came later, when I had to admit that much in life is not determined by one's choice, that the silent inner currents of the self, the good as well as the dark, determine them. No baby chooses her parents, or chooses when and where she is born, or when and where and how she will die. Clearly, life is already defined from its very beginning by invisible fences of fate. Looking back, I was forced to ask myself if I had ever escaped any of the fences that had surrounded me, if I would ever escape the ones that still do. Was it possible to escape from between, or survive outside of them? Can anyone anywhere escape and yet survive? Was this a story not merely of this oryx, but that of all animals? Was it not my own story, or Africa's, or even perhaps the story of anyone anywhere? Fences are no doubt seductive metaphors, imbued with the dichotomy that confinement resides within them, freedom without. Was there not always tension between inside and outside, between unique individuals and their social niche?

Though my story contains elements of everything it is not, it is easier to define what it is not rather than what it is. It is not an autobiography. Neither is it a family history, nor a history of Namibia. It covers only a part of my life, from the years after my birth in 1937 to the time of my departure from Namibia in 1970, a departure that was never intended to be final. Each chapter is a window into life at that time, a snapshot that shows particular people, and their experience in a particular place at one moment in time. However, the singular moment, by itself, although ultimately only my family's, or mine, is at the same time representative of the life of many people in Namibia. For example, the story of the one rainstorm represents the overall importance of water in the lives of not only my family, but of everyone in the land. In the same way each chapter is a timeless condensation of many people and places, but is ultimately my own story, only mine, bedrock of lasting emotions and perceptions that rise like islands out of the sea of my life. The Oryx was the first story. Others followed, though never with the intention of writing a book of one whole story. That came at the end, an arduous task of melding the many into one.

When writing, each chapter also had a definite, even defiant tendency of suggesting its own content, of following its own course, of finally expressing that search for myself. I was forced to ask myself how I got from Omburo, my family farm in Namibia, to where I was in London in 1973. How had I dealt with separations and separateness within my family, as well as its existence in the society of my childhood? How did my family get there in the first place? And how did their beliefs, be they political, religious, or personal, contribute to the fabric of my being now?

The subjects of my story cast a light not only on my personal experiences but also reflect emerging changes while I lived there. Much more changed after I left. Most importantly, the country gained a new constitution, by which all citizens are subject to the same laws, laws that impart a sense of equal worth to all its citizens. It did away with at least legal Apartheid. Might it do away with Apartheid altogether? Or, for that matter, with racism?

Back when I lived there, I did not know much about my country's past. I had not learned about it at boarding school, not even through studying history at university. Little did I know I would discover much that had become unmentionable, that was at best forgotten but later on I did want to know about, what life had been like "in the good old days", before my time, how that compared with the present I knew. I wished to possess this past, even its secrets, because then, I believed, I might also know myself better.

This wish meant I had to attempt to recover at least part of the story of those who came before me. I had a copy of my mother's paternal family history, "Vorfahren der (Ancestors of the) Familie Redecker 1528–1960," which her mother, my grandmother Diederike Redecker, had laboriously put together, and which I had typed up for her in 1959. This history interested me then, but I forgot about it because at that time it did not impress me emotionally. That came later, when I wanted to know not just the history as such, but wanted to discover how it affected my own life.

My search for records and sources of my great-grandfather Johann Wilhelm Redecker, the man who established my family in Namibia, brought little to light. In most of the documents kept in Windhoek in the archives of the Rhenish Mission Society (RMS) for which he had worked, he was rarely mentioned beyond a brief comment in connection with his job as chief domestic economist. The RMS archives in Barmen, Germany, sent me copies of two curriculum vitae, a numerical record by the RMS of him and his family, and copies of eight reports he sent from the Cape and

Otjimbingue (its early spelling, I believe, was Otyimbingue) concerning annual harvests. I also received copies from various sources of four letters he wrote to family members: a letter to Caroline Gronemeyer, his bride-to-be; a letter from his daughter-in-law, my grandmother Redecker, to her own father after she arrived in Swakopmund; a letter from Johann Wilhelm's first wife, Caroline, to her father; a circular Johann Wilhelm sent to friends and family about Carolina's death; and, last but not least, a copy of his obituary.

This small treasure-trove of documents was expanded considerably when, after my mother's death in 2000, I found Johann Wilhelm's diary among items she had squirreled away over the years in a box. In his diary he notes his trip in 1866 to Cape Town and his experiences over the eleven months he spent at the Cape, as well as the first few months after his arrival in Otjimbingue in 1867. In this same box I also found thirteen meticulous diaries written by my mother's maternal grandfather, my great-grandfather Heinrich Wilhelm Kaufmann, during his thirty-month visit to Namibia, from 1913 to 1916, as well as a notebook in which my mother had attempted, albeit briefly, to transcribe Ur-Opa Kaufmann's old German script. I referred to her transcript only initially, when I myself was unable to decipher his handwriting. Sometimes my mom had been so baffled by his hand that she simply left blanks, leaving me to unravel the mysteries of his words on my own.

Transcribing my great-grandfathers' letters and diaries was an uncanny experience. The act of rewriting in my own hand what they had written so long ago was to momentarily be them, stepping into their shoes and footsteps, feeling their feelings, seeing what they had seen. Though once I stopped re-writing and simply went on reading, the experience became more distant, less emotionally involving. I no longer lost myself. The act had helped me dip into their way of thinking and feeling, to understand them better and see more clearly where I came from.

And so, inspired by these documents, I recovered my own story from the layered landscape of rough sediments of memories. In the act of their retrieval, these memories were reshaped and reintegrated, deepening the perception of their emotional colors and meanings. Though much in my heart remains unspoken, I am myself within my context, my mind having sprouted and grown in this particular society, having been forged by its forces and breathed in by me like air without realizing it happening. It is a context that includes past and present, family and culture, time and place. My story is my testimony to this place, to its people, to my family, and especially to those who compelled me to write about them because they were most important to me.

Getting to Africa

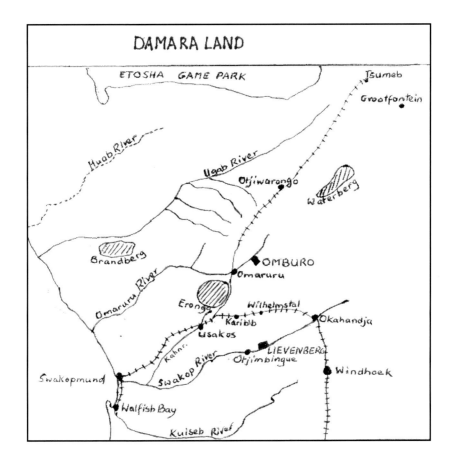

I N 1939 MY father bought a farm in Damaraland, in the heart of the central highlands of South-West Africa, a country now known as Namibia. The name of our farm was Omburo, a Herero word meaning "the place of constant water." It was named for the hot spring that bubbled up in the sand of the usually dry bed of the Omaruru River, a spring not known to have ever dried up.

Dad liked to tell my brothers and sister and me the story of how he and our mother came to Omburo. Unlike Mom, he was a newcomer to the continent. Born in 1901 in Bönen, a small coal-mining town in the Ruhr area of Germany, he was christened with an impressive list of names: Erich Richard August Hellmuth Staby.

He was always called Hellmuth. Twenty-seven years later, on New Year's Day 1928, he left Bönen to work for his cousin Hans Lühl, who owned a farm named *Garib* east of Windhoek, the capital of South-West Africa. He worked on other farms as well, on *Dordabis* and *Audabib*, before returning to Germany a year later with the hope of taking over his family *Hof* (farm). His dreams were dashed almost instantly as the Hof was sold. After learning to make cheese and butter he returned to South-West Africa, yet instead of using his new skills to make a living, he drove the "chocolate" truck at night, emptying Windhoek's outhouses. The pay for this job enabled him to rent the grazing of the Rooiwater farm in 1930 for his first one hundred Karakul sheep, taking the step toward being an independent farmer, all the while realizing the meaning of his name: "spirited courage." In 1931, he found work as dairyman on the Westfalenhof farm, where part of his payment, as was usual in those days, was grazing for his sheep. It was while working there that he met my mother, Anna.

Anna Katharina Redecker was born in German South-West Africa in 1908, a part of Africa claimed as colony by Germany in 1884. Her grandfather, Johann Wilhelm Redecker, had been the first of her family to settle there. He arrived in 1867 to work as chief domestic economist while also helping to run the mission's trading post for the Rhenish Mission Society in *Otjimbingue* in Damaraland, a station established for the RMS by missionary Johannes Rath on July 9, 1849. The *Damaras* were a people who herded their cattle, who also hunted and gathered. They lived in that part of country called the *Kho-mashochland,* the highlands of central Namibia. They were subdued and partly enslaved not only by the Herero but also by the Nama who arrived at a later time in this part of the world, around the beginning of the nineteenth century.

Mom's father, Friedrich Eduard Redecker, was Johann Wilhelm's youngest child. Friedrich (Fritz) and his older brother, Wilhelm (Willy), inherited their father's land, land he had gained through payment of a debt owed at what became his trading post in 1873 by the people of Herero chief Zacharias Zeraua. At first the brothers farmed the land together, but toward the end of World War I they divided it: one half, Westfalenhof, for Willy and the other, Lievenberg, for Fritz.

When I was a child, I liked to pester my grandmother to tell me about the "good old days" on Lievenberg, where she and my Opa Fritz raised my mother and her seven other siblings. Grandma was baptized with the wonderful name of Diederike Susanna Kaufmann. For me she was simply Oma Dieta.

I always felt close to Oma Dieta. She had taken care of me for half a year from the time I was fourteen months old while my parents traveled to Germany by way of salvaging an inheritance Dad had received there. My brother Hans-Erik, a little more than a year older than I, went with them. Though my parents had planned to stay longer than just six months, they hurried back to Omburo because of political developments in Germany under Hitler. I discovered only much later that Oma Dieta had been a staunch supporter of Hitler, though that did not matter when I was little. What mattered then was that she had taken care of me. What mattered later was that even so she had taken care of me. Her positive qualities mattered still more, balancing her darker side that included these political views.

Even after my parents and Hans-Erik returned from Germany I visited Oma Dieta frequently on Lievenberg in the early years of my childhood. Her house stood about two miles from the banks of the Swakop River, twelve miles east of Otjimbingue and about 120 miles east of the seaside resort of *Swakopmund* where I was born. I usually spent the day's noontime rest reading in her living room. Its solemnity was such that even the flies, if any dared to be there, stopped their buzz. I barely moved while lying on the carpet by the sofa, looking around at the rest of the furnishings she had assembled as part of her trousseau: a table, two regal armchairs and four regular chairs, a cupboard with decorative columns, a tall mirror, and a grandfather clock whose heavy brass weights on brass chains sounded the passing of time every fifteen minutes. All of the furniture was intricately carved in a traditional Frisian style, the oak wood stained black, the chairs and sofa upholstered in the same green-gold velvet that draped the large, grand windows. It was a somber room, cool and quiet in its eternal dusk, even in the brightest and hottest hours of summer. Its awe-inspiring formality made a fine backdrop for the world of Grimm's Fairy Tales.

Through the years Oma Dieta taught me much about the world that made it a larger place for me than the square miles I grew up on. She was born in Emden, in Germany's Friesland, and in her youth had traveled widely at home. She had also visited France and England and mastered their languages.

She regularly read the *Allgemeine Zeitung*, the German newspaper published in Windhoek. She read much more than my parents ever did. I don't recall the actual books, but she always had one or other on her desk that she was reading. I remember my parent's small dark oaken bookcase in our living room on Omburo, holding several hefty volumes of Winston Churchill's life, four volumes telling the story of a Lithuanian family over several generations, and a few other unremarkable books. That was the library complete.

Oma Dieta knew many people—family members, friends, even representatives of state. After she died and after I read her diaries, I realized she had always possessed this intense curiosity, this desire for involvement with life. She simply seemed interested in everything that came her way. Not surprisingly, she became a teacher for elementary classes. She was the only woman in her family with a profession, quite an accomplishment in her day and age. It turned out to be a handy one, especially after she went to German South-West Africa to marry her Fritz.

When I was about five, I spent three months with Oma Dieta at the seaside. I'm not sure why we stayed in St. Antonius, a hospital in Swakopmund run by Catholics, and not in a hotel. An old man with a long white beard used to go up to our floor on the same staircase we also used, carrying his cup with hot water he needed to shave in his room. He died during our stay; I took a never-to-be-forgotten forbidden look at his body in a coffin that stood among ferns in the gazebo behind the building, trying to grasp what it was to be dead. He lay there absolutely still, his face ghostly white, his eyes closed as if asleep, emanating an uncanny silence that scared me into rushing back to my grandma to make sure she still talked and moved. I didn't tell her what I had seen, but she sensed my fear and simply hugged me.

Opposite the hospital was a kindergarten where I played with other children. The yard was sandy, and the only toy around was a small wooden house in which lived a wicked witch: according to them that witch was I.

I remember the day Oma Dieta took me to the beach for the first time just below the lighthouse to show me the Atlantic Ocean and to tell me of her journey to Africa.

"See," she said to me, "that's the Atlantic!" I clung to her hand, keeping a distrustful distance from its waters. I had imagined a *vley*, a peaceful pond with ducks, spanned by a white curved bridge, not a mass of thundering waves that came crashing at me as if in attack.

"Don't worry," she comforted me. "The waves stay where they are. But never go too close, even if you could swim! The undertow is dangerous. Some good swimmers have drowned here because they could not deal with its fierceness and the force of the waves." I needed no further reminders. Seeing and hearing the waves were sufficient warning.

"Let's walk over to the *Landungsbrücke* (bridge for landing boats, i.e. a jetty)," she suggested. "Let's look out over the ocean from there." This "bridge," as it was generally referred to, was built to assist surfboats with the loading and unloading of ships that had to anchor far out on the waters.

Several such jetties had been built along the 800-mile long coast where only two or three harbors were to be found. The streets of Swakopmund were not macadamized in those days; they were covered with salt. The moisture of endless days of fog dissolved the salt that glued the sand into a solid surface, making walking and driving easier. The town eventually planted an avenue of palms lined with beds of Livingston daisies that ran along the beach from the lighthouse to the "bridge." It was customary to climb the steps of the "bridge" and walk out above the surf. It was not only exciting and fun but also scary to watch the waves breaking underneath, thundering in my ears, spraying me with cold, salty foam. Indeed, it was only much later that other real bridges were built across the colony's rivers. For a while

Oma Dieta and I stood at its very end, looking out over the ocean, mesmerized by the waters crashing against the pillars and onto the beach in roaring rhythm.

"Over there, about half a mile away," she said, interrupting our reverie, while pointing out to sea, "the boat I came on, the *Adolph Woermann,* finally anchored. Our trip was a long one. We left Hamburg on May 25 and arrived here on June 16, 1907." She explained how everyone aboard had to climb into a wooden crate, four people at a time, the women wearing long skirts! She laughed. "That wasn't easy, but somehow we managed. Then a crane on the ship lowered us in the crates into a small boat. *Kroo* boys rowed us – I think they came from Nigeria, black men hired by the Woermann shipping company because of their experience with boats. The waves kept slapping the sides of our little boat, spraying and drenching us. Over here, right here where we are, stood another crane. It hoisted the crate up out of the boat." Her recollection was punctuated with habitual little clicks of her tongue. "Ts-ts! Eventually, we clambered out, and, wet as we were, we walked to the beach. This was it—Africa! German South-West Africa! Without palms or flowers, just a lot of sand. Finally! I was so thrilled to be here. And your *Opa* Fritz was there to meet me! We hadn't seen each other for a whole year!" I took her hand and leaned against her, happy that she was by my side, like she was happy to see her Fritz again.

I asked her to tell me more about Opa Fritz when she and I were drinking tea one day while she visited us on Omburo, some years before she came to live with us in 1949. I was about ten, she in her early sixties. She was no longer as slim as when she was young. Time had wrinkled her face and threaded her dark hair with gray. Even so, she was a beautiful woman. Although her back was beginning to show a hunch, her posture still expressed the assurance and determination of her youth.

She drank her tea the way Frisians liked it: extremely strong, with cream and *clontjes,* those large translucent lumps of dark brown sugar. She sipped it in silence, lingering over her cup as I waited for her to begin the story of her life with my grandfather. She still misses him, all these years later, I thought. Opa Fritz had died in 1933, the year before their daughter Anna, my mom, married my dad.

"Yes," she began, not answering my question just yet. "Yes, he was such a loving *Vater.*"

Oma Dieta had called her mother and father *Mutter* and *Vater*, the same as my mother called her parents. I could not imagine doing this. It was a strangely distant address, not at all affectionate like *Mutti* and *Vati*, the way my siblings and I called our parents. Still, similarly, my mom usually called my dad Vati when we children were around, not by his name, thus keeping their relationship private. Still, when my grandmother spoke of Opa Fritz as Vater, I knew she meant a loving husband.

"It all began over Christmas in 1905," she resumed, remembering the year she turned twenty-three and was teaching at a junior school in Biebrich, a small town near Bonn. "My father had mentioned many times meeting some young man from German South-West Africa, a fellow who some years ago trained in Gütersloh, Germany as carpenter, specializing in making ox wagons. This time round the young man had come to gain business expertise at a commercial school in order to be able to take over his father's shop, the general trading post in Otjimbingue. Father had told me he had invited him to stay because he liked him so much." Her father, Heinrich Wilhelm Kaufmann, owned a factory that made brushes—hairbrushes, paint brushes, shaving brushes—all marketed as Adlerpinsel (Eagle Brushes). He was a wealthy man from a family of sea-faring captains who traded across the Atlantic, and had him self visited both American continents.

She paused briefly. "You must know it was quite unusual for my father to invite a stranger that quickly into our home. 'Remember to be careful of strangers,' he'd tell me. 'You have to know them before asking them to enter your house.'" She fixed her blue eyes on me for emphasis, her tone strict. Having reminded me how to behave sensibly, she continued.

"He also mentioned that this young man loved music, and that, after seeing our *Hofberg* harmonium, he wanted to buy it and take it to Africa." I knew that harmonium. It stood in Lievenberg's dining room, against the wall opposite the door to the veranda. My Aunt Gudrun, Oma Dieta's youngest child, used to play it often when I visited there.

"You know," said Grandma, smiling, "I had a strange feeling that my dad was plotting something. When I finally came home that Christmas, there this man was, right in our back yard, helping my younger brother Diedrich make a birdhouse, as if he already belonged to the family.

Oh, was he ever so handsome!" she exclaimed, heaving a deep sigh and clicking her tongue. "Ts-ts! I was smitten at first sight!"

She shook her head. "That father of mine! He first actually told us no, absolutely no wedding!

But in the end, just before Fritz went back to Africa in 1906, my father agreed to our engagement, despite his concern that I was going to live in a country where there was so much fighting, initially between Herero and Nama over land and grazing and cattle, subsequently between Herero and Nama against the colonizing Germans. I knew we would never have been happy without my father's consent. We needed his blessing. We had to keep the fourth commandment and honor God." About a year later, after having assembled an immense trousseau with which to make her new home, she followed her Fritz to German South-West Africa.

She placed her cup on the tray and asked me to take it to the kitchen. I knew she would say no more, private as she was about herself, shrouding all else in silence.

Years later, after she died in 1973, I learned from the family history she had written that soon after Fritz returned to Africa, he began repairing the house on Lievenberg for his bride. It was a house built in 1903 that had been partially destroyed during armed skirmishes in 1904, at the start of the uprising of the Herero against the German occupation. At that time, about three thousand German colonists lived in South-West Africa. In 1907 Gottlieb

Redecker, the oldest brother of Fritz and a master builder, created a design that incorporated into the original house two more rooms and a large veranda. While Opa Fritz crafted new floors, windows, and doors, Mr. Paul Hoppe, my Aunt Amanda's father, laid the bricks. Together they renewed the old roof. Hard as they tried, however, they could not get everything done before the wedding day.

After arriving in Swakopmund in 1907, Oma Dieta and her Fritz still had a long trip ahead before reaching Lievenberg. Her luggage was loaded onto a horse-drawn trolley and taken to the railway station, where she and Opa Fritz boarded the express train to Karibib. "Express," mind you, turned out to be a whole day's travel, but it was better than another several days by ox wagon, the arduous way Ur-Opa Redecker had made his two-week trip forty years earlier. My grandparents were lucky to have seats, and a roof over their heads to protect them from the sun, the dust, and the engine's sooty smoke. The train stopped for lunch in *Usakos* before continuing the last miles to Karibib.

There, on June 23, they married in the state's district registry. They proceeded by donkey cart to Otjimbingue, spending a cold night on the hard ground under a starry sky. They were married on July 4 in the settlement's church. At the ceremony Pastor Johannes Olpp read from the Book of Ruth: "Where you go I shall go . . . and your people are my people."

Otjimbingue weddings were bright moments within long, dull stretches of weeks of mostly hard work. Everyone helped to prepare for the celebration. The church and the couple's small three-roomed home were decorated with palm fronds and flowers. Presents were piled up. Pigs had been slaughtered for making sausages and ham. Three sheep and bags of rice were given to the black people so they too could celebrate. Some women made sweets. Still others set a long table on the veranda for the white people to have coffee and cake after the ceremony. Amazingly, even a German Hock was served (white wine from vineyards in *Hochheim,* where the wine ostensibly came from, was called "Hock" by the British as they had difficulty pronouncing "Hoch"). Over dinner that evening letters and telegrams of congratulations were read; someone took photos, and the younger generation entertained everyone with sketches. It was truly a joyful day, filled with singing and happiness and excitement.

The newlyweds began their life on Lievenberg in August.

Nine months later, on May 6, 1908, my mother, Anna Katharina, was born. Ruth came along in 1909, Wilhelm in 1910, and Renate in 1912. In February 1910 a great storm uprooted hundreds of trees in the area and ripped away much of the roof of their house. As many times before, the good rains of one year were followed by several of severe drought. *Rinderpest*, a cattle disease, devastated their herd, and many people died of malaria. Fritz's father, whose health had been ailing, died in 1911. His community buried Ur-Opa Redecker next to his first wife, Caroline, in Otjimbingue's graveyard.

The worst of my grandparents' trials on Lievenberg coincided with a long-promised visit in July 1913 from Oma Dieta's father, whom she had not seen for six years. Ur-Opa Kaufmann had planned on a year's stay; he wound up staying two and a half. Although they were thousands of miles from Europe, and although World War I had not yet broken out, the colonial government of German South-West Africa had requisitioned spans of oxen and all ox wagons for transportation purposes in support of the colony's defense before the war actually broke out. By August 1, no goods, not even rice or wheat, were reaching the country by sea or by land. The colonists had to do anything and everything to grow food. Opa Fritz did his share by enlarging the garden in the Swakop River for vegetables and tobacco, even planting a second garden while continuing to grow wheat in the riverbed as before, the same way his father had in Otjimbingue.

In October 1914, Opa Fritz was recruited to prepare to fight in a possible war. First he joined the Ninth Company of the Schutztruppe in Windhoek. Later he was sent to Aus in the south to prevent South African troops from entering the country in support of Great Britain. But the troops had already landed in Luderitz Bay and taken the harbor, and when thousands more landed not much later in Walvis (Whale) Bay to march inland, he was recalled from Aus to join the local defense positioned along the railway to Windhoek. The small number of recruits and the few German soldiers were unable to hold back thousands of advancing South African troops.

Once Fritz was recruited, his brother Willy continued the gardening. Willy had recently moved his family from Lievenberg to Westfalenhof, though now, with the outbreak of World War I in August 1914, they moved back to Lievenberg. Under the circumstances it was considered safer to remain together. However, very soon the whole clan trekked with their cattle to Annenhof, a farm near Grootfontein in the far north of the country, while a few cows, sheep, and goats were taken to the Windhoek area closer to home.

Ur-Opa Kaufmann did not go north with the family.

He wanted to stay on Lievenberg, hoping that the presence of a white person there could prevent the farmhouse from being looted or destroyed. Everyone advised him against it, claiming it would be too dangerous to live there alone. He followed the advice, only to regret it subsequently. Having remained in Otjimbingue, he was the first family member to go over to the house after three thousand South African soldiers had passed through on their way to Windhoek. In his diary he described for his daughter the devastation he encountered:

> Eventually I sorted through the keys, found the right one, and unlocked the door. I hesitated, still prepared only to look. Filled now

with fear, my eyes more closely ranged over the destruction I had glimpsed moments ago through the window. Finally, I forced myself to step inside.

The large oak dining table lay in the middle of the floor, upside down, torn in half. The sideboard's doors had been hacked open, its contents of glasses and crockery shattered, scattered all over. I saw the clock lying on the floor just under the spot where it used to hang on the wall, its clockwork ripped out. The pictures were shredded; frames smashed; the sewing machine dismantled; documents, books, photographs torn into pieces; clothes in shreds! I stood there, frozen in disbelief. Everything had been demolished. Debris! Nothing but debris there, six inches thick, covering the floor, remnants of memories, of love, of comfort, of identity.

I picked my way across into the living room. There, I stopped dead in my tracks, once more deeply shocked, even if for different reasons. It was absolutely amazing.

The room had remained almost untouched. The black furniture was all there. The table stood in the middle of the room, as always, surrounded by its chairs like a hen with chicks. The sofa still invited me to sink away in its comfort. The sideboard, standing in a far corner, was still intact. Its doors were swinging, open; I could see that the books that once filled its shelves had been removed. The large mirror serenely reflected opposite parts of the room. The grandfather clock stood silent. No one had thought of rewinding its weights. Nothing but the books had been touched. Even the greenish velvet curtains still hung in their places. The harmonium stood in its usual spot, inviting me to play. I thought of music, but only Chopin's funeral march, songs of death, came to mind. I could not play.

This has always been a cool, quiet space embraced by dusk, a place of rest for us, where I sometimes felt I should only whisper. At that moment, standing there and surveying it, it seemed an apparition from heaven, an entirely new place of solace and peace and wholeness, especially given the destruction all around. I pondered what sentiments had prevented its destruction. Had the soldiers been awe-inspired by the room's atmosphere? Had the captain's love of beauty moved him to order his subordinates not to touch anything? Had it simply been the order to leave at once that had kept it intact?

The corridor, the bedrooms, the bathroom, the kitchen, the storage room— were a complete shambles. Beds had been stripped to their frames. Umbrellas were mere skeletons, the zanella torn off their metal ribs. The medicine cabinet had been thrown on the floor, all the bottles and vials broken, the precious medications spilled. Our beloved books were scattered all over the place, their pages torn; doors were splintered, drawers thrown randomly in all directions, boxes opened. Everything that could be opened had been opened, even part of a wall, all in a frenzied search for treasure.

Everything I myself had brought with me or had collected so far during my visit, my books, letters I kept, my diaries, my African treasures, the carefully collected silver-backed jackal and the leopard pelts, everything was gone. Taken! Nothing remained.

As I stood there glancing through the gloom, I noticed the picture over the sofa, still in one piece, that painting of the destruction of Jerusalem, you know. I had no idea why you had chosen to hang it there. I had not thought about it before this moment. Did you think you were building that New Jerusalem here in Africa? It spelled such irony at that moment! I then noticed, for the first time and just before I intended to leave, the picture of your mother hanging there. She looked sad, I thought, or did I see my own feelings reflected in her face? Maybe it was really my own sadness about the state of affairs, or maybe I missed her because her picture forced me to remember her death when you were only four. I turned on my heels and left quickly, overcome by my feelings. I locked all the doors and went back to the cart. . . . The driver, sitting down so the basket with the intact items I had collected was between us, cracked his whip. The oxen strained and slowly set the cart in motion. We began the tedious and fearful trek back to Otjimbingue into an uncertain future.

Incredibly, Willy's house on farm Westfalenhof had remained untouched. When World War I broke out, it not only prevented Ur-Opa Kaufmann from leaving in August 1914 as planned. It also decisively altered the history of the colony. Because Germany lost the war, the colony was handed over to South Africa as a mandated territory. From then on it was known as The Mandate of SWA. Already existing differences in the colonial population were continued. Differences of languages and cultures remained, the status quo gradually cemented into law, most specifically in 1948 when South Africa's National Party won the elections, keeping all power in the hands of the whites.

My grandparents persevered with making a living on Lievenberg, facing years of strenuous efforts just as Fritz's father had done after he came to German South-West Africa in 1866 to work for the Rhenish Mission Society, first at the Cape, then later in Otjimbingue. By 1867, when Ur-Opa Redecker arrived in Otjimbingue, a place about seventy miles south of our farm Omburo, it had already become the headquarters of the RMS in Damaraland. It was conveniently located on the northern bank of the Swakop River and fairly central in the land's expansive area. It had also become a point of convergence for all the main traffic, public or private, to and from the coast.

Next to providing the settlement with wheat, oats, maize, many kinds of fruits and vegetables, Ur-Opa also helped run a trading post set up by *Eduard Hälbich*. The mission saw the shop as serving a twofold purpose. The first was to protect black people, mostly the Herero, from being exploited by traders, and hence squander their cattle or land as payment for "silly" things like glass beads and "bad" things like guns and brandy. The second was to put the indigenous nomadic people in touch with European influences through trading in order to further the process of their acculturation, thus inducing them to settle in one place and so, it was hoped, to be converted more easily. So far, at the time of his arrival, in all the years of the mission's hard work since 1839, not a single convert had been made. However, not only because of opposition within the RMS to the idea of a trading post, but also because the post was economically unsuccessful, it was transferred from the mission to my great-grandfather in 1873, making it his private business. From then on it was called *Kolonial u. Manufacturwarenhandlung*: Colonial and Manufactured Goods Trading Post. Its outlet in Karibib remained in Eduard Hälbich's hands.

Ur-Opa Redecker had worked for the RMS for three years before he married Carolina Gronemeyer, a woman from his hometown of Jöllenbek in Westfalen, who joined him in Africa.

In the next nine years, apart from helping in the shop, helping with the gardening, and feeding and clothing her family (and also the workers), Lina, as Carolina was called, gave birth to seven children. Two died in infancy. She herself died a sudden death in 1882, three days after having moved some heavy furniture. Desperately needing help with raising his children, Ur-Opa sent his oldest son, Gottlieb, to relatives in Germany; his youngest daughter, Maria Louise, was sent to live with a family in Walvis Bay. Opa Fritz and his older brother Willy were cared for by their oldest sister, Louise, and lived in the home of Missionary *Johannes Olpp* in Okahandja. The family was reunited in 1885, when Ur-Opa wed *Anna Maria Husemann*, another woman from *Jöllenbek* whom he had not known before but who, like Lina, had been recommended to him by trustworthy sources. Anna Maria was ten years younger than Ur-Opa; together they had three daughters. She died in 1917 in Otjimbingue at the age of 70, six years after her husband died.

Ur-Opa's chief customers had been the Herero people of Chief Zacharias *Zeraua*. They lived in their domain around Otjimbingue. Over many years he and his people incurred a great debt of about forty thousand German marks at the shop. Since they had no money, they could pay for their debts only with either cattle or land. Two centuries before, when the Cape was settled by the Dutch, the Khoi Khoi (first known as the Hottentots because they were perceived to be stammerers) and the Khoi San (previously called Bushmen) quickly realized that, by allowing the "visitors" to use their communally owned land to raise cattle and crops, they were losing not only their land but their way of life. It took the people of Damaraland many years to realize that by buying the goods the westerners had to offer, they were selling not only their land, but also, unavoidably, their identity and independence.

It needed a good deal of persuasion by many people for Ur-Opa Redecker to eventually insist that Chief Zacharias Zeraua pay off his incurred debt at the shop. Zeraua and the elders of his tribe finally deeded about 27,000 hectares of land, known as *Omaningerere* and *Ondukatjikende* (approximately 69,000 acres) of his domain along the Swakop River to Ur-Opa in 1896. My great-grandfather thus gained the land in a way typical during those decades. When he became too frail to run the shop, his sons, more especially Willy, operated it until it was finally given up after Ur-Opa died in 1911. With his death his two youngest sons inherited the land.

Fritz, Willy, and their families returned from Annenhof in September 1915. By then my grandparents had had two more children, Viktoria and Hildburg. Hans-Dietrich and Gudrun followed in 1920 and 1921. The debris in and around Lievenberg was cleared; still useable items were retrieved, windows and doors were repaired. The gardens were reestablished and the wells cleaned. New hand pumps were installed on both wells in the river and on the bore at the house. Staple food was scarce. A few goats from Westfalenhof supplied a little meat, and from time to time a kudu was killed for the pot. Once the sheep and a few cows returned from Windhoek, milk was again available. Nine months later the cattle returned from Annenhof, despite the Rinderpest (a viral disease) raging in many areas. Opa Fritz even built a new ox wagon.

Having returned from the north to Lievenberg, Willy built a second veranda and added one more room to the back of the existing house, a room in which he started making Limburger cheese. He continued his cheese making after moving back to Westfalenhof in 1917. Years later, in 1931, he hired my dad to do this work.

In 1918 the Spanish Influenza, known as the black plague—the same influenza that raced through Europe that year—also ravaged German South-West Africa. Brought in by the South African troops, it spread mainly along the railway lines. The Redecker families were spared because they lived far from the tracks, and they also had not sent their children to a public school, hence avoiding contact with the disease. Each year, from 1918 on, one or more of the families' children attended the home school that Oma Dieta had started for my mother. Desks became available from a school in Otjimbingue that had closed at the start of the war. A blackboard and a map of Europe were donated. Books were borrowed from anyone who had any.

When the end of World War I was finally sealed in 1919 with the Treaty of Versailles, South Africa was handed the administration of German South-West Africa, and from then on it was called officially "The Mandate of South-West Africa", otherwise simply known as South-West-Africa. Oma Dieta's home school was recognized by the new government and each year an inspector paid a formal visit. From 1926 to 1929 a teacher was hired, but after she left, Oma Dieta taught both families' children until 1934, when the school was closed. During the last five years of the school's existence, and, fortunately for her, her husband's youngest stepsister, Auguste, a fully trained housekeeper, helped run the household.

In 1923, after years of fairly dry seasons, good rains finally came—rains that also brought locusts that denuded the land over the next three years. Despite these difficult times my grandparents decided to sell their ox wagon and buy a three-quarter-ton Dodge. Then, in 1930, the government decreed that all the farms in the country had to be fenced in. I have no idea where the money came from for the fences or, for that matter, the new car, the children's education, and everything else that was needed. I suspect that the families back home in Germany contributed large sums or that money was borrowed from them. This is probably a correct assumption, as I discovered many years after writing this that Oma Dieta's trousseau cost 32,000.00 D-Marks in 1906 – an enormous sum of money in those days. However, she never mentioned money in her diary. To my knowledge no accounts of spending, or of bills paid have survived from those years except for the details of her trousseau. She never complained about their hardships. They were facts of life. It was simply how it was.

Another year of unforgettable drought hit in 1931. Throughout the country, cattle died by the thousands. In 1932, after a better rainy season, my grandparents exchanged a number of heifers for three hundred Karakul sheep, hoping to finally make money instead of continue losing it. But 1933 turned out to be yet another year without rain. The Redecker families and everyone else lost still more cattle. Rather than sell the lean animals to a meat factory in Okahandja for a paltry seventeen shillings a head, Opa Fritz went north with what was left of his herd. During the trek he developed phlebitis, an inflammation of the veins, and pneumonia. He was taken to hospital in Swakopmund and never returned home, dying there that spring on May 3.

More than two hundred Nama and Herero, as well as all the white people of the neighborhood attended his funeral on Lievenberg. He was buried in the farm cemetery next to his daughter Ruth, who had died a terrible death of abdominal tuberculosis in 1913 at age four. To their lifelong regret, neither my mother nor her sister, Renate, could come home for their father's funeral. Both were working in South Africa, my mom as nurse to the children of a wealthy English-speaking family in Paarl. There just had been no money for the trip. My mother often mentioned with great sadness that she had so missed being with her family that day.

On December 12, 1934, after she returned from Paarl, my mother and father were married on Lievenberg, that is, after my mom had made quite sure my dad really wanted her, only her and no other woman. She told us kids many a time how Dad proposed to her three times before she accepted. Five years later, he bought Omburo. It was to become the center of my life, the place where, for me, everything began.

PART ONE:
CHILDHOOD ON THE FARM

Fences

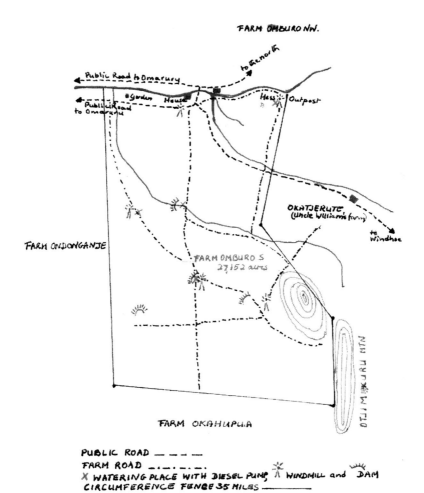

FARM OMBURO NW.

to the north

Public Road to Omaruru

Public Road to Omaruru

Garden House

HQ Outpost

OKATJERUTE
(Uncle William's farm)

to Windhoe

FARM ONDONGANJE

FARM OMBURO S
27,152 acres

OTJIMAKURU NTN

FARM OKAHUPUA

PUBLIC ROAD — — — —
FARM ROAD — . — . — . —
X WATERING PLACE WITH DIESEL PUMP, ☼ WINDMILL and ‿ DAM
CIRCUMFERENCE FENCE 35 MILES —————

ARLY ONE SATURDAY morning, when I was about ten, I was chatting with my parents at the breakfast table when a truck pulled up in our back yard with a fusillade of bangs. It was *Heinrich* in his battered and rusty Chevy, a colored man who worked as foreman on a farm further east - I think on *Otjikoko*. He stopped by on his way into town, as was the custom for everyone living along this road, offering to bring back mail from Omaruru, or pick up something that was needed. My dad went out to greet him and to find out what he wanted. They talked for a while, and when Henry sputtered off with a few explosions, Dad came back to the kitchen with a note in his hand. "It's from Uncle Wilhelm. He says he wants to come over midmorning." Dad sat down with a sigh. "It doesn't suit me at all to wait for him," talking more or less to himself. "I need to go over to the Hess outpost and check the windmill and the kraals, and that part of our fence bordering his farm. The oryx scramble under that fence a lot, and I think it might need mending." He turned to my mother, saying, "Your dear brother has complained about problems there before," as if my uncle's complaints were her fault.

"Well," Mom offered, "why don't you leave now? When he shows up later I'll just tell him you had to leave. I'll ask him to stay for lunch, so he'll be here when you come back."

"That's a thought," Dad muttered gratefully.

My father was not particularly a keeper of schedules, so I wondered why he didn't want to wait for Uncle Wilhelm. He and my uncle were good friends. At least that was my understanding. Yet I always felt some unspoken tension between them. Maybe Dad felt he should have done something about the fence before now. Maybe Uncle Wilhelm felt envious about Dad having a bigger farm. I also wondered if it might have something to do with taking sides in World War II, either with faraway Germany or with our own South-West Africa. I really had no idea then.

The English-speaking people, in power at the beginning of the war, had supported Britain, while the Afrikaans-speaking Boers stood behind Germany. The German-speaking population was indeed strongly anti-British and anti-South African government, our "them." German colonists had taken down the South African flag in Windhoek in 1933. In 1934 the strong organization of Hitler Youth was banned by South Africa. On the whole, the twenties and thirties were filled with censorship that divided the "races" both in South

Africa and in South-West Africa in order to keep control over the territories and remain in power. The South African government clearly feared that the German men might revolt, that perhaps they might even enlist the support of the Boers. So they locked them up. The first men to go were those active in a Nazi group; next came those who had served in the German army; then those on the list who participated in or supported the National Party. Uncle Wilhelm spent six years in *Andalusia* in South Africa. Most men from South West Africa were imprisoned there, some at two other camps: *Baviaanspoort* or *Koffiefontein*. While Uncle Wilhelm went to Andalusia, Dad remained at home. He, as well as a number of other men, was not summoned for internment. They had always been totally anti-Nazi and supportive of the United Party as well as the South African Party. Some women were interned on their farms, remained behind, having to manage them on their own. And Oma Dieta was one of them.

Dad was a gentle man, quite emotional, and passionately loved us, his children. I always trusted him. He liked many different people. He was a friend of Mr. Gie, the Jew. He liked Mr. Cilliers, the Afrikaner, and Padre Schlottbohm, the Catholic priest. It did not matter to him that he himself was a Lutheran and the padre a Catholic. It was more important that they both came from the Land *Westfalen* in Germany. The Padre ran *Waldfrieden*, a farm and Catholic mission station halfway to Omaruru, with a school for black children. Dad supported his work. Like others, we bought vegetables he grew to help cover the costs of the enterprise. Dad accepted people who had different political views also. And he certainly treated those who worked for him well, whether black or "colored." The only "them" for him I knew were the Nazis. And they were German, like us.

At the time I wasn't terribly clear about any of this, but I knew better than to pursue my curiosity with probing questions and get rebuffed for asking about what I was not supposed to know. Still, it didn't stop me from trying to figure out what was going on. I was aware of similar tensions at school between German-speaking and Afrikaans-speaking children. Afrikaners were different. They had different customs. Their children at school were usually much older than my German class friends and I. They were also not terribly smart — so I thought. Except, of course, for *Augustinus* E, the boy who was Hans-Erik's chief challenger for first place in his class. These children were our "them". They spoke a different language, which we were forced to learn after 1945 so we could continue our education. They ate different foods, like *koeksusters,* a tooth-curlingly sweet donut. Grrrr! Besides, I thought the barriers had to do with likes and dislikes, but still, I never quite understood how having a different language would make one set of people so dislike another. Maybe the tensions had to do with something else. Were people afraid? Of what? Were they perhaps afraid of us? On the other hand I also could not understand how you could be loyal to a country where you had lived long ago, like so many Germans did, a place so different and so far away, unless, of course, you did not like the place where you lived now. Maybe you could feel such loyalty if you were intensely attached to the old place, or if you thought life were greener elsewhere. Were we not always hoping for greener seasons? It was beyond me to understand such thoughts at this time in my life.

My dad pottered around the yard and workshop for a while, asking me not much later: "Do you want to come along?"

"Of course! Right now?"

"In about five minutes."

I skipped away to tell Mom that I was driving out with Dad and went in search of Foxy, who also loved rides. Foxy was a mongrel dog, mostly fox terrier, who had arrived in our yard from nowhere on a hot day a few years earlier, mincing along on three legs. After some time we discovered that nothing was wrong with his legs. He just had the habit of using three, any three. Hans-Erik had been the first to take care of him, thereby turning Foxy into his ferocious guardian. We couldn't get near Hans-Erik for fear of Foxy's snarls and growls. It did not take us long to discover that he was a meticulous snake killer as he barked only once he had discovered a snake. It always felt safe to have him around.

I found Foxy curled up in his usual spot, in a corner of the garage on the loam floor where he had turned many circles to create a cool and dusty hole in which to lie down comfortably. I gently scratched him behind one ear, telling him to come along. Together we joined my dad, who had already picked up his hunting rifle from his office, a .303 Lee Enfield. He always brought the gun along, just in case he ran into a kudu or an oryx to shoot for the pot. It was less trouble than going on a special hunting trip.

The track to the Hess outpost followed the south bank of the Omaruru River eastward. The outpost was named after the fellow who supposedly had first lived there, who had dug the well on the riverbank and had kept his sheep on that land, and who had left long before we even moved to the farm. It was a good area with low bush on which sheep liked to feed. Along the way we briefly stopped at the hot spring. We wanted to see how much water had accumulated in that sandy expanse. As in most of Africa, and the world over, water is life's sustaining elixir. For us there was always a worry about having enough, even with the spring right there.

We liked to visit this spot also for its special setting. Huge dolomite boulders were stacked into a towering *koppie* (hill) on the bank beside the spring, the oxidized iron showing in the deep, rusty red-brown of the rock.

Over the years kudus had created a trail across the hill down to the spring in the dry riverbed, one that we now followed. From the top we could easily see where its hot water bubbled under carpets of green and yellow algae, meandering downstream in a narrow, silvery band. All of this had been there for many thousands of years.

"Let's go search for the rock art, Dad," I suggested, tugging his arm after a few pensive moments of gazing down on the river. With Foxy close at our heels we moved away from the trail and soon found the shelters that had been built on top of the hill by peoples long since extinct, perhaps used even more recently by the many hunters who completely decimated the area's wild life within two decades after 1860. Each shelter was no more than a circular hollow, the rocks from its center piled around its rim. Perhaps four people could hide there from view and find protection, at least against wind. Strange homes, I thought. Not very comfortable! Though the site was still the same, life had been different then. Those ancient rock art peoples had hunted and gathered, maybe 600 years ago, maybe even before then. Everyone used the land and the watering places. In those days there were far fewer people. They had far more space. Not like now, when fences everywhere created possession, islands of isolation and heart-eating envy.

We looked around for a while for the only rock art on our farm. The engravings were hard to spot in the jumble of boulders. They could be seen only if the angle of light at which it fell on them was exactly right. We often showed them to visitors with pride, as if they bestowed upon us the dignity of an African lineage, right back to the cradle of Olduvai Gorge. I found the giraffe first, its image scraped out in a dull reddish color on the flat surface of one of the larger boulders. "Here are the others," Dad called out. "Here's the hyena and the antelope, maybe an oryx, right next to it." What we thought looked like a hyena had a polished surface, while the outline of the antelope had been chiseled into the hard, flat stone.

After the rock people, the Herero came here with their cattle. They chose a good name for this place—*Omburo,* the "constant water." And the river they named *Omaruru,* meaning "bitter milk." Evergreen bitter bush (*Pechuël-Loes-chea Leubnitzae*) grew along the banks, on which cattle would browse during the dry time of the year, giving their milk its bitter taste. Like the rock people and the Herero, we also thought this place to be a good spot. Had it not saved us with its plentiful water in many a dry year?

Dad interrupted my thinking. "In those days more game was around than we see here today."

"You mean right here?"

"Sure. Some of the early hunters, missionaries and traders wrote about large numbers of elephants, rhinos, antelopes of all kinds, lions they had seen here just a hundred years ago. You name the animal, and here it roamed. Hunting for profit was big in the late nineteenth century, especially a group of hunters under the auspices of the Swede, Axel Eriksson, killed wildlife here in our area, almost exterminating it." I loved the animals, loved to watch them in the veld. How could people simply shoot thousands of animals when simply seeing them was such an exciting and gratifying experience? We, on the other hand, shot an animal only for the pot, and that was hard enough.

It was difficult to imagine all these animals ever having been here as I looked across the riverbed to the bushy hills on the other side dotted with white thorn and black thorn acacias, then scanned the banks and hills of the other two rivers, the larger one named *Otjimukuru*, draining the area of the Otjimukuru Mountain, the place of god, and which joined the Omaruru River here. Clumps of enormous Ana acacias rose from their expansive beds of sand. The morning sky was a rich forget-me-not blue. Wisps of clouds floated above, writing their own message of clear weather. All was dry. I could see nothing that moved. No birds, no antelopes, not even a jackal or a baboon, as if all life had also been consumed, now, by the murderous whiteness of the sun.

I looked over at my dad, sitting there on one of the rocks on the hill by the spring. He wore fawn drill trousers and a gray short-sleeved shirt, both made by my mom, and old veld shoes that got cleaned once a week by Lendina, one of our shepherd's girls. A floppy hat shaded his lively gray eyes, wrinkles of laughter skirting their edges under his bushy brows. Dad was a stocky man, his muscular hairy arms a reddish tan, his hands broad and strong. He was not very athletic like Uncle Wilhelm. My mom worried about his appreciative love of potatoes with gravy and their effect on his waistline. That never mattered to me. And people liked him. He was an elder in our church in Omaruru. He was warm and chatty. I admired him for his sense of adventure. I admired him as the best storyteller I knew. His stories were different from those Oma Dieta told. Hers were about events and real things; his were made up. We children loved it when he gathered us around him in the evenings on the living room sofa to tell us his robber-thrillers, exciting tales he created on the spur of the moment, something like robbers hiding deep in threateningly scary dark woods, sitting around a fire, waiting for a good moment to steal some treasure, bloodhounds eventually tracking them down so the thieves could be jailed and justice be done. It was most important to us for the room to be dark during his storytelling. Mom never joined us. She shut herself out with her light, sitting dutifully at the sewing machine, working away instead of joining us.

On this particular visit to the koppie, for me Dad, sitting on a rock, had become part of it. Here, in this place, time seemed to stand still through long dry and short wet seasons. Here, change was barely measured by the slow erosion of soil and wildlife. Like this piece of land, my dad seemed unchangingly present. I knew that he loved this arid place fiercely, the way he loved us, like we loved him. I also loved this spot. *Because he loved it?*

My dad seldom talked about his past. He spoke little about his experiences during World War I or the years afterward. At age seventeen, he (and many youngsters like him) was required to leave school before gaining his *Abitur*, his certificate of school completion, and join the German army. Fortunately, the call came only months before Germany capitulated, so he never saw a battlefront. In the early 1920s he joined the cavalry of the famed *Hussars* of Kassel. He rarely spoke of the terrible years of the Depression, of the time he worked on a farm in East Prussia, or of his later trip to South-West Africa, where he stepped off the boat in the country's only port, Walvis Bay, and onto the shore of a new destiny. What he did talk about was his arrival there, the moment of setting foot on African soil.

"I just walked to the end of that quay, sat down, and cried," he told us kids. "It looked such a hopeless place." Though his voice was calm, his eyes betrayed emotions that still moved him almost two decades later. I knew the place and understood his feelings. It invited no one to continue inland, not now, not then and certainly not sixty years earlier, when my great-grandfather, Ur-Opa Redecker, arrived from Germany. Even now many shipwrecks, more than 350, dot the Atlantic West Coast between the Kunene and Orange rivers. The bones of humans and animals still bleach in the searing sun, hence the ominous name of Skeleton Coast.

Ur-Opa had thanked God many times for having delivered him safely to Africa, and although he did not cry, he too sighed toward heaven after reaching Walvis Bay. The trip north from Cape Town aboard the ship "Lightning" had been a rough one, taking ten days instead of four. Huge post-storm waves had slowed the ship's way. He had to remind himself that wherever God sent him, it would be the right place. Once ashore, it took courage to press on. For him, as for everyone else, this first wagon trip inland of almost two weeks must have been bone-jarringly tough, an extended test of endurance. Days were extremely hot. There was no shade. Nights were cold, and spent lying on the sand or the hard-baked soil, too uncomfortable for anyone to find sleep. After a long stretch up the *Kuiseb* River to avoid crawling through the dunes, he and the other missionaries still had to cover the long haul northward over to the Swakop River, across a rough, burned moonscape, land blackened by the sun and ravaged by the wind, followed by many miles of trekking along the Swakop River until they eventually reached Otjimbingue.

I wondered how many people had cried like Dad on arriving in that dismal harbor, marked then by only a few corrugated sheet iron barracks. Nothing much more there meets the eye even now but a sea of sand along an endless ocean. Heavy mists often roll in from the cold Atlantic, hiding the sun so that you freeze in the very middle of summer, while underwater volcanic eruptions fill the air from time to time with the pungent odor of sulfur dioxide. To visitors it has rarely looked even remotely like paradise. They wonder what has kept those who live in this country, where the land is hard as the Camelthorn tree, where the rivers are dry, and where the sun chars even the rock. All of us—the Herero, the Nama, the colonists from Ur-Opa to my father—all had been as tenacious about survival as the animals and plants, as the land itself. What did keep anyone here? Was it a way to survive, or was it merely the great skies, the freeing sense of space? Was it the wish to belong to some place, any place? Did owning it enhance a sense of power in the face of all the hardship? Was it the shared earth and the bones and blood of ones own buried people that entitled and attached everyone to this beautiful, cruelly difficult place?

"Let's go," Dad said, abruptly bringing my wandering mind back to the present. As we stood up we heard the hum of a car coming along the track. We turned and were surprised to see Uncle Wilhelm. He stopped his late 1920s Dodge behind our truck, got out, and waved. "Stay there, I'll join you!" he shouted. Taking a shortcut, he clambered over the rocks, wending his way through the *vaalbos*, a thorny gray-leafed bush common in our veld.

I liked Uncle Wilhelm. He was the older of my mother's two brothers, tall, lean, tanned, and terribly strong. He loved athletics and tenniquoit, a game much like badminton but played by throwing a rubber ring instead of hitting a birdie with a racquet. I fondly nicknamed him "Kudu," though I never called him that to his face, because his flyaway ears reminded me of the animal. Like Dad, he too had lots of wrinkles around his closely set eyes. They often twinkled as if some secret thought amused him, sustaining him in his loneliness. Sometimes their blue gaze was icy, with a sting that made me shudder.

Despite my grandparents' constant lack of money, they sent all but one of their children to school in Germany, at least for a while. Uncle Wilhelm, the family's deep thinker and math wizard, went to Berlin in 1921, when he was barely twelve. In 1923 his sister Anna, my mother, was sent to a colonial school in Rendsburg, a city in Holstein, where she trained as a nurse for children. By 1939 all of my mother's siblings had gone to Germany for further education, except for my Aunt Gudrun, the youngest.

I remember Uncle Wilhelm telling us about his impressions of Berlin when he first saw the city as a ten-year old boy. "I found Berlin simply amazing," he said. "So many big houses, so many cars, so many people, and so many things I had never seen before! One day my uncle and I went to the railway station to meet someone. While we were waiting for the train to arrive I looked around and saw something very peculiar: a door that went around and around, and people walking around and around inside it."

"Why do they keep walking in a circle like that?" I asked him.

"It's not the same people! With every turn of the door different people go through!"

"It can't be different people," I argued. "It must be the same ones all the time."

"Why do you think that?"

"Because there are not that many people in the world! Of course, I can see now why I thought this. Even now here are only a million and a half in this country that is much larger than Germany!"

He chuckled. "Thousands of people lived in Berlin at that time, so many more than here. And it is such a different world from here, so very, very different!"

I gasped with admiration. I had little idea of what just a thousand was, never mind a million. And I had yet to see a revolving door, an escalator, or even an elevator. I knew only a few people, like my family, the employees on our farm, friends and neighbors, people at school and in the village. What did people do in a city like Berlin? Did they know each other? Berlin sounded big indeed, bigger even than our own capital, which I had not yet set eyes on so far.

Uncle Wilhelm had to give up studying engineering in Berlin in 1933 to help Oma Dieta run the family farm on Lievenberg after Opa Fritz's death. But while he was interned in Andalusia in 1940 he studied math and Hebrew. He also acquired great skills in making leather goods: handbags, satchels, and purses that he sent to us as Christmas presents during those years. It was in Andalusia that he became such a good tenniquoit player. After returning from the internment camp in 1946, he made up for the loss of a career as an engineer by running Okatjerute, the farm his mother gave him, with great precision. He calculated everything down to the last millimeter. Every fence, every gate, every water trough was made according to exact measurements. My dad, on the other hand, didn't worry too much about a few inches more or a few inches less, so long as it functioned, whatever "it" was.

Because my dad and uncle often disagreed about how things should be done, I sensed that they also deeply disagreed about other things, like their political views. I sometimes overheard them talk about Hitler and Nazis and Jews. I didn't know much about Hitler or Nazis then, but I knew about Jews from the Bible. And the only Jew I had ever met was Mr. Gie, who owned the farm *Omapyu* some fifteen miles away. He and my dad were good friends. No doubt politics was a serious matter, one the grownups did not mention when we children were around. Just like sex! There was something secretive about it. But then, there was much the adults did not discuss when we were present.

Despite their disagreements, my dad and my uncle were helpful and dependable neighbors to each other. They had to be. I often wondered how under these circumstances they could also be the friends they seemed.

Uncle Wilhelm sat down with us on one of the boulders as Foxy resumed his scramble over the rocks, sniffing out and chasing lizards from their hideouts. Uncle Wilhelm looked around, nodding. "This really is a fine spot, Hellmuth," he said. "Wish I had all that water down there." As he stared at the spring, I could feel his yearning for something more than water, his disappointment that there so seldom was enough of what was needed. After some silent longing he looked at my dad. "Anna told me you had come this way. I'm glad you're still here." There was a ring to his voice that made the silence that followed uncomfortable.

"Yes," Dad replied, "we just wanted to enjoy this place and see how much water there is. I'm actually on my way to the Hess boundary fence."

I waited silently.

"I hoped you would be," my uncle said. "It's about time. The fence is broken along your part in several places. I thought some of my cattle had strayed over."

Dad grimaced slightly with guilt. Fences were shared by neighbors: one half was yours, the other theirs. They brought trouble when not maintained properly. Wooden posts, about eight inches wide and eight feet high, were set into the earth at ten-foot intervals, more or less. Six or seven thick steel wires are strung from one post to the next, kept in place by seven *droppers* (smaller posts) tied onto the wires, stabilizing them, as well as rendering them visible. Fences often broke when animals got tangled in the wires while trying to push through, or under or over, and when termites devoured the wooden posts or when lightning slashed the wires. Fences had to be tended regularly, their gates checked and kept shut at all times, protecting your grazing and water, keeping in what belonged to you while keeping out what belonged to others.

"I noticed that some of my animals had not shown up for two days or so," Uncle Wilhelm continued. "When I searched for them, I finally tracked them to a gap in one of the gullies that course under your stretch of the fence."

I sensed his anger, though I had yet to see him lose his temper openly. The grownups I knew didn't lose their tempers, ever. It was we, the children, who had the fights, even though we were not supposed to. When we did argue, my mom usually threatened to leave and go into the bush, where surely she would perish. It wasn't fair!

"Yeah, I know," dad said. "I should have checked it long ago." He was silent for a while. "But you know what it's like, Wilhelm. There is always something more pressing to see to. And I am on my way," he pointed out, trying to mollify him.

"Well, now my cattle are grazing on your land as there is not much grass left on my place. You should have taken care of the fence sooner. Don't blame me if they eat your last blade."

"No, no, don't worry. I'll get Paul to round them up as soon as possible. Maybe we'll even come across them later on today. Then we'll drive them back onto your side and fix the gap temporarily." Dad hesitated before finally putting forth his question with a worried voice. "If you have no grazing left, Wilhelm, what are you going to do?"

My uncle narrowed his eyes, focusing his gaze on my dad. "You probably have guessed why I wanted to see you. I'm wondering if you could keep about fifty animals for me."

Dad hesitated even longer before replying. "I thought you might ask that. But you know how difficult an issue it is to take on more animals."

He seemed torn between wanting to say yes while knowing he had to say no. It was such a hard question to answer. Being a Christian required my dad to help, I knew that. We all had been raised in the Lutheran faith, which meant always having to be selfless. But survival required him to say no. After a while of sighing and shaking his head he said, "Even one animal would be too many, Wilhelm. You know it's no good, overgrazing. The land is bad enough as it is. I'd like to help out, but I don't think I can. I might barely make it through to the next rains with just my own herd."

"That so? Your place is so large, Hellmuth. And yet you still don't have enough?" He sounded mad, unwilling to accept the answer.

Dad sighed, but repeated his answer. He couldn't do it. It would not be right.

"I sort of thought you might say that," my uncle said eventually. "Still, I had to ask, to make sure before making that long trek north to Soris." Soris was a farm far to the Northwest, land that belonged to his in-laws, and which he had bought. He shook his head and stared back at the spring. "This damned weather! Always this uncertainty about rain! And my place never seems to get as much as yours. Somehow it rains everywhere but where I am. I often wonder why Granddad came to this godforsaken part of the earth!" he said, his voice splintering with despondency and anger over such foolishness.

"He was fulfilling his mission," Dad reminded him. "You know that! He came here to help pacify and convert the heathens by teaching them skills."

I shifted around on the rock where I was sitting, attempting to ease the discomfort between us, scrutinizing the two men as they stared across the river into the distant bush. I wanted to know more about my great-grandfather's mission, but no one in my family talked much about it. Nevertheless, I admired Ur-Opa Redecker. I admired Opa Fritz and Uncle Wilhelm and my dad, the women who went with them. I admired every pioneer anywhere in the world for setting out into the unknown. I am sure Ur-Opa gathered quite a bit of information about Damaraland before coming to Africa, but knowing about something and experiencing what it was all about were two exceedingly different propositions.

Uncle Wilhelm changed tack. "You're so lucky with your place. Remember how I thought you were crazy to buy it? The chutzpah you had to purchase it four days before the outbreak of World War II!" He shook his head, still marveling in disbelief.

"I'm glad the bank auctioned this farm off," Dad agreed. "I'm glad I bought it, even if you and everyone else thought I was crazy to do so with war that imminent. It sure was my chance, maybe my only one, for actually owning land. I was so tired of moving around. Anna and I had moved farms three times in five years, first to Erora, then to *Otjua* six months after our marriage, then from Otjua to *Okandura*-South."

All of us children were born in different places: Hans-Erik in 1935 in Otjua, I in 1937 in Swakopmund, Karen in 1939 in Windhoek, on the day Dad bought Omburo, and Jürgen in 1941 in Omaruru, the village named after the river. A fifth child aborted in the third month, but that remained a secret until shortly before my mom died. Moving to Omburo meant that at least now we were settled on our own soil.

My dad chuckled on recalling that great day when he bought Omburo, on July 29, 1939, the very day my sister was born. "Remember? I had to borrow the whole down payment."

I knew he would be pleased if I asked him more about that. I didn't mind, even though I knew the story well. I always liked to please my dad.

"Dad," I joined in innocently, "Dad, you really had no money then?"

"No, I didn't, and I needed a fortune. Hardly anyone had any money at that time, especially not forty-five hundred pounds. Considering that an ox cost only three, it was a huge amount. I had to borrow a third of that for the down payment from the Karakul Association in Kalkfeld. And then there was the mortgage to be paid for the rest of the sum. We are still paying it off."

It must have been a lot of money. All I knew about money had to do with my savings book at the post office. Although I got just two shillings pocket money a month, I happily deposited a few now and then into my account and watched the clerk deftly plant his stamp on the page of my book. Maybe one day I would be able to buy something with my savings, but I wasn't sure it would be a farm. I liked life on Omburo, but it was so difficult. My parents always worried about rain. They were always working to pay for that mortgage and for what we needed. There wasn't much left for what we wanted. I had often heard them talk about farmers who were deep in debt, owing the bank or their siblings a lot of money, working, working, working to pay it off. No, I probably would not buy a farm with my savings, I told myself.

"Well, that way I got these eleven thousand hectares," my dad said, looking about him with pride. He was luckier than Moses, who had been allowed to only glimpse Canaan, the Promised Land, with longing! "Remember, I came here with nothing in 1928. Absolutely nothing! Now, this is everything!"

"Yeah, you've been a lucky man, all right," my uncle muttered. "You got this land and didn't even get interned! That United Party Smuts government . . . they thought of sending us all back to Germany!"

I bristled. The conversation was shifting from the family's invisible minefield toward more open and accepted division and animosity. My dad was a firm supporter of Jan Christiaan Smuts, two-time prime minister of South Africa and, indirectly, ours as well. Here we go again, I thought. Would anyone really have had to go back to Germany? Did anyone want to go back? Maybe Uncle Wilhelm wishes he could have. I had no idea. I had not been to Germany, not yet. But I knew my mother yearned for it. She often spoke about walking in the forest of the Harz, the woods near Bad Lauterberg that she had so loved. There were no woods in South-West Africa. As for my dad, he seemed to feel perfectly content to be here, in this land he had chosen, not inherited.

"Come on," I said impatiently to my uncle. "You're here. You've got so much." He fixed his blue eyes on me with a stare of annoyance that shut me up instantly. I was so sure he minded that he didn't get Oma Dieta's place, even though she had bought him Okatjerute. His brother Hans-Dieter inherited Lievenberg. I knew that their father, my Opa Fritz, had inherited half of my great-grandfather's land. And once Ur-Opa had that land, he passed it on to his children, who were burdened with it and its hardship. They had no choice but to stay, given circumstances and family expectations, even though they did not necessarily want to.

For a while we sat in silence. I looked at my father and my uncle, sensing again their unexpressed feelings about the land and about being here. I respectfully liked my uncle, but he seemed weighed down by expectations of gratitude and duty toward his family. Although he was here and had a lot, he seemed to yearn for something else, for something he really wanted, whatever that was. Here my dad had found something new, something he could not find back in Germany that would satisfy him for a lifetime.

"I have to get going, Wilhelm," Dad finally said. "I'm so sorry I can't do anything for you."

"Well, I guess I'll just have to move up north again with the cattle," Uncle Wilhelm thought aloud. "What else can I do? It's my duty. It's our livelihood. And I'm so tired of it."

My dad remained silent. Whatever could we have said? Living here was never easy. We all knew that.

We got up and slowly and silently picked our way across the rocks back to the trucks. As I walked along behind the men, African style, with Foxy at my heels, I pictured my uncle moving north with his cattle for two hundred miles or more, negotiating for grazing and water. It would be a long and difficult journey, a lonely trek of obligation along roads divided by fences. Would he ever be able to thrive, or would he just survive?

I kept looking at the ground while making my way across the koppie. As I walked I saw rusty pebbles, iron rocks strewn all over, a bit of rough-grained sand in between, hardy vaalbos eking out an existence, clumps of lion-colored grass keeping a precarious hold in the sparse soil with their tenacious roots.

The Farm House

ALTHOUGH I WAS born in 1937 in Swakopmund, the coastal desert town just north of Walvis Bay, and by age two had already moved with my parents several times from one farm to another, Omburo is the farm I remember. Like a nut, the Herero word Omburo contained more than merely a kernel. It contained the essence of our farm, that secret magic of Africa that is an amalgam of both eye and mind. This piece of land cast a spell over me, a spell that emanated from each grain of sand, the barest hue of green, the wisp of a cloud, the slightest snap of a twig. And the heart of this land was the house.

My earliest memories of Omburo stem from the first days after we had moved there, shortly after my dad bought the farm in July 1939, a mere four days before the outbreak of World War II. I remember my mom squatting by a small Primus stove in a room of the farmhouse that had one small window facing south. The house had been empty for some time, so the floor was covered with a thick layer of dust and shards of glass, porcelain, and other debris. Mom had cleared a corner, creating a clean space for the Primus so she could boil water for tea and cook our food.

The crates my parents had used for moving remained unpacked for six months. They had been concerned that Dad might be sent to an internment camp in South Africa. Should that happen, as it had to Mom's brother Wilhelm and many other German-speaking men in the early days of the war, she wanted to move back to Lievenberg to live with her mother instead of remaining alone on Omburo.

The lower parts of the walls inside our house were painted a murky green, the doors a horrible brown, colors that remained for many years until others were available that we could by then afford. Green should have been a pleasing color, given that the world outside was usually so dry. But that particular green reminded me of cow-pats, not pastures. A band of gold separated the ghastly green from the white expanse that stretched up to the ceilings of reed covered with a two-foot-thick mixture of mud and straw carried by dark red-brown Camelthorn acacia beams. I remember Mom saying that this was such a large house. "Whatever will we do with twelve rooms?" she asked, rhetorically, when we moved in. We had little furniture then, just a few tables and chairs, beds, and some cupboards. Once my parents unpacked our belongings, Dad turned the rough, wooden Pegasus boxes, previously used to transport petroleum cans, into storage shelves.

Oma Dieta's house was lavish by comparison. Her living room on Lievenberg was furnished with a majestic set of carved furniture. We had nothing as posh as that. Even so, our house was special, not only because it was our home, but also because it had its own story. Although other similarly constructed houses dotted the country close to sources of water, not all of them had been designated as mission stations like ours.

This part of Damaraland, where Omburo was located, had been the domain of Herero chief *Tjiharine* and his people since about 1845. In the 1870s he requested the RMS to establish a station on his land. When the missionary Eduard Dannert finally arrived there on May 16 in 1876, Chief Tjiharine designated a few acres just south of the spring in the Omaruru River for their home.

The mission house was built in stages, the first stage being the two rooms facing east, in one of which my mom had set up the Primus stove. The house was expanded bit by bit toward the west until there were a dozen rooms altogether. As it grew, the house became wider at its western end so that no room was either a standard square or rectangle. The walls were about eighteen inches thick, made of mud-and-straw bricks, later smoothed over with cement, afterward whitewashed. The end walls were arched. Each wall had two round openings for ventilation. Both supported a roof of corrugated sheet iron. This combination: the arched roof with a good deal of space between it and the ceiling, with thick walls and small windows, made the house comfortably cool in summer and cozily warm in winter.

It wasn't long before the missionaries discovered that after heavy rainstorms water flowed through these first two rooms. They had indeed been built in the dry bed of a small river. So Chief Tjiharine had his people dig a new channel for the river. In the years that followed, the water sometimes still filled its former bed. Even now, decades later, with heavy rains, the water tended to flow through our yard, between the garage and these two rooms. One of these two rooms became a bedroom that I shared with my younger sister, Karen, the other was shared by my brothers Hans-Erik and Jürgen.

In 1908 the lands around the mission station were surveyed and divided into smaller farms: *Ondongandje* 1, Ondongandje 2, Omburo NW1, Omburo NW2, Omburo NE, Omburo South, and *Okahupua*. Omburo South and Okahupua remained farmlands of the RMS. The government leased the Ondongandjes to private individuals. Omburo NW1, NW2, and NE were sold to private individuals. From then on the downsized mission farm raised cattle to support the RMS financially. In 1915 Omburo South was occupied by South African troops for some months, though the resident mission farmer, Martin Werner, stayed on to manage it. Eventually, in 1920, the government required the RMS to pay off its debts. As they could not come up with the money, they finally, in 1924, had to hand over the land in lieu. Perhaps other individuals leased it from then on. All I know is that my dad bought the South lot at an auction held by the local Barclays Bank that day in 1939. The bank auctioned it off since Mr. Cartwright, a Dutchman who had occupied it for some years, had accumulated large debts, possibly also owing the mortgage for the land. He had vanished, leaving the Bank to deal with his debts. Although our farm was known from then on as Omburo South, to us it was simply Omburo. The only one!

Our house stood, like a fortress on the banks of the Omaruru River, an oasis in a clearing of the dense and savage bush, fenced in against the dangers that might be lurking beyond the open space of the yard.

Fears of such dangers, real or imagined, could terrorize the heart even in the light of day. Inevitably, the dark of night intensified these, allowing the perception of Africa as "that dark dangerous continent" to loom even larger.

Each night as I lay in my bed, safe inside the space created by the thick walls of my home, I took in the loud silence of the tropics, a silence thick as the blackness itself. It pressed in on my ears, down upon my soul. It enveloped me until I fell asleep. Yet it was steadily interrupted by strange noises: a black-backed jackal calling eerily from upriver, another answering in reply from somewhere closer to the house. Back and forth they'd send their fearful crying, like a conversation. I used to pull my blanket tightly around me, sealing myself against their ghostly voices until their calling stopped and the ocean of silence once again washed over me.

Occasionally a screeching flock of Blacksmith plovers in the river would startle me awake. Trying to stay alive, they were always jittery, always ready to take flight. Once they stood on safer ground, their raucous shrieks gradually settled into short *pik-piks*, soon smothered by the velvety night-blue mantel spread over the bush. Sometimes it was the hollow hooting of a prowling owl or a muffled thudding outside my window that penetrated my awareness. I would then listen intently, trying to make out what I was hearing. Yes, I was sure the thudding was a hoofed animal racing around the house.

Was it an oryx? No, an oryx wouldn't get into the yard by jumping a fence. It would dig a ditch underneath and creep through. It was probably a different antelope, a kudu.

Kudus could jump fences easily, even though fences were intended to keep them out. Whatever it was, the fleeing animal must have entered the yard in a panic, vainly and ironically seeking safety in the presence of humans. A pack of dogs, probably including ours, were steadily following it, paws softly padding in pursuit, lungs rasping. I stiffened, barely breathing. On and on the chase continued around the house until a crash tore through the night. Fence wires reverberated loudly while, shivering, I pulled my blanket yet more tightly around me. The dogs gave a few low yelps and crept into the night while ours once again curled up by the backdoor steps, now and then erupting into short spells of barking. Sometimes they barked at porcupines, whose quills rattled loudly as they fed on sweet Prosopis pods stored at the back of the open garage. Or they barked at the kangaroo-like springhares that entered the garden in search of greens. Sometimes they barked for no apparent reason, perhaps having dreamed of chasing *meerkatte,* (prairie dogs) or having perceived moving shadows in the moonlight as intruders.

Otherwise I heard only the wind rustling the palm fronds or the leaves of the Prosopis outside my bedroom window, the gentle sounds soothing me back into dreamland. Feeling safe within the fortress of my home, I inhaled the night's noises with fear and excitement, alert to a life that vanished into hiding with the dawning of day. Always, the light of day with its different measures of silence and sound was a relief. At least then you could see if only within limits.

Every morning Francolins shattered the barest of light with their screeching, the first sounds to wake me, announcing the break of day. Not much later the glossy blue-violet Cape starlings would start chattering noisily, while flocks of black-masked yellow weavers continued making their intricate nests that dangled from many a palm frond. From my bed I liked to listen to these morning sounds, to watch the sky grow lighter, to wait for the first burning arc of the sun somewhere along the silhouette of the Otjikoko Mountain. On seeing the sliver, I jumped out of bed to stand at the window and witness the moment when the rays would strike the earth, daubing the white walls of the garage with a rosy hue, then lighting the large fenced-in yard with a rich golden-red glow.

The shade of many trees formed a cool, green oasis of about four acres in the otherwise thorny dry landscape of yellows and browns that surrounded our house. Three impressive palms, already about sixty years old when my dad bought the farm, stood a few yards from the back door, their fronds and trunks swaying in the wind. Being so tall, they were visible from afar. Two of them were females. During summer they each bore enormous bunches of juicy, oblong yellow fruits, which with time shriveled into sweet, delectable brown dates. One year the smallest of the palms, too heavy with fruit, was toppled in a big storm. A few more grew farther over on the bank of the river and around the well.

Beyond the palms closest to the house stood a grove of Casoarinas, their trunks making useful posts for our washing lines. Their branches were covered with segmented scales, the sharp point of one fitting neatly into the hollow of the next, a string of them making up a pine-like needle. The trees produced hundreds of half-inch-long prickly cones that often covered the ground below. Walking barefoot there was not advisable. It was difficult not to step on them, their sting causing you to curl into contortions, as if walking on burning coals.

Many other trees stood in our yard. Here and there a black thorn or white thorn acacia stabbed the air with its enormous spikes. One of these stood near the garage, supplying the starlings with the thorns and twigs they needed to make their messy nests. Over time a cactus had sneaked up along the acacia's trunk to enchant us once every summer with its ethereal white blossoms and their sweet, sensuous fragrance. We carefully monitored the gradual thickening of the buds to make sure that we did not miss the moment of one night's viewing of these exciting beauties the "Queen of the Night" brought forth.

On the side of the house opposite to our bedrooms a gracefully drooping pepper tree grew close to my dad's office. In the early summer it was covered with clusters of tiny yellow flowers that turned into bunches of green peppercorns popping out of bright red membranes. To the right of the door to this small room was a cupboard made from the Pegasus boxes that Dad and Mom had used for moving. It held a few rolls of black and white twine, pipes and pouches of tobacco, shoelaces and shoe polish, matches and other oddments. Next to it, under the window and looking out over the back yard, was a table serving as a desk. Its top had a faded red oak color, patterned with ink and many scratches, a surface with its own history to be surveyed. There my dad would sit, signing checks to pay our bills, or writing letters in his heavy hand to his mother and, not often enough, to my siblings and to me when we were at boarding school.

To the left of the door was another rough but lower Pegasus cupboard. On it stood the scales and its many glowing brass weights. As a child I especially liked to help weigh the brown sugar: such large crystals, such a delicious honey color! I often sneaked in there, licking my fingers before dipping them into the two-hundred-pound bag to savor the sweetness, feeling guilty despite knowing that no one would notice a few crystals missing. Several more Hessian jute bags leaned against that wall: one with raw coffee beans, one with *mielie* meal (corn flour), another with salt, all supplies we needed for at least one month. I loved the indefinable smell of this office, the crunch underfoot of what had been spilled.

Behind the garage, a space once used by the missionaries for services aimed at converting unbelievers, its bells now ringing from a church tower in Tsumeb, stood an enormous Casoarina next to a drooping pepper tree. Both shaded the outdoor workbench with its heavy cast iron anvil and vise. Behind the bench, and somewhat hidden by the trees, was the place where our firewood was chopped. A chunk of a tree trunk bore marks of the heavy blows that Uibeb, one of our Herero farmhands made as he spliced and chopped the dry trunks and branches collected and brought in from the bush. Close by and around a corner at the back of the garage was a room for storing the chopped wood. The outhouse was there too, a scary place, tucked away, out of sight as if shy, permeated by the smell of ashes and turpentine and much more. Snakes liked to hide there in the gloom, alerting us to their presence with a hiss that sent us scrambling into daylight with pants or knickers flapping around our knees. Along a wall and a fence that extended from the storage room toward the river my mom planted a row of prickly pears, green ones to savor in the heat of the day once peeled and cooled, red ones for making a tasty syrup for desserts and cool drinks.

Several evergreen Prosopis (*prosopis juliflora*) grew along the yard's fence, their yellow puffball flowers attracting bees, eventually delivering a protein-rich harvest of long, juicy red-brown or green pods. Every fall the pods were raked and stored at the back of our garage as a bit of extra feeding for the chickens, the milking cows and calves, or any sick cattle or sheep. Most of our animals loved to eat them, just as the porcupines did.

At first my father raised Karakul sheep, not especially for their wool, which was short and wiry and hard to use, but for the softer pelts of their lambs. He also raised a herd of Red Poll and Shorthorn cattle for meat, initially using their milk to make cheese and butter and kasein (dried whey). Ten years or so later he gave up the sheep and the milking, raising only cattle for meat to be sold on South African markets, eventually upgrading his herd with the genes of hardy Afrikaner cattle.

During the first few years Dad also grew a garden closer to the Omaruru River. The missionaries had already dug a well on the edge of its bank, perhaps ten feet across and maybe twenty feet deep. Its upper inside was lined with several rounds of large, neatly cut rocks, while lower down a wide tube of corrugated sheet iron kept the sides from collapsing. We often looked down into the well to see how much water there was. Usually it was so clear that you could see right to the bottom, small whirls and bubbles indicating the spots where it came seeping in. You could even see a few tadpoles cutting through its coolness or mistake a frog for a floating leaf.

A windmill over the well pumped the water into a small tank raised close by for our use. My dad laid a pipe from the tank to the house, setting up a regular tap in the yard and a well-polished, proud brass tap in the kitchen. These were the only taps around for many years.

Although the Omaruru River was dry for about 362 days of the year, its sandy bed was a perfect reservoir. There was also the hot spring upriver that flowed all year round, supplying the little stream that usually vanished in the river opposite the yard, but sometimes flowed even farther than that. And so the well never dried up.

In this garden my dad grew mostly lucerne. He used it to feed the chickens, the sick sheep, and the few milking cows. With its clover-like leaves and purplish blue flowers it attracted bees and butterflies. I loved to follow the clear water flowing along the main furrow he had made, the long beds stretching away on either side. I watched it pass into the beds through the openings in the furrow, first seeping into the soil, changing its color into a muddy darker tawny brown while filling the beds slowly. The plants showed their gratitude with each watering, lifting their flower heads higher while their leaves seemed instantly greener on soaking up the moisture. Through the years in which the lush green lasted, the Easter Bunny enticed us often to search there for the colorful eggs it brought.

Alas, the pleasure of so much green did not last long. Each year, mysteriously, maddeningly, despite plentiful water and organic fertilizer, the lucerne grew to lesser heights until my dad stopped bothering to grow it. As so often happens in Africa, this garden vanished into dust, forcing us to create a potted version of it. Only barely discernable ripples of soil remained, vaguely suggesting the green that once had been.

On the bank of the river, behind the well, stood an enormous Camelthorn (acacia giraffae), bearing long, white, deadly pointed thorns, the tiniest of pale yellow round flowers, and a harvest of velvety, crescent-shaped gray pods filled with shiny brown seeds, each in its own little pocket. It was underneath this ancient tree that we buried Pasha, our first German shepherd. Also near the well a Prosopis had fallen at an angle, providing us children with good opportunity for climbing. Many a time Mother would call us back to the house. *"Hände waschen! Mittagessen!"* ("Go wash your hands! Lunch is ready!") In the event that we did not heed her command, she'd call, *"Gleich rufe ich Vati!"* ("I'll call Daddy in a minute!"). It was enough of a threat to send us scampering.

Mutti was always there, like the earth, the bush, the farmlands. Sadly, she was always working. She had helped take care of her younger brothers and sisters from age seven on, getting them up and ready in the mornings, looking after them during the rest of the day. I think she forgot then what it was like to play. I don't remember her ever playing with us children. Sometimes she brought her mending or knitting to the river, sitting close by, intermittently watching our imaginations taking shape in the wet sand and the water. Now and then she came to see our creations from stones, lined up as houses, streets, and villages. Occasionally, on a Sunday, when the sap of the *wag-'n-biejties* (wait-a-bit bushes) began to flow in September, she would take us into the veld (bush) to search for the fresh drippings of their resin, glowing like gold among the thorns. She detected the minutest details around us— the tiniest flower, the smallest ant, the most colorful pebble like a diamond in a wilderness of drab stones. As a child, I suspected she could see even my thoughts.

She was a slim woman, only an inch or two shorter than my dad's five-foot-nine. Her dark brown hair, when loose, reached halfway down her back, though she always wore it plaited and pinned into a bun at the back of her head. She never cut it until two years before she died. Of all the dresses she wore over the years, the only one I recall, the one I thought most beautiful, was made of chintzy crepe with a beautiful pink-and-blue floral print, short wavy wide sleeves, and a ruffle around the neck. In the late forties, when fashion shortened the hemlines of dresses from mid-calf to just below the knee, she got embarrassed when men commented on her lovely legs. She was shy about her body. Talk about the body, let alone show it? Never! Oh, the sinfulness of the flesh!

She was reliable, quiet and tough. When we had visitors, she never said much. My dad did the talking. She did not express her political views, and, looking back, I think her views were conservative and straight-laced. Duty excluded imagination and that free flow of creativity, which is what you need to be able to play. Duty sets boundaries. Mainly she was intensely religious and pious. She never criticized her parents and expected the same from her own children. The main purpose of living was to be good, and to believe in Jesus as your Savior. Her silence was lifted after my dad had died: then she never stopped talking, not giving others much chance of having their say. Still, she was also enterprising. She learnt to drive in 1954 before my dad went to visit his mother in Germany for six months. She also learnt to speak Afrikaans so she could communicate with the Afrikaner man, Abraham Cilliers, who helped her run the farm during my dad's absence. She was definitely conscientious in creating a well run household, careful with money and all else, a bit like the sparse earth all around us, though at times soft like the wet soft soil after the rains.

Near the fallen Prosopis tree and next to one of the palms stood the cage where the beautifully black-coated Karakul lambs were kept before they were slaughtered when four days old. I sometimes sat there in the branches, watching with deadened heart how Gideon or one of the migrant workers, an *Ovambo*, (tribe in the north of the country) slit their throats. Their helpless, protest-kicking legs eventually lay still, their pitiful bleating dying away once their veins had run empty, their bright red blood covering the metal sheet, soaking the soil, forming dark clots in the sand. As I watched, I shut the doors of my soul, paralyzed by the togetherness of the tender and the terrible. As if by way of an explanation, my mother would laconically remark, *"Des einen Tod ist des andern Brot"* ("Death of one is bread for another").

In the early years the cattle *kraals* (corrals) were still attached directly to the house. Whenever the first rains came, be it in November, December, or January, the yard melted into a smelly, squelchy mass of dung and dust with myriad small brown puddles. I had great fun squeezing the soft mud through my toes, making worms. But once my dad had moved the kraals farther out, the rains quickly washed it all away. Then the true surface of the hard-baked soil was exposed, subsequently covered again with a mixture of gritty sand and yet more dust.

In those days the bed of the Omaruru River just opposite our house was about 150 yards wide. It was a serene sleepy sight in its dry state, yet terrifying when it came rushing down with the full force of its floods. Its source was farther to the northeast, in the foothills of the *Etjo*, a table mountain that was an unusual geological formation in our part of the world: exposed petrified dunes, sand from the far-off Kalahari Desert. The Etjo, the *Oserameva*, the *Otjikoko*, and the Otjimukuru Mountains edged the eastern horizon, pearls strung on a giant's necklace, landmarks of orientation and origin of many tributaries to the main river. Some low, long ranges of dolomite and a few chalk hills lay to the north while the granite *Erongo* massif faded far into the sunset.

The river formed the northern boundary of our farmlands. The Hess outpost nestled on its bank in the northeast corner where Mr. Hess had once dug the well. From there the fence ran south to the Otjimukuru Mountain, where it turned to cut west at a ninety-degree angle for another five miles, then turned another ninety degrees north and back to the river's bank. All in all, the boundary covered about thirty-five miles, marking and securing our very own patch of about 11,000 hectares—27,500 acres—on the vast continent.

This was Omburo, our land, one island isolated among the many. This is where the house stood, where we children spent the first years of our lives until we had to attend the public boarding school in Omaruru, twenty miles downriver. This was Omburo, site of my memories, dwelling of my desires.

Christmas on Omburo

WHEN I WAS a child, time as such did not exist in my mind. There was no clock to strike the hours. There was only the sun rising and setting, day followed by night followed by day in secure succession, days stringing upon days into years. Life was imbued with time. African time meant there was always time to have time. Only a few calendar markers—Christmas, Easter, and birthdays—interrupted its endless stride through the bush. I awaited these special events with great impatience, but that did not make them take place sooner.

On one long-awaited Christmas Eve in the mid-forties, when I was about eight, my father sat at the head of the dining table, as he did every day.

My mom sat to his left; my sister Karen next to her, I faced my dad, and my brothers, Hans-Erik and Jürgen, sat to his right. This was our usual seating order, each one always in the same place. The annual Christmas wreath, made with cypress or pine branches from a friend's garden, hung over the table, its four candles now burning low, having spent much of their light on previous Advent Sundays. We had just finished our traditional Christmas Eve meal: a bowl of chocolate soup with baked islands of sweet whipped egg white floating atop the sea of brown. The crisp cold of the soup was a welcome contrast to the hot dry day, dry despite our eternal hope for green on the day of Christ's birth.

The soup was more than enough for us at this hour. Any mutterings from our stomachs evaporated in our excitement about the approaching dark, when all those unimaginable secrets in the bedecked sitting room would be revealed.

We searched for the right tree that morning, cut it and placed it in a pail filled with sand in a corner of the sitting room. My parents then decorated it, keeping its beauty a surprise for us children. Besides, this night was for us the beginning of a few days' unlimited access to cookies and rare delicacies such as marzipan and pecans. We certainly did not wish to spoil our appetites for sweets yet to come!

After the meal we had to wait until the clock in the entrance hall chimed seven-thirty. Around that time the sun dipped below the horizon, allowing night to fall rapidly within thirty minutes over our world of the bush. At last my brothers and sister and I were allowed to huddle excitedly by the door of the living room, whispering, shifting from one foot to the other, elbowing one another for front space. All day long our patience had been tested and now we would reap the reward. Ever so finally Dad struck the first chords of a Christmas carol on the piano, the tune to which we traditionally entered the room of rooms. Mom opened the door while we chimed in:

Ihr Kinderlein kommet, O kommet doch all,
Zur Krippe her kommet in Bethlehems Stall!
Und seht was in dieser hochheiligen Nacht
Der Vater im Himmel für Freude uns macht.

Come little children, oh come you all!
Come to the manger in Bethlehem's stable
And see what in this most holy night
The Father in heaven such joy for us makes

There, in full view, stood the glorious, perfectly decorated acacia for which we had searched that morning, cutting it down late so its leaves would still be fresh and green in the evening. The tree's thorns and tiny leaves gleamed as the white candles on its branches filled the dark room with warm light. Silvery lead *Lametta* (tinsel) shone and twinkled and cascaded from every branch. White folded paper stars swung gently in the air, stirred by the heat of the candles' flames. As always, my parents had placed a transparency of the Holy Family—a framed silhouette of the scene in the stable cut out in black paper and pasted on to white translucent paper—on the white sheet beneath the tree, lit by a candle from behind. While gazing in rapture at our tree of hope and survival, we sang all three verses of the carol.

Christmas Eve was indeed a special time, when all of us who lived on Omburo spent a few hours together, just this once each year, to celebrate the birth of Christ. Earlier in the day, before we ate the chocolate soup, before my parents lit the tree, and before we children marched into the room of rooms, all the farmhands and their families gathered with us on our veranda to bow heads in prayer, sing Christmas carols, and exchange gifts. Only afterward did we as family celebrate on our own.

71

Although the workers were in many ways an intimate part of our daily lives, we did not share our table with them. We spent our work time together, but lived separately. We never visited them, nor they us. That was simply how it was done.

My parents taught us children to treat the farmhands respectfully, the way they did. They were interested in them as people, asking about their health, their families, and their desires. My mother and father rarely shouted at them. They certainly never beat them. We children had to say "please" and "thank you" when we wanted them to do something for us. We had to tidy our own rooms before they were cleaned. No one ever picked up after us. There were many times when we did the same chores as they did. At times we also fetched food from the coolers and wood for the stove. We peeled carrots and potatoes. At times we set the table and cleared it after meals, washed dishes, helped with the laundry. Sometimes we cleaned shoes and paraffin lamps. My brothers sometimes helped in the house, but mostly did chores in the yard or on the farmlands. There was no job we could escape from performing, and our parents set an example by doing many of the same chores themselves. We were not served hand and foot. All of us were required to do our part in the process of making a living under their guidance. We were a truly patriarchal family.

On this particular Christmas Eve *Petrus Engelbrecht* and his wife, Sara, were the first to arrive. Petrus was our shepherd, quite a tall man for a Nama. I often wondered about his surname. Engelbrecht was so European. Perhaps it was German, or maybe Dutch. Was it the name of a former white boss who was perhaps also his father? Petrus had joined my dad on the farm *Rooiwater* in the Windhoek district back in 1930 and worked for him till the day Petrus died in the late forties. Initially Dad had been his own shepherd, but he quickly hired Petrus so he could have time for the many other chores involved with running a farm. Petrus and Sara and their six children subsequently moved with Dad to all the farms he rented. On Omburo they built a group of traditional circular huts next to the road that led to the spring, farther away from our house than those of the other farmhands' dwellings, perhaps a quarter of a mile or more.

When herding the sheep, Petrus searched for the best feeding places and fended off jackals, either black-backed or silver-backed, or, more rarely, other predators such as leopards or cheetahs, perhaps a lynx or two. He kept the newborn lambs in the safety of bush kraals, reported the loss of an animal, any sickness, or mishaps concerning them. Now and then he brought the herd down to the house to be treated against worms and claw sickness in the dip by the chicken coop.

Dipping day was always filled with great commotion. The sheep were forced into the deep end and swim through the milky medicated water in the dip, loudly bleating their protest, eyes bulging with fear, legs flailing, seemingly expecting to die. They'd scramble out at the shallow end, visibly relieved. Poor things—to have to pass through such an ordeal! I sympathized with them. My own ordeal had been to swallow many teaspoonfuls of whale's liver oil, eat pounds of chopped raw liver, and drink port laced with raw egg for the sake of my iron-poor blood, pale child that I had been.

I knew only the three youngest children of Petrus and Sara: Lena, Lendina, and Gideon. The older ones lived I knew not where. The three that were around could speak Afrikaans, a little German, and, of course, their mother tongue. Petrus himself spoke Nama and some German, but Sara used only Nama. My mom spoke Nama too, as if she had imbibed it with her mother's milk. She had grown up on Lievenberg together with many Nama children. Learning their language while at play was by far the easiest way to master this four-click tongue. I myself could barely count in it. The clicks were so difficult, and without the opportunity for ample practice it seemed best left alone. But all of us children had quite a large Herero vocabulary at our disposal. For a short while my parents tried to get us children to speak one language at a time making us pay a penny for every foreign word we'd use, without much consequence and very few pennies handed over.

In the early days on Omburo, clothes and household linens were not only expensive, but also hard to come by. We could not afford ready-made items. My mother knew all the tricks and details of sewing, knitting, and embroidering. She taught Lena all of them so she could assist her with making trousers and shorts and shirts for Dad and the boys, dresses and blouses for her self and for us girls. Lena also helped with knitting socks, later with darning them. She knitted cardigans and sweaters. She helped sew sheets and pillowcases. Whatever we needed, Lena helped my mother make the item. She often added the finishing touches such as sewing on buttons, making buttonholes, and edging seams, the very tasks I detested.

Lendina's job was to clean the house every day. She swept all the rooms, washed the floors, made the beds, scrubbed the pots, and washed the tableware after meals. On Saturdays she cleaned the paraffin lamps. The methodical task involved washing the cylinders, trimming the wicks, polishing the brass, and refilling the lamps' bellies with that acrid white liquid. Saturday was also the day for Lendina to clean all shoes and sandals.

Gideon helped my mom with the garden, watering the Livingston daisies, the cacti, the Prosopis, the bougainvillea, all in their separate beds, as well as the potted plants—the ferns, the shrimp plants, and the geraniums. He raked the yard every Saturday and often gave my dad a hand with odd jobs.

Petrus, Sara, and Lena eventually died of tuberculosis, a disease prevalent in South-West Africa until the middle of the twentieth century, later almost eradicated. All of us in my family had, in fact, contracted TB at one time or another, probably from cow's milk. But each of us developed immunity to it. I still recall the moment when in 1948 all children at school were inoculated, and my looking at this patch of red spots on my left arm while the nurse told me that I did not have this disease. Adults were not inoculated as far as I knew. Many years later, in 1964, my dad died of the disease.

For the time being, however, Petrus and his family were with us on our *stoep* (veranda) on Christmas Eve. The women squatted down, carefully arranging their floor-length and voluminously wide, colorful Victorian skirts like flowers around them. The men stood farther back, leaning against the veranda's low wall, wearing their best: long pants, white short-sleeved shirts and ties, shoes polished into mirrors. Quietly they waited for everyone to arrive.

The veranda was not large, so people had to squeeze closer to make room for Paul, our Herero cattle herdsman, and his extensive family of many children and grandchildren. The little ones sat on laps, wriggled around, then settled and hushed after whispered admonishments. They all lived some miles away at the Jakobus outpost. On this day Dad brought them over on our pickup for the Christmas celebration, a great treat for the little ones.

Paul was a short fellow with very black skin and a wrinkly face. The wrinkles didn't mean he was old; faces here wrinkled early in life under the strong sun. No one knew Paul's age, not even he himself. Maybe he was fifty years old, maybe seventy. His age didn't matter. He was a man of the timeless bush. He knew our cattle so well that they were his, even though he did not own them. I often walked with him, especially around the watering places where he scrutinized the dust that collected there. "Hmm," he would mutter, "that Red Poll cow that was about to calve hasn't been here for a few days.

I have to go search for her because she probably has had the calf by now. I have to bring her here so the cheetahs won't get the calf—or her."

Often he'd pause, majestically leaning on his walking stick while surveying the kicked-up dust around the water troughs, and proclaim, "Only twenty came to drink yesterday. Wonder what happened to the rest of them." In my childhood I used to marvel at Paul's ability to know such things. Where he was focusing I could see nothing but stirred-up dust. And yet, despite being impressed, in a far recess of my soul I had daring doubts. Did he really know this? Yet somehow, invariably, he turned out to be right. This was Paul. He lived the veld. And knowing it, he was a comfort to us in the bush.

Jan, his oldest son, was the only child of the family to have completed eight years of junior school. He later became foreman for my brother Jürgen when he took over the farm. Jan liked to work and be paid on a daily basis.

"Why don't you work all week long and have a monthly salary?" my brother had asked him once.

"Why would I do that?"

"Well, you could gain more experience and earn more money that way."

"And when would I be able to spend time with my friends? When could they come to visit? When would I be able to visit them? No, I don't think I want to work all the time. I like to sit in the shade of my house, move around with it to stay cool, play my records, and have fun with my friends."

Nothing could persuade him to exchange this leisurely life for a long week's work, not even the promise of hard money. He had a point, not so? Living was more than working for pay, unless, of course, you liked your work. Perhaps the more goal-directed activity of work—an ordered life of regularity, punctuality, constancy, and industry—was alien because of his peoples' free-roving past. Perhaps you could live the way Jan did if you could afford it, or if you were prepared to make do with very little and yet survive, or if you had no desire for power or greatness, no vision of something you created that lasted beyond death, something you might be remembered by.

Alwine and her partner Uibeb, a childless Herero couple, came, also wearing their best outfits, Alwine joining the women, Uibeb the men. Like Petrus, Alwine had also worked for my dad since Rooiwater. She did our laundry every week while Uibeb chopped wood to fire the kitchen stove and did odd jobs in the yard and around the farm. They lived on a hill beyond the cattle kraals, first in huts plastered with mud and dung, later also in a house made of concrete bricks with a corrugated sheet iron roof. Only in the mid-seventies, after Jürgen had taken over Omburo, did the farmhands have running cold water. Decades later they also had hot water when it was possible to have solar-powered heating.

In addition to employing Petrus and his family, Alwine and Uibeb, and Paul and one or two of his children, my dad also employed two migrant workers. They were Ovambos, men who came from the north of the country without their families, and who contracted their labor for eighteen months, after which they returned home for six. The government not only regulated the length of their stay, it also regulated their salaries and their rations of mielie meal, sugar, salt, and fat. All of our workers also received milk, meat when available, and occasionally vegetables.

The Ovambo migrant workers joined everyone else on the veranda. They lived to the east of our house, first in one building, and later in two, each with two rooms. They also carried their water home in pails before they had running water. They did not carry them on their heads, the way Alwine did, but in their hands. Occasionally these workers were permitted to extend their stay for another six months. Sometimes they returned after a visit home because they liked working for my dad. I don't remember most of them. They never stayed for long, and once I was in boarding school I came home so rarely that it was hard for me to keep track of them.

I do remember one of them, though. He was Alfred, a young man who steadfastly saved his wages. One day he asked my mother to buy him a pair of shoes, specifying their color and size, a size too large to fit his own feet.

"Who are they for?" Mom asked him.

"My father."

"But I thought you had no father. You told me so when you first came. You said he was dead."

"Oh, yes! He died, but I still have a father!" Alfred insisted.

"Well, so is your father dead or alive?"

"My father is dead, but my other father is alive."

"What do you mean, your other father?"

"I have many fathers, not just one."

"So your other father is an uncle?"

"No, no! He is my father, not my uncle!"

Mom gave up. She didn't know how to respond. It was difficult for her, for us all, to grasp his family relationships. The families of black Africans were often so different from ours, our cultural dissonances so extreme, with seemingly unbridgeable gaps. Their families were extended and communal rather than nuclear. Anyone could be your father and your mother. Everyone was your mother and your father. Raising children must have been easier under those circumstances, losses felt less severely, or so I thought. In varied ways time was different; work and possessions were different - if they ever were discrete concepts of living.

There was also a "colored" man, Jakobus Claassen, who worked for my dad. I almost forgot about Jakobus! He was a great fixer of things: he made new handles for old tools, put locks on gates, repaired fences—he fixed anything that needed fixing. He made toys for us, blocks to build with, a pram for taking our baby-dolls for walks. On top of that he was a good bricklayer and helped make water troughs and cement bases for the water tanks. That Christmas Eve he also joined the men already standing by the wall.

When at last everyone was present, all children restless and wide-eyed, the adults quiet and patient, my dad finally lit the candles on the tree even though the sun had not yet set. He read the chapter from Matthew about Christ's birth in German. Together we sang several carols, they in their language, we in ours, Dad accompanying all of us on the piano. Sometimes we also listened to "His Master's Voice" records on a gramophone playing carols and other music.

At Christmas every employee received a special gift. One by one they stepped up to my mother, who handed the men shirts or pants, sometimes a pair of shoes, while the women received eight or twelve yards of fabric for a voluminous new dress. Everyone was given some small gift as well, perhaps a tool, or a leather belt, a brooch, yarn, a toy—usually something useful or something they had specially requested. At the end of the celebration, everyone received a loaf of bread, made at home or bought from the baker, sometimes also oranges or other fruit, perhaps some sweets, peanuts, or even a precious slab of Cadbury's chocolate. Having received their gifts, each employee shook hands with my mother. Each one said a thank you, and "Merry Christmas," then stepped outside where they showed each other their gifts, inspecting and comparing them, chatting and laughing. Occasionally they brought gifts for my parents—a chicken, a few eggs, a live tortoise or a shell they had found. Afterward Dad drove Paul and his family back to their outpost.

The candles on the tree were snuffed after this ceremony and when Dad returned, the six of us sat down to eat our chocolate soup. We still had to wait for darkness to fall, for the candles on the tree to be lit again, and for Dad to strike the first chords of *"Ihr Kinderlein kommet!"* before we could enter the decked room, singing. Only then did the hours of waiting end. My dad read the story of Christ's birth yet again. We sang more carols. Each child had to contribute something to the evening's celebration: a tune played on the piano or on the recorder, a poem, a verse or two from the Bible said by heart. Only then did our own time come for the pleasure of presents. We took turns unwrapping them, beginning with Jürgen, the youngest (how could he wait so long?) and ending with the oldest, usually my dad, or Oma Dieta while she lived with us. The gifts were usually something we had made ourselves for each other: a shirt, a lace hanky, some small embroidered cloth, hand-knitted socks, a painted plywood figure from a fairy tale. Sometimes we received a book, a pen or writing paper. Meanwhile we stuffed ourselves with our once-a-year moment of unlimited cookies, marzipan – forever the most special symbol of Christmas indulgences - walnuts, almonds, pecans, dates, and other delicacies from our heaped plates. We children exchanged what we did not like for something we liked better with someone else. Bedtime was whenever we were ready to crawl under our sheets to rest our weary heads, full tummies, and happy hearts.

Over the years, this was how Christmas Eve passed. Our annual gathering was surely curious and unusual: all these people, congregated on our veranda, members of different cultures, speaking different tongues, all, supposedly, Christians sharing a few festive moments in the name of God, together representing in miniature the mix of the wider but to me yet unknown world. Although I was always aware of these differences, they did not matter then. They did not matter ever. To me Paul and Petrus and Alwine were individuals, people who were part of our life. I knew them and was fond of them. Only much later in life I wondered about what we shared beyond our working life, beyond our faith, beyond that day. What did we ever share that lasted beyond this one silent night of the year except our humanity? Yet these childhood experiences remained the bedrock of my life, because they included this one silent night of the year, and because my parents cared about these people in the isolation of our life on the farm, a life that at least for us created lasting bonds. As in "Dances with Wolves" we depended on each other, making a living, making life possible, together.

Alwine Katjikoro

XCEPT FOR THE migrant workers, the farmhands all stayed on Omburo for a long, long time. They became a landscape surrounding me, their faces like the hot noon or the cool dusk, their smiles like the wet summer rains or the dry winter winds.

I remember Alwine best of all. She was the one who spent the most time in and around our house, the only older adult woman apart from my mother, that is, before Oma Dieta came to live with us. She often stayed with us children when our parents went to Omaruru, or were invited out for an evening meal, or had to attend the occasional funeral. It was always Alwine who stayed with us until they returned, even if only at midnight. I felt comfortable and safe having her around. We were her *"kanatjes"* (children).

Years later, when I went to boarding school, friends would ask me who Alwine was. I didn't know how to respond. Well, I told them, she lived on our farm and she did our laundry, from Monday to Friday, every week of the year. Alwine had been doing laundry for my dad since he settled on Rooiwater, which meant that by the time I was about eight she had already worked for him for fifteen years. What more could I say? She could talk a blue streak. She was ageless. Like the bush and the land she was always there. Life without her was unimaginable.

Yet she remained a mystery to me. What did she think about? Did she have dreams? Did she feel lonely at times? Did she cry? I cried, and my brothers and sister cried, but I never saw Alwine cry. Nor did I ever see my mother or my dad cry. Maybe grownups just didn't cry. Did she love Uibeb, the man she lived with? Did they kiss? They certainly lived together like my mom and dad did. Yet they had no children. For us that meant above all that we had no one else to play with other than our siblings.

Despite all these mysteries, one thing, however, was certain: Alwine was most important to me. She seemed to love me, to love all of my family. Sometimes I felt we were her family.

When I was little I often waited for Alwine to arrive for work on a Monday morning. Here she comes! I'd tell myself as soon as I heard her voice in the distance. I then dashed to the gate in our yard, forcing my feet under the wire mesh that covered its frame so that I could stand on the bottom bar and swing on it as I waited for her to appear. I watched her as she walked down the footpath that led from her home through the kraals and past the chicken coop to the gate.

As I stood swinging and waiting, I heard her voice undulating across the distance with intense emotion. I knew some Herero, the language she now sent out in a rapid stream of words, her voice rising and falling, moaning like the wind when it came down the river valley. She understood German but spoke it in a broken way, the way I spoke Herero. Even so we managed to communicate with more than merely words.

"Riro . . . I . . . ome . . . moro . . . " I caught only fragments of words she uttered, so I could never make out what she was shouting. Who was she talking to? Was she upset? Just talking to her self? I wasn't sure. No one else was in sight. I was convinced she wasn't addressing me since she had not seen me yet, or so I thought. Perhaps she's letting Mom know that she's on her way to work.

As Alwine approached she appeared at first as a distant blue patch with a loud voice. Once she came closer I could see her dress more clearly, her skirt draping to the ground, dragging through the dust. It was the proud length of a Herero woman's long-sleeved Victorian-style dress that always deeply impressed me. Only Herero women wore such long dresses. Nama women also had long ones, but theirs were different, reaching no further than their ankles. Alwine usually made her dresses from a blue cotton fabric with a patterned print of darker blue or white. During, and even after World War II, this was often the only fabric available, hence commonly used. Her Singer sewing machine stood on the smooth, firm mud-and-dung floor of her home, a solid hand-operated machine instead of a treadle operated by foot like my mom had.

Every day she draped a piece of the same cloth as her dress around her head in a high turban. Young women draped their turbans in a dashing style, angled forward like the horns of cattle, as if to shade their faces from the sun or shield their eyes from intrusive glances of men passing by. The rounded height of Alwine's headdress acknowledged that she was an older woman. Her turban kept her hair and ears covered, and I sometimes wondered what her hair looked like. Was it a mass of peppercorn curls, like Uibeb's or Gideon's?

Her chocolate brown face looked soft and wrinkled, chiseled by the unforgiving sun and dry air. Her brown eyes peeked out from under the lids, disappearing in their folds when she smiled, which was not often. Her nose was wide and a little flat. Her lips curved softly, flexibly, and she had the best pout

I ever saw. I sometimes tried to copy it, but I couldn't quite manage to mold my lips into the same shelf-like shape under my nose the way she did.

As she stepped closer, her feet bare and dusty, her shouting muted into mutterings. She knew then that I was waiting for her. She smiled at me.

"*Moro! Moro, okatiti* (Good morning, little one)!" she greeted me. "*Warara nawa* (Did you sleep well)?*"

"Moro, Alwine. Iiiii (Yes)!" I replied, extensively expanding the yes. "Warara nawa?" I asked her back.

"Iiiiiiiii . . . nawa, nawa," was her even longer drawn-out reply.

I swung to open the creaking gate so she could step into the yard. I did not take her hand but kept a small distance between us, a sign of the awe I felt in her mysterious presence. This gesture of respect generally appeared to satisfy her.

"*Onguaje tjimbis'o okungura ngunda ambin'o vinamuinjo?*" she asked me. (Why did she have to work when she was a rich woman with livestock?) I had no idea. Maybe she just liked my family, was my first thought. But then another came to me.

"*Weil Du meine Kleider gern sauber haben willst* (Because you like my clothes to be clean)!"

"*Hapo* (Of course)!" she said, smiling broadly.

From the moment she entered the yard I followed her around, watching her perform the various chores connected with washing. My curiosity about her transformed me into her second shadow. Sometimes I helped a little, if she allowed me to. Doing our laundry was her only job, and it took her all week to wash and iron everything to perfection.

She loved to have coffee. Before doing anything else, she made a small fire to boil water for the sweet-smelling brew she would drink all morning long. "*Koviungura mevaza pumbara zere,*" she said. ("I'll get to the work when I get to it.")

That was fine with me. I closed the gate, first hopping impatiently around her, soon running ahead while she padded over to the corner of the yard to make the fire where Dad dumped the dry wood for Uibeb to chop into pieces usable for the stove. Over the years the small wood chips had formed a foot-thick layer, so there were plenty of bits for making a fire.

It looked so easy when she started it. I watched her collect a handful of dry grass and cover it with a small hut of chips over which she placed a few larger pieces of soft wood that burned easily. Then she struck a match and held it to the grass. Sometimes she used a few live coals from the kitchen to light the fire. It fascinated me to see the sudden burst of flames and sparks as the grass caught fire, then quickly shriveling into dark worms of ashes as the chips began to glow.

At this moment Alwine took a deep breath and blew gently into the glow, fanning it. I helped. I filled my lungs and, with my lips rounded, blew out the air from the depth of my small being in a long, thin stream. The glow increased. We blew faster and faster until, suddenly, with a little pop, flames began to leap upward, still a bit blue but turning yellow as the tongues became larger. A wisp of smoke rose from their tips, up and up. The flames now licked over the larger logs, blackening them until they too sent up tongues of fire, spitting sparks all around.

Once the fire got going she walked over to the only tap in our yard to fill her blackened kettle with water, after which she placed it carefully on three rocks that lay around the flames. She squatted on her heels, tucking her blue skirt under. Next she reached into a pocket hidden in the folds of her dress for her pipe and a pouch with tobacco. She plugged the pipe and lit it. My mother disdained smoking, but I was fascinated. My dad smoked a pipe. Sometimes, when he felt rich, he allowed himself a cigar. And now, here, Alwine was also smoking a pipe!

We squatted, waiting for the water to boil. We seldom spoke. I watched the dancing flames and followed the pale puffs of smoke as they rose from her mouth. I loved the warmth of the fire on my face while I still felt the cool morning air on my back. Soon, she added several handfuls of ground coffee to the boiling water. The air immediately burst with its aroma, especially when she poured the brewed liquid into her enameled tin mug, adding milk and lots of brown sugar. It was a dreamy, peaceful time for me: the fire burning, Alwine smoking and drinking coffee, the two of us just sitting there together. There was no rush. Tomorrow was whenever. Now was the endless moment of Africa.

As we sat there, her man Uibeb arrived, waking us from our daydreams. He looked sleepy.

"*Ove ndino weya rukuru!*" Alwine greeted him. Indeed, Uibeb had come early today. "*Okokuwa* (That's good)!" she said. "*Nambano kake ozongune* (Now please chop some pieces of wood)!" She royally extended a hand toward the heap of dry branches.

Uibeb squatted. *"Ohakahana oyaye* (What's the hurry)?"

"Konokutjiwa kutja mbis! Okungura? Nu mehepa omuriro!" she impatiently told him. He knew she had to work and that she needed the wood for the fire. I looked over at Uibeb. He didn't move despite this exhortation.

"Basuvera okosiva jandje muhuk'omunene," he said with a big grin. He also loved his coffee first thing in the morning. She simply had to smile while she poured some into her mug and handed it to him.

When he had emptied the mug he gave it back to her. He got up, stretched, and said, *"Nambano opuvo* (Now this is it)!" He walked over to the big block of wood, picked up the axe, placed a branch on the block, swung the axe up over his shoulder, and brought it down with resounding force, shouting: *"Ka ekuva* (Chop, axe)! *Ka ekuva!"*

She began energetically to pile more wood onto the fire. She shifted a large iron tripod over it. The pot was filled with water, which needed to heat so the sheets could be boiled. Meanwhile we ambled over to our bathroom and began taking out the clothing we had soaked in the bathtub the night before. Soaking was an important part of the process of washing. I marveled on seeing the dirty brown water that remained after we had removed all the soaked items.

She then carried the sheets back to the fire, where she dumped them into the tripod together with a cotton bag filled with leftover pieces of soap my mom saved for doing the wash. For a while she stirred the pot with a long wooden pole. Afterward she pounded the sheets in machinelike fashion with a metal bell. Once they were boiling, she settled in the bathroom beside a smaller tub to begin hand-washing our clothes with a bar of cream-colored homemade soap, afterward rinsing them. It took at least two days to complete the job of washing and rinsing everything.

When she was done with some items, we carried them in pails over to the Casoarinas. There I handed them to her so she could pin them with wooden pegs to the many wires that were strung from one tree to the next. Everything dried quickly, usually within half an hour. As she took the dry pieces down, she piled them into my arms for me to carry to the bathroom table. Sometimes she took a rest in between taking down dry and hanging up wet items. She'd squat there by the trees, taking out her pipe for a brief smoke. When she got up and walked away, she left behind a big round wet spot. I stared at it. Did she really do that right there? Does she not wear knickers? I gazed at her long dress. Perhaps she doesn't. It might be too hot to wear those under such a long dress. We all used the bush for our needs when we had to, so it surprised me that she did that right there in our yard. Oh, well, in a few minutes the spot would again be as dry as the dust that lay all around.

Once all the dried laundry was collected, the real fun began: we sprinkled each piece—and sometimes each other—with cold water, then rolled it tightly and packed it into our old baby bath. My mother had kept this bath long after we children had outgrown it. She had washed our dog Pasha in it. She made soap in it from donkey fat when no soap was to be had in the forties, soap that was sold as far away as South Africa. In those days about a thousand donkeys roamed our farm, decimating the grazing we so desperately needed for the sheep and cattle. For a few years my dad bought a permit to shoot them. Every scrap of the animals was used: the skins, the meat, the fat, even the bones. Nothing was wasted. And now, once the bath was filled with many rolls of clothes, Alwine covered them with a hefty towel to keep them from drying out.

Only too soon it was past noon and hot. Time to eat lunch and have a rest! Alwine took some *omaere* (sour milk) in a small pail from our cooler outside and placed it on her turban, balancing it adeptly. She left, saying, "*Ovikohua vondova embi vendji urisa ejuva arihe.*" Yes, I thought, doing laundry all day long is tiring. I watched her walk through the little gate amazed she could carry the pail on her head like that. I had tried many times to carry an empty pail on my head, yet could not manage to balance it for more than a step or two. But now I was tired also, so I went over to the kitchen to check what my mom had prepared for lunch.

In the afternoon, when Alwine returned and had sprinkled the sheets with a bit of water, she and Mom had some fun. First they folded the sheets in half lengthwise.

"*Nambano menana omasa* (Now pull hard)!" my mom told her.

"*Menana* (I'm pulling)!" she replied. They stretched the sheet a couple of times, lengthwise as well as diagonally. Then they folded it and stretched it again, giving it a final tug at each end.

"So, *nambano yanga* (Now let's fold it)," Mom said to her.

"*Iiiiii, yanga nana* (Fold it right)!" she told Mom.

Suddenly my mom gave a strong tug. It surprised Alwine, but as she teetered to regain her balance her eyes twinkled with laughter. The two of them often played this trick on each other. You never knew who would play it when.

"Onana nomasa! Mondji wisa!" Alwine told my mom not to pull so hard. They both giggled and laughed. This in itself was remarkable. Mother was usually unemotional. It wasn't until the end of her life that I discovered she even had a sense of humor. Until my dad died, she had been a quiet person. She started to talk much more after he was gone, unfortunately without – ever - intending to stop.

So now they continued the work in all seriousness. Suddenly Alwine gave the sheet an unexpected tug and it was Mom's turn to laugh while trying to regain her balance. But soon they were serious again, stretching each sheet back into a proper rectangle, neatly folding it, stacking all into a pile, covering them until they were going to be mangled.

I was always eager to turn the big wheel of the mangle. At first I looked on as Alwine fed the sheets between the two rollers. Then, still turning the wheel, I leaned over and watched them come out on the other side, smoothly pressed.

"Kann ich das jetzt machen? Bitte, bitte (Can I do it? Please, please)!" I begged her when we were alone.

"Ts, ts, katiti," she'd say disapprovingly, but moved over to let me do it. *"Pass auf Deine Finger!"* she'd add in German. ("Be careful. Watch your fingers now!")

She then turned the wheel while I struggled to pass the sheets through without a single crease. I so worried about my fingers, imagining them getting caught and coming out on the other side, flat, just like the sheets. I focused intently until the last bit of cloth had almost passed through the rollers, rushing quickly to the other side to catch the piece and hang it on the triangular wooden stand to dry completely.

Days of ironing followed days of washing and drying. The irons were pointed at the front, hollow, with vents on the sides and a handle on top to lift the scalloped lid and place red-hot coals inside. I watched her with admiration as she flicked the coals from the fire outside into the irons with her bare hand. Shuddering, I grabbed it to check that she had not burned herself. She smiled at me.

"Ts, ts, katiti," she clicked, shaking her head in amusement.

She usually filled three irons with coals, carrying only one back to the table where she began the ironing. She'd spit on a finger and lightly touch the iron's bottom to check if the heat were right. A sizzle meant she could begin.

Since I couldn't help her with ironing, I visited her again only toward the end of the day to assist with folding the ironed pieces that had dried on the stand, carrying them to wherever my mom told me to. Occasionally I noticed a yellow or even a brown iron-shaped patch on a vest or shirt, signs that the iron had been too hot. It was truly an art to iron the fabrics without creases and burns. She did it so well.

At sundown each day, she picked up her pail of water, put it on her head, and walked a slow, tall, proud walk along the path through the kraals back to her home at the top of the hill. Through the weeks and years, laundering melted in my memory into one long process from soaking to ironing and folding, all inextricably linked with Alwine.

My parents told me once that they had asked about her birthday, but that she could not tell them when or where she was born. Maybe birthdays were not as important to her and her people as they were to us. The Herero certainly used to recall time differently. They did not keep track of years by counting them; instead, they remembered events, such as "the year of the terrible drought" or "in the year of the great rains." We had no idea who her parents were or if she had other family. It had been rumored that she was a niece of the great Herero chief Samuel Maharero. Who knows! No one ever visited. As for me, she was part of my family.

I remember studying her face, trying to see beyond the brown surface of her skin. Sometimes she had bloodshot eyes. They scared me. When I asked my mom about them, she'd say, "Guess she had too much beer last night!" I had seen such beer in Alwine's white enamel pail standing in the shade of her house. People made their own beer with mielie meal, sugar, peas, and water, but they were not supposed to. It was illegal. The mixture became a milky liquid, tickling the nose with its pungent smell. Some people said it was good. "It has many vitamins!" Others said it was simply bad to drink. "Too much alcohol!" they'd add critically. My dad was the only one I knew who drank "real" beer, Windhoek Lager, or Hansa Lager, from a large brown bottle. I surprised him one afternoon as our siesta ended when he was sitting in the verandah, drinking Lager from one of the bottles. I rushed away, scared, thinking he was an alcoholic. But really he never drank much as I discovered on carefully scrutinizing his consumption. Perhaps beer was expensive, or, more likely, my mom didn't like his drinking it, influencing him with her ascetic pietism.

Compared with other workers, who also kept animals on farms, Alwine was a rich woman. She possessed about thirty head of cattle and a large herd of goats. Her animals were her pride and she usually took no more than milk from the cows. She rarely sold an ox or even one small goat. My mother had to persuade her every now and then to do so in order to buy herself some things she wanted—a good chair, more colorful fabric, or perhaps something she needed, like shoes. Although she sometimes did buy fabric or shoes, she never bought what I thought was real beer. Instead, she brewed it in her enamel pail.

Alwine kept her home spare and simple. My dad had built her a small house with concrete bricks on top of the stony hill beyond the kraals next to her *pondok,* the traditional circular hut made with dry branches plastered over with a mixture of mud and dung and a floor made of the same. The brick house had two rooms covered with a corrugated metal roof. Inside one room was a steel-framed bed with a mattress, perhaps a chest with drawers, and a chair. A few dresses hung on nails in the wall. In the other room an enameled basin and a jug stood on the floor next to smaller enameled dishes and plates, and some utensils—a ladle, spoons, forks, knives—lay around.

The pondok had only one entrance, but it was cool inside, cooler than the concrete house ever was. In front of the hut was her "kitchen": a fireplace with three large stones on the edge of a heap of ashes. A blackened tripod stood in the ashes, a coffeepot on one of the stones, while a few more pots hung overhead in the acacia branches. She had no bathroom for washing herself or her clothes. There was no toilet. There was no running water. She had to carry it all the way from our yard, about a quarter mile, pail by pail, balancing each load on her head. There was no garden, not even a potted one like ours. A few acacias provided meager shade.

I don't recall ever visiting her on my own, only occasionally with my mother. I had a vague feeling I was not supposed to go there, as if some invisible fence existed between our house and hers, something other than the fences of the kraals. I never questioned this, so I did not visit her alone. Alwine and Uibeb had slowly worn the footpath from their quarters to our house all by themselves, walking back and forth day by day, over a long time.

Years later I once visited the ruins of her home, filled with memories while sitting on a nearby rock. Some acacias and wag-'n-bietjie (wait-a-bit) thorn bushes were still around, a few tufts of grass rooted in patches of softer soil. Most of the roof of the building had disintegrated, as had the pondok. It must have been terribly hot in summer in that concrete house, very cold in winter. And lonely, ever so lonely, just like a green tree in the desert.

Apart from the rumor that Alwine was the great Chief Samuel Maharero's niece, there was also one that claimed she was a witch. This was supposed to explain why she had no children. "Witches don't like children," the grapevine whispered. Supposedly that was why other adult Herero and their children stayed away from our place: to avoid the witch. But apparently my brothers and sister and I were immune to her spells, though it left us with no other children to play with. To me, in the years of my innocence, she was simply Alwine, the woman who washed our laundry and who sometimes took care of us when our parents were out on an afternoon or evening.

On finishing my junior school years in Omaruru, I left South-West Africa to attend high school and later university in Cape Town. In all those years I was able to come home only twice a year. On one of these visits I noticed that Alwine was absent. My parents told me then that she had taken her cattle and goats and had moved away to another farm. They had tried, unsuccessfully, to locate her after that. I hoped she had not moved because of unhappiness, or because others envied her riches. Nevertheless, she may have been unhappy or lonely and just wanted to live with her own folks. Our cattle herdsman, Paul, who himself had also moved away but still occasionally visited my parents, mentioned on one of his visits that he heard she had died.

It saddens me not to know where her grave is. Graves remind us of the departed, of those we have known and loved, whom we remember even when they have turned to dust because they took us by the hand and helped us become what we are. Our grief and tears recall our past, reminding us where we came from, while also forcing us to consider where we are heading.

I have a large, beautiful portrait of a Himba Herero woman done in pencil. From the wall near my piano, she looks from under a traditional leather headdress over the living room and out to my garden. It is not a portrait of Alwine, yet every time I look at it I think of her, wondering what became of her and how her life might have ended. Life in Africa tends to vanish without a trace. Everywhere dust returns to dust only too easily. So it was with my Alwine.

Neighbors

THE TELEPHONE IN the entrance hall stabbed the air with our Morse code signal on the farm line we shared with eight other neighbors. Short-long-long! Short-long-long! Short-long-long! The sound easily punctured the thick walls right into my bedroom. Outside you could probably hear it miles away.

I continued to read, trying to keep my attention on the pages of Grimm's Fairy Tales. But the code was persistent. It seemed to say, impatiently, "Where are you? Short-long-long! Why is no one answering? Short-long-long! Come on now! Hurry up! Someone answer!"

I was getting impatient also. Where was Mom? Short-long-long! Why didn't she answer the phone? Short-long-long! My irritation with the interfering sound grew but I didn't budge from my bed. "Someone else can get the stupid phone," I growled under my breath, turning another page. I don't want to. I'm busy! But as it kept on ringing annoyingly, I finally felt compelled to answer.

I glanced at the clock above the door in the hall that led to the dining room. It was just four in the afternoon. Where is everybody? My dad had gone to Omaruru as he did every Friday to do the shopping and run errands. It seemed to me he had been away all day, probably getting little done as he always stopped for a chat with anyone he met. Going with him always meant waiting for him to stop a conversation before continuing to get to the next item on the shopping list. And the chats could last quite a while. So, that was where he was now, but where was Mom? Where was Hans-Erik? He liked to answer the phone. What was he up to? Short-long-long! I rushed out to the yard and yelled, "*Mutti! Muttiiiii! Hörst du nicht das Telefon* (Don't you hear the phone ringing)?"

No sooner had I called her than I rushed back to where the brown box of the handle-operated telephone hung behind the wide door. I grabbed it. "Helge, *wo ist Mutti* (Where is Mother)?" my dad asked on the other end of the line. "I think we have a veld fire! The bush on Omburo is burning. There is a pillar of smoke by the Otjimukuru Mountain!" The urgency of his voice struck like a fist into the hollow of my stomach. I dropped the receiver, dashed back into the yard, and screamed even more loudly for my mom. "*Ich komm ja schon!*" she exclaimed, already running down the path from the chicken coop toward the house.

"Where on earth have you been?" I scolded her. "Did you not hear the phone ring? Dad says there is a bush fire on our farm!"

She ran into the hall and grabbed the dangling phone to listen. She instantly gasped, fear making her small blue eyes as big as they could get. Dad told her to call Uncle Wilhelm and Brian, our closest neighbors, and to ask the operator to alert the police as well as the whole neighborhood.

As she began making the calls for help, I ran into the yard to look for the pillar of smoke Dad had mentioned. There it was! Puffs of powdery gray paint brushed up against the blue of the sky, like a signal from James Fenimore Cooper's Indians in his book "The Last of the Mohicans." No orange blaze appeared yet on the horizon. My heart pounded with excitement and fear, my imagination already in flames.

My brothers and sister joined me, and together we speculated how the fire could have started and where exactly it was burning. There had been veld fires before this day, only far, far away, like the one that had crawled through the dark of night over the Oserameva Mountain, a thin, glowing yellow worm against its black belly. Clearly this smoke was rising from somewhere along our southern border, or from somewhere beyond it on Okahupua, the neighboring farm. That meant it had not yet reached our farmlands. Impatiently we waited for Dad to come home. He said he'd hurry, but the hour that it took for him to drive along the bumpy, curvy track home seemed to last much longer.

Thank goodness no one lived on Okahupua. It had no well or bore, just a *vley*, a shallow pond that provided water for a short period during the rainy season. And now in July, in the dry season from June to December, this vast fire was racing across its acres toward our farmlands.

Our neighbors were racing their way toward us as well. We saw Brian Enslin and Uncle Wilhelm often, but the rest of our "neighbors" were merely acquaintances. They lived several miles away, each on their own fenced-in space, neighbors of a more distant kind. We met them on occasion in Omaruru while shopping, or picking up mail at the post office, at church on a Sunday or in town at auctions, bazaars, and occasionally at the bimonthly bioscope.

Although we did not see our more distant neighbors that often, we knew all there was to be known about them, just as they knew all about us. We heard how many pounds a neighbor was paid for his cattle, or how deep his debt was. We heard about other, more embarrassing things, messes, such as the social indiscretions of fights, or of romantic affairs. We knew every greasy spot on their tablecloths, they probably ours. Nevertheless, we all helped each other out whenever necessary. We needed our neighbors, especially on days like today. It was good to know they were there, that they could be depended upon. Decades later, under Namibian law, everyone had to help in such times of disaster as there was no fire-brigade in this large country.

The homestead of our closest neighbors stood on the northern bank of the Omaruru River, a mile-and-a half upstream, just opposite the hot spring. Their farmhouse had a tall square tower, its pointed red roof glowing from afar like the beacon of a lighthouse across the stands of gloomy acacias. Although it was relatively near, we rarely had contact with the families who lived there. Even without water the river proved more of a barrier than actual fences.

Word about our fire spread as fast as the fire itself. Uncle Wilhelm and Brian were the first to arrive, long before my dad did. The homestead of Uncle Wilhelm, Aunt Amanda, and their six children was seven miles to the east. In all the years I lived on Omburo I walked over there only two or three times. Sometimes we visited each other on a Sunday; sometimes they stopped by on their way to town to ask if my parents needed errands done. When stopping at our house on his own, Uncle Wilhelm usually had a long chat with my dad. The two of them would scan the weather of the moment, the weather that was expected; they'd discuss how grazing and water resources were holding up, how the cattle and other animals were doing. Inevitably, they would also explore the political landscapes.

His wife, Aunt Amanda, was a beautiful woman. Her fine hair was dark, a little wavy, stray wisps escaping the tight little bun at the nape of her neck, softening the edges of her bony face. Her skin was translucent, peachy soft, the cheekbones high. She was as jittery as the plovers, her eyes blue pools of panic as she stepped out of the truck only to exclaim, "I don't have the time! I can't stay!" After exchanging a few sentences with my mom or dad, she'd rush off to do all those many chores she felt she had to complete. She had planted a large citrus garden by the nest of small buildings that were their home. Frost came rarely, but when it did, it brought great excitement with the lighting of nightly fires to save the fruit. She also kept geese, ducks, and other waterfowl, selling them as roasters, especially over Christmastime. And she baked the best Stollen I ever tasted, richly pitted with almonds and raisins and orange-ade, her annual Yuletide gift to family and friends.

Life on the farm was work, too much work for her. Above all, it was isolating. Uncle Wilhelm was frequently away, taking care of their cattle up north on Soris. That left Aunt Amanda too often alone with the children. Raising five boys and a girl was more than she could accomplish comfortably. During the six years of her husband's internment she had lived with Oma Dieta on Lievenberg. Later, while the children were still under age seven, and before they attended boarding school in Omaruru as we did, their two oldest boys,

Sieghart and Manfred, (the two in the check pants in the photo) came to stay with us to be taught the three R's by my grandmother, like my mom had taught Hans-Erik and me.

From time to time Uncle Wilhelm went hunting with Brian. Sometimes they shared the meat of a kudu or an oryx they had shot. Brian helped Dad and others clear the unpaved tracks all across the farm and along the fences with one of his scrapers, helped mend fences, and dropped off loads of dry wood he'd collected. Now, however, they studied the billowing pillar that darkened the late afternoon sky, indicating that the fire was moving closer. Even from this distance the sight began to strike terror in our hearts.

"We need to get hold of Uibeb, Petrus, and the two Ovambos, and pick up Paul on the way," Uncle Wilhelm suggested.

"Yes, everyone that is here has to come along," Brian agreed. "Does Staby have empty sacks around? We should also take as much water as we can. He must have some old milking cans around. They can easily hold about twenty to twenty-five gallons each. And what about some axes?"

Uncle Wilhelm showed Brian the milking cans, their sides dented through years of transportation, now rusty and dusty from standing around for the longest time. Brian began carrying them out to the tap in the yard, filling them for the task ahead while my uncle summoned the farmhands. They gathered as many axes as they could find, as well as empty Hessian sacks, those roughly woven bags that held sugar or salt and other staples. They would put all items to good use.

Brian was a big, strong man, irascible, balding, wearing glasses. You could tell he loved machinery. He was always tinkering with his trucks and tractors and bulldozers. He looked happiest when he wore his dirty, oily overalls, when his hands were covered with grease, his nails all lined black. He was away often, building dams for farmers and for the government around the country: dams across rivers, dish dams (saucer-like hollows meant to catch rain water) and weirs. There was even a time when he made bores. I was wary of Brian, having more than once seen his eyes flashing, his voice booming in anger, seemingly ready to raise a fist, though I don't know if he ever really lashed out.

Brian owned thirty acres adjacent to our land, about three miles from our stead, land the neighbors a few miles farther west along the road to the village had sold him. Brian called this patch of alluvial soil "Peter Pan." He turned the bush of that plot into a lush green garden, growing mostly lucerne for fodder, selling it as far away as South Africa. He marketed various kinds of vegetables in Walvis Bay, selling a truckload every two weeks during the summer season. His wife, Hermine, planted many fruit trees, oranges, pomelos, clementines, lemons, figs, peaches, and apricots, and yards of vines for grapes and, most importantly, a jungle of flowers that glowed in the sun and ended up in our vases. The building of dams came later.

Brian and Hermine were a hospitable couple, fun to visit and the best of neighbors, always prepared to help, always generous with a ready gift from the garden. Three miles was close enough for us to venture on foot over to their home along the river's bank many a time, a bank quite overgrown with grasses, acacias, thorny bushes, and brush. Occasionally we'd get caught in a barely visible yet enormously strong cobweb, its strands spun from one tree to another, obstructing our way. The strands stuck all over you and were hard to remove, the terrifying, nameless large black spider, a glowing golden cross on its back, lurking somewhere, ready to pounce on any prey that might get entangled in its web — including humans, I wildly imagined.

Coming upon animals such as leopards or cheetahs on the trip was a constant worry. It seldom happened, although one day my mother and Jürgen, on returning this way from Peter Pan, breathlessly bubbled with excitement about the cheetah they had encountered along the way. They and the cheetah had frozen in surprise over the unexpected meeting, staring at each other for what must have seemed eons, until my mom, stepping forward with a loud "Wah!" caused it to take off across the riverbed with long, loping strides, its tail high, stopping at a distance to look back and make sure it was not being pursued. As nothing more disastrous than this ever occurred, the bush kept luring us for the walk, beckoning us with both hopes and fears and excitement of adventure, with the warmth and safety of Peter Pan or our home embracing us at either end of the effort.

Brian's mother tongue was English, but he also spoke German and Afrikaans and some Herero. As he and Hermine spoke three and four languages they would sometimes converse in all of them. *"Ag jene man, hoe gaan dit nou* (How are you now?) Would you like a glass of water? *Ich habe ganz kuehles Wasser im Eisschrank* (I have really cold water in the fridge)." Neither of them ever seemed to notice their gliding from one tongue into another. However, their way of talking seemed to be still somewhat more reasonable than my cousins' and brothers' conversations. One day Sieghart and Manfred came over to show off Manfred's newly acquired motorbike – and although its make eludes my memory, their conversation did not.

Manfred, after stopping with a roar and cloud of dust in our backyard, exclaimed:

"Man, jesses, die pad ist darrem lellek! Da ist so viel Wellblech und kein Padskrapper zu sehen! *Jees man, the road is really terrible. So much corrugation and no road scraper in sight.* Zum Glück ist das Bike nicht gekalbt, dann hätten wir noch futsam laufen müssen. *Luckily the bike did not break down, then we would have had to walk the rest of the way.* Dazu sahen wir noch mehrere ohorongos die pad überqueren, und ein paar doowe beester lagen sommer mitten auf der pad. *We also saw a number of kudus cross the road, and a few stupid cattle just lying in the middle of the road.*

Sieghart: Ja man, ich bin dabei amper abgefallen. Der Mankie hatte solch einen spoed drauf. *Yes man, I almost fell off. Mankie drove so fast .* Ich dachte auch das bike fällt sommer so in pieces. *I thought the bike would break up.* Und papwiel hätten wir auch noch haben können. *We could also have had a flat* – Man, der outjie reit darrem schnell. *Man the guy rode fast!*

Hans-Erik: Yes, man! Es macht so baie krach, da kann man schon denken das fällt auseinander. *Yes man, it's so noisy one could easily think it might fall apart.*

Trotzdem denke ich das ist schon ein kwaies bike. *But I still think it is a great bike.*

Und wie baie marieba hat dich das gekostet? *And how much money did it cost?*

Sieghart: Zu stief. Wragtig zu stief! *Too much! Far too much!*

Jürgen: (ganz der mechanic) (quite the mechanic)

Ich hätte das bike nooit gekauft. *I would have never bought it.* Du musst unbedingt die schocks checken lassen, *You really need to have it checked.* Ausserdem scheint die gearbox ziemlich geschtrippt. *And besides the gearbox seems pretty used up.*

Nee man, wragtig, und du willst das auf der plaas gebrauchen? *Want to use it on the farm?* Keine Kahns! Das kannst du net vergessen. *No chance! Forget that!*

Yes, really, and so the conversation continued for hours. You get the gist!

Well, back to the fire. When my dad finally returned from the village, everyone in the yard was talking in this mixed-up way, their voices filled with foreboding and excitement and speculation. Was it a fire started by lightning? By someone dumb enough to throw a cigarette butt out a car window? Heads were shaking at such thoughts as all hands hurried to finish loading the trucks. Although everyone expected it to be a long night, the determination written on the faces expressed the hope for a short one. A few men had to make a running jump onto Brian's truck, as he was the first to pull away in a hurry.

Even more neighbors arrived to help battle the blaze. Our yard was soon filled with parked trucks. Men shook hands or waved them about as their raucous voices filled the air like smoke. They had brought with them as many farmhands as they could muster, as well as axes for chopping branches to help beat out the flames, to clear a wide strip of grass and brush to stop the flames from spreading. They also brought more sacks and countless barrels of water. After giving them all directions, my mom left with the last vehicle. Silence now settled over the yard like a thick, suffocating blanket. The roar of the trucks faded slowly into the dusk. I stared after them, toward the mountain where the glow of the seemingly slowly advancing fire began to light up the sky. Fires are flashy, my dad had said. They are fast, devouring the grass like a hungry monster, eating sticks and branches and brush, lashing out in all directions, suddenly leaping ahead with a puff of wind to yet untouched veld. How I wished I could see all of this!

Left behind, I was no longer afraid of the fire. I was mad for not having been allowed to go along to witness excitedly its taming. My brother Hans-Erik went "because he was older and more capable and could help." Boys! They always got to do more exciting things than girls. Was I not as capable? Obviously neither Karen nor Jürgen could pitch in. You have to realize they were still really little. But I was only fifteen months younger than Hans-Erik. I crept into my parents' bed, sulking and staring into the dark while their bedroom clock boomed away the timeless minutes.

The next day I woke in my own bed before dawn, having missed all the commotion of people returning from saving our farm from the fire. "It took us most of the night to put out the flames, just inside our fence," my mom told me. Feeling cheated yet relieved, I felt lucky and grateful that we had such helpful neighbors. Together they helped limit the damage our land might have suffered. This time our loss was small compared with that which others had suffered in times of bigger fires, in times of other disasters like drought or floods or sickness.

In Africa that is how all people have survived ever since Olduvai: together and depending on each other. Here, no one could survive alone in this endless, unforgiving space. Yet even with good neighbors light and shadow, fire and rain, all fall differently across the expanses of being. In our corner of Africa this was simply the way of life.

The Smell of Life

R AIN IS AN unreliable and usually unexpected visitor in South-West Africa. Summer's clouds spell both promise and privation. Beautiful and bulging as they might be, they are forever pregnant with the uncertainty of which it will be: rain, or no rain. And although the hope for rain was not always fulfilled, hope remained the rain of our souls, the nourishment of our endurance to survive.

When rain did come, it often brought disappointment because it was either too little or too much, too early or too late. After the end of the dry and cold season that began in May or June, when the implacable blowing of the east or west winds stopped, and August came upon us with its dry and searing heat, the tiny yellow flowers of acacias announced spring for no more than two weeks in September. Their fragrance moved everyone to yearn for the little rains to fall in October and November to at least renew the green of the bush. Only too often, though, the months till December remained bone dry, dream as intensely as we might of a green Christmas. Then the waiting for the big rains intensified. But whether little or big, rain seldom came as needed, even though that was what everyone expected. At times either its floods, or their lack and the accompanying drought, simply swept away any dreams of abundance anyone may have harbored. Rain here has rarely been kind to life of any sort.

On a Saturday early one December, I woke up when it was still dark. As I lay there I felt the hard horsehair mattress underneath and the warmth of the sheet around me, protecting me against both the crisp cool of the morning and the sting of mosquitoes that began their buzz at this hour. Karen was still fast asleep in her bed in the opposite corner of our room. It was silent next door where Hans-Erik and Jürgen slept.

Mom and Dad are probably awake and worrying, I thought. At this stage of the dry season everyone was concerned about rain. Each year the same tensions arose. By this time my father carried with him an air of such intense worry that it invaded our whole family like a cancer that quietly permeates a body. Water was so precious around here that the Batswana in neighboring Botswana even chose their word for rain, pula, as the name of their currency.

I wriggled around on my mattress to find the hollows that best fit my body. It felt as hard as the baked earth outside. I wondered if one could do something to that earth to soften it, the way my mother occasionally opened the blue-and-white-striped cover of my mattress, took out the balled-up horse hair, teased it into soft clouds, and stuffed it all back in. Rain definitely could transform the hard earth into a soft, nourishing womb.

As I looked out our bedroom window, I thought of Oma Dieta, who had told me that, to some of the Khoi San, the stars were hunters. The greatest hunter was the morning star, "Dawn's Heart." I whispered its name, feeling certain that by speaking it I could cast a spell that would bring rain. Oma Dieta had also told me that the San were really clever about storing water: they filled ostrich eggshells with it, buried them, and were always able to find them again when they needed to. I imagined that where they lived in the Kalahari they had to know all the waterholes and the places where they had buried eggs, just as we knew the bores and wells on our farm. I often wondered how the San survived the searing desert heat in their flimsy shelters of sticks and grasses or skins. Our thick roof made of mud and straw, covered with sheets of corrugated iron, kept us cool. Still, I felt they were lucky to be able to follow the rains and the game wherever that might take them, while we were fenced in and had to stay put. I marveled at their ability to survive with so little in such a terribly uncompromising and sparse place as the desert. Our farm was not a desert, but at this time of the year it was close to being one, cruelly beautiful.

As the sky became visibly lighter, I quickly dressed and slipped into the yard to skip to the kitchen without going through the house and waking my siblings. The sand felt cool under my bare feet, the smooth grains pushing up between my toes. Mom was already in the kitchen making oatmeal porridge. As I breakfasted alone with my parents, I listened to them talk and worry and make plans for the day.

"Very little grass is left in the Okamen camp," Dad told us. "Paul came by yesterday to report that the water in the tank there is very low. Perhaps the bore is drying up."

"Oh, I hope not!" Mom exclaimed anxiously. "I know this year's been a hard year, with the rains stopping so early, even at the beginning of March. Maybe we will have to rent grazing in the north—they had better rains up there last season. But I'd hate for us to do that. I'd hate for you to leave this farm. What would I do? Go with you? What about the children if I did? Perhaps it would be better if we all stayed and only you go—but then what about you?" She sighed heavily, burdened with the thoughts of such choices. I quietly prayed that it would come to none of these, that we would just stay.

"Well, its no use worrying," Dad said. "We'll just have to wait and see and hope and live with the uncertainty. But I'll drive over to Okamen after lunch to check if it is the windmill that has broken down, if the bore has really dried up, or if it is a different problem."

"Can we come along, Dad?" I asked immediately, and was jubilant when he nodded. We children cherished rides on the back of his truck, when he went out on trips to check the bores or other watering places, to mend the fences, or to shoot an oryx or a kudu for the pot. Sometimes we walked to the spring or to one of the dams. My brothers often prowled through the bush with enthusiasm with their air gun or the .22 in search of doves, guinea fowl, or francolins to bring home for a meal. My parents had nothing against Karen and I shooting. Still, I had no interest in killing, except for flies or other bugs, and poisonous creatures such as scorpions or snakes.

I made a round through the house with my dad as he took down the screens, letting out the mosquitoes that were buzzing against them, closing the windows to keep in the cool of the night. Once this had been done, I joined my mom to water our potted garden, a collection of geraniums, Livingston daisies, shrimp plants, hibiscus, ferns and cactuses, more geraniums, and boldly purple bougainvillea. We had wondered for some time why the water from the well by the river stunted the growth of flowers and other plants. When finally my dad had the water analyzed chemically, we learned it contained too much fluoride. That's why the first garden died. That's why my mom potted all the plants. That's why we collected rainwater in a huge vat as it came running down from the roof, and used it to water the pots.

I fetched a watering can. On my first trip to the vat I knocked with my knuckles against its metal ridges. Each knock elicited a hollow echo until I reached about two feet above base. Not much water was left!

While walking back and forth between the vat and the pots, I caught glimpses of my dad doing his Saturday chores. He checked the tools. He checked whether Uibeb had chopped enough wood for the kitchen stove and for hot water for a week. He checked his office, where he stored yarn, tobacco, sugar, and other goods that he sold to the workers. He checked the drying room to look over the lambs' pelts, which he sold to traveling traders back when we still had sheep, until about 1952. It had become difficult to find herders after Petrus had died. No one liked herding. It was too lonely a life.

As Dad moved about, he often stopped to look at the sky. I knew he wanted to see those towering flat-bottomed clouds that might give rain. But so far, that Saturday, the sky remained a relentlessly shimmering blue.

At the end of each week, one of the farmhands had to rake the yard. This morning it was Gideon. First he raked the debris into little piles: dead twigs covered with long, white thorns, a mess the starlings made when building their nests; bits of bones or skin the dogs had chewed; Prosopis pods, dry leaves, rotten dates and palm fronds; scales and cones of the Casoarinas. I followed him around, watching him create islands of dead stuff in the sea of sand. While raking, Gideon muttered, "*Te veël droë goed, dit moet maar gou-gou reën* (Too much dry stuff, it better rain soon)!" I nodded and looked up to see only the pale dome of the glaring sky, unable to detect even an insinuation of a cloud.

Once he had raked all the debris into little piles, Gideon fetched the wheelbarrow and shoveled them onto it, taking the load along a narrow track down to the river's edge where he tipped the gatherings. There they lay until water would fill the riverbed and sweep everything downstream. From where we stood only sand was to be seen. Most rivers of the country were simply beds of dry sand throughout the year.

On returning, Gideon performed my favorite part of the yard cleanup: he pulled the rake through the sand, designing circles, waves, and grids. The surface looked beautiful, a peaceful expanse of patterns. No debris. No footprints. At least not yet! *"Ek wens die reën wou dit als uitwis* (I wish the rain would wash it all away)," he'd say. Even without rain this pristine condition was short-lived. Soon you could tell where my dad and others had walked, where the dogs had run and the birds had hopped about. Soon even these prints would vanish. In the shifting sand, nothing lasted.

The sun now was almost overhead. I was feeling hungry. Good, I thought, soon we'll have lunch and be off to Okamen. Impatiently I watched my mom cleaning the two coolers standing in the yard a few feet from the kitchen by the tall palm trees. Each cooler stood on four legs in a cement pond filled with water, which was meant to keep out ants and other bugs in search of food. Each cooler consisted of a wooden frame, with walls made of two layers of chicken wire, the space between them filled with charcoal. Twice a day the charcoal was saturated with water, its evaporation keeping the insides cool. My mom used Vim to scour the shelves, and boiling water to kill the cockroaches and wash away the dirt. She also checked what vegetables we would need for the next week. Potatoes, beets, carrots, and cabbages were all one could get at this time of year. She made sure that not all the milk had turned sour and skimmed it for the cream. She's so meticulous, I thought, irritated about having to wait for her to finish before we could have lunch.

When she was done we went inside. I silently grumbled at the ritual slowness of the meal: of having to wash our hands, of assembling at the table, of prayers having to be said, of oryx stew and yellow potatoes and boiled white cabbage to be ladled out to each person before any one of us could eat. We all ate in a hurry and even skipped the dessert: sweet cottage cheese with sugared tomatoes, my favorite. Instead, the four of us children rushed to the entrance hall to grab our hats, dash outdoors, and climb on the truck. I stood in the spot I considered most desirable: right behind the driver's seat.

When Paul, our herdsman, and my brothers and sister and I all were aboard, my dad drove south along the winding track to the bore at the outpost of Okamen. Despite our worry that it had not yet rained, not one of us would miss a trip out to the farmlands for anything. I knew every bend of the tracks, every dip, all the sandy spots where the truck might get stuck. Knowing this and seeing its sameness was reassuring. But everywhere the bush looked black, a wasteland created by the death-dealing force of the sun. Not even dry grass was to be seen. Along the way a few skinny kudus were scared out from the sparse shade under a grove of acacias. At another moment a duiker (a small antelope) rushed off into the distance with huge leaps. A lone oryx just swished its tail against the flies, refusing to leave his spot in precious shade. Cicadas shrieked everywhere like the glare of the sun. As the truck came to a stop at the bore we had to squint against the pall of thick dust it had stirred up.

We children hopped off and raced over to the open tank to stand on the edge of its cement base. As we were still too short to be able to look into the tank, and as there was no ladder, we scrambled with our feet on the ridges of the corrugated metal to get higher while hanging on for dear life to its edge to see how much water was left. It wasn't much. The windmill firmly stood still. All was silent. The lack of the familiar creaking of its wheel or the clank-clank of its piston signaled trouble. But my dad couldn't find anything wrong with the mill; it simply seemed to lack wind. So he started the diesel pump. At first it sputtered for a bit. Then, as it fell into a regular throb, a precious thin stream of clear water spouted out of the pipe, informing us that the bore had not yet dried up, relieving our anxiety with the very first burst. "I hope it will give water at least until January," Dad said.

After we watched the stream spurt for a while, we took turns at taking a drink. The water was cool while the earth all around was hot and scorched. The water from each bore and each well had its own special taste, pure and smooth like rainwater, or chalky, with a touch of minerals, like the water from the spring. And we knew which was excellent for making the tastiest coffee, a perfect tea.

Gradually the light of high noon drained the world of its color. Everything alive went into hiding. A few dragonflies skimmed the greenish surface of the water where rust-colored islands of algae drifted. Slowly the watering trough filled. All along Paul plodded through the dust surrounding it. It was hard to imagine that even with very little rain the yellow "morning stars" with their thorny seeds would cover the area with beauty. As he checked the cattle tracks in the kraal he muttered and frowned, no doubt imploring the great god *Omuhona* to make *ombura*: rain. The dry white heat burning and searing the already blackened veld filled us with dismay. The drink had been its only brief relief. I watched my dad, his face shadowed with concern as he yet again surveyed the blank sky. Then he suggested we drive a little farther south before turning back home. We often drove along this track for about another mile to a favorite spot by the southern fence that opened on a magnificent view.

When we reached the top of that rise, Dad turned the truck to face the way we had come and switched off the engine. While the dust settled we stood on the back of the truck, looking around in silence, the remote solitude overwhelming us. The dead-looking thorny land gradually sloped down to the river by the house a few miles away, melting beyond it into the undefined distance. We could not see the house itself, although I thought I detected the green dots made by the cluster of palms and Casoarinas around the yard, now an oasis in this desiccated landscape. Under the fiercely blinding cloudless sky we could barely see the tabletop of the Etjo, the Erongo in the distant west, or the closer mountains in between that stretched along the northern horizon and receded into faded purples and blues. The view erased even the memory of rain.

"Dad!" I suddenly yelled. "Look!" I proudly pointed to the northeast. What I had spotted there, far away, was a wisp of a cloud, merely the size of a hand, yet heavily pregnant with hope. We all stared at it, mesmerized. I waited for a response from the others. There was none. I felt cheated. Had I not just made a most important observation? Had I not just discovered a cloud, and, what is more, a cloud that we had been awaiting for months? The others' silence brushed away my discovery. Oh, well, I thought as I shrugged off everyone's disappointment, it was merely one cloud, one tiny, distant white cloud. Not much to hope from. I knew without words that we all thought this: not much hope for rain. After a while my dad started the car. We drove back to the house in heavy silence, tortured by the withering heat.

By the time we reached home, however, the tiny cloud had become many. Large and gray they scudded across the sky from the distant horizon, rolling and racing along. Within the hour they obscured the sun. Dad was pacing around the house and yard. He checked all the buildings, made sure that doors and windows were closed firmly. The air was electrified, prickling our skin, making it feel like an overly tight membrane. Would it really rain? Or would we be cheated yet again?

Not more than half an hour passed before the first lightning flashed and claps of thunder sent the dogs scurrying for shelter. We scampered around the house, checking in every direction to see where the rain may have started to fall. I had just reached the back door when the first drops struck the sheet iron roof with deafening noise, creating huge wet pockmarks in the dust and sand. I watched them as they blasted away the remnants of Gideon's raked patterns and the various tracks. Then, from the moist dust, there rose the smell of wet earth, the smell of all smells: the smell of life.

I stood in the doorway, filling my lungs with the cool and vibrant air. I watched the drops fall faster. More flashes of lightning tore through the sky, followed by peals of thunder and strings of rain. Soon the yard was filled with small puddles. Quickly they merged into larger puddles, joining with yet more puddles, rapidly forming a vast lake.

Some fifteen minutes later a stream started up between the main house and the garage. It followed the old riverbed in which our house had been inadvertently built. We children resumed moving from window to window to see the rain all around. I don't remember exactly when our excitement turned into fear, but I do remember standing at my bedroom window, staring at the sheets of water falling from above and the brown flood rising below. Its flow was gaining in momentum and depth, the sight filling me with dread.

I ran to the hall to check the clock. It had been raining for only half an hour, and already there was so much water. Already the current was terribly strong. Might it take away part of the house, or all of it? I rushed around in search of my father and clung to his hand. He still looked happy, so I felt safe again. We wandered from room to room and gazed out every window. When we reached my room once more, I noticed that he too was looking worried. It continued to rain in torrents. And the water kept rising, rushing ever more swiftly through the yard. Dad sent us all to the kitchen, where Mom made us cocoa. I hadn't noticed how cool it had become. The hot sweet drink warmed and soothed us. But Dad did not join us. He continued to make rounds. As long as he was there, I felt protected. He would know what to do. Had he not always known?

For about an hour we watched the water rise on our dry earth, our fear rising with equal measure through our bodies. Then, finally, the clouds closed off their streams. For a while we waited for the water to drain away a bit before racing out barefoot to the rain meter where it stood by the chicken coop, splashing through the icy puddles that sent shivers up our legs. We lifted the funnel and took out the measuring glass to read how much it had rained. Seventy-seven millimeters! We were stunned. Even we children knew that that was an unusual amount. "Three inches!" we yelled back at Dad. "Three inches!" He had followed us out more slowly. His eyes shone. He was all smiles!

The sky was still gray, a little lighter overhead, while all around us it was still raining. We grabbed his hands and formed a long line, dragging him down to the river, sloshing through the cold brown water, chanting "No school on Monday! No school on Monday!" Dad laughed and took his turn dragging us along behind him. The dust had turned into mud, now deliciously squelching up between my toes.

As we stood on the riverbank, we saw what Gideon and I had seen earlier in the day: the expanse of sand with a narrow meandering ribbon of water, a few bulrushes growing alongside it, and plovers still serenely stalking the wet sands. We scrambled up and down the steep bank, waded in the streamlet, betting how long it would take water to get here and how much it would be. "It will be really full," Dad said. "Just you wait!" This rarely happened, but if he were right we would definitely stay home from school for at least one day. Luckily for us there was no bridge across to the opposite bank, at least not then, to where the school stood twenty miles or so downstream.

It was some hours before we first heard a low rushing noise, surging, like a big wind coming down the valley. It advanced slowly, growing into a dark growl. Shallow water began to lick the sand in tongues, as if uncertain about its way, soon followed by a massive brown wave. As the flood filled the riverbed and gained momentum it either thrust everything out of its way or simply swept all along. The water swirled and eddied, frothing up yellow clusters of foam tossing wildly on its surface, only to be swallowed by the ever deepening and frighteningly powerful current almost as soon as they were created. Bushes tumbled around, trees lugged along by its force. We huddled near my dad. Looking on, I wondered what else would be swept along in the murky floods. Perhaps cars were being dragged away, drowned animals, maybe even people.

I could not stand this terrifying sight for long. I dashed back to the house to seek refuge in the kitchen with Mom. She had kept the fire going in the old stove by feeding it with pieces of the red and white chunks of Camelthorn that Uibeb had chopped. The kettle on the inch-thick stainless-steel plate was spouting a steady cloud of steam, its lid rattling away. In the growing darkness she lit the paraffin pressure lamp, its sock becoming a brightly glowing center, casting shadows all around the room. She had brought a small round table into the middle of the kitchen, her never-empty mending basket on top: socks to be darned, torn hems re-sewn, seams fixed, lost buttons to be replaced. We gathered around her in this comforting space against the fear of floods and darkness. Jürgen, then about four, was lolling around on the floor, asking endless questions, scrunching up his brow with worry.

"Why is Dad staying down at the river?"

"Where does all the water come from?"

"Will it take the house away?"

"Where would we go then?"

He rolled over on the floor to look up at Mom. She put down her darning and hurriedly answered his questions. "No!" she replied, trying to stem the rush of her own anxiety. "No! I've never heard of such a thing happening before, a river taking away a house." After a tense silence she added, "We'll go to Okatjerute if we have to go anywhere. Uncle Wilhelm's house is miles from the river and safe from these floods. But I hope that will not be necessary!" My own fears were allayed, if only briefly.

"Does Hans-Erik have to go to school on Monday?" Jürgen went on.

She did not answer. "Oh, shut up!" I said, giving him a good kick. I did not wish to know about school. I wanted to stay home at least one extra day, more, if possible. Just then Dad appeared in the doorway. He set down the lantern on a sill. "You're right," he exclaimed, having heard the question. "You won't be going to school for quite a while. But let's hope we can stay here!" Almost at once we felt no elation at the thought of staying home. We were too concerned about having one. Then Jürgen began again. "Mom, can I have some more cocoa?"

"Please, Mom," we all chimed in.

"Oh, all right!" She got up, poured milk into a clean pot, put it on the stove, and added a few tablespoons of cocoa and sugar. Soon the sweet smell filled the kitchen. My dad gulped down his, grabbed the lantern, and was off again.

I watched the light swinging at his side as he receded into the dark, his shadow dancing alongside him. Even at midnight he was still going back and forth between the house and the yard, watching the edge of the water, trying to make out if it were rising or receding. He continued the debate with my mom about what we would do if it became necessary to leave. She had cut slices of bread and buttered them, but we all were too nervous to eat. I kept hearing the ominous roar of the water. We had wished for rain, but not this much! We had not wished for a flood that might destroy our home.

We children remained with Mom in the kitchen. I returned to reading Heidi. I had read the book at least ten times before, though that did not matter now. Its familiarity was calming, shutting out the turmoil of the immediate threat. Hans-Erik continued to paint the plywood picture of *Rumpelstiltzchen* he had been working on, while Karen leaned against our mother, clutching her favorite rag doll. Mom picked up her darning again, and Jürgen continued to shift around restlessly on the floor while Dad kept an eye on the water level that had risen to half-way between the river's edge and the house.

Finally, long after midnight, Dad sauntered into the kitchen, the expression on his face telling us that the worst was over. "Off to bed now, all of you," he told us. "The water is receding. I think everyone will now sleep well." We were almost too exhausted to respond. While he hugged us and took us to our rooms, Mom came to tuck us in and kiss us goodnight.

As I drifted off into sleep, the sound of rushing water in my ears, I wondered if I would wake to a green day and the fragrant smell of life exuded by the soft, drenched earth.

PART TWO:
CHILDHOOD EXPANDING

7 Hostel Life in Omaruru

IT WAS DARK and long before dawn one Monday in July 1944 when my dad set the paraffin lantern down on the floor next to my bed, quietly stroked my hair, and whispered so as not to wake my sister, "It's time to get up, my sweet." I had heard his footsteps before he entered the room and knew what he had come to say: "Get up, my dear. It's time. I have to take you to school. We have to go." My heart contracted with pain, my lungs froze. I stopped breathing and squeezed my eyes tightly to stop my tears. "It's time to get up," my dad repeated softly, taking my face into his hands, brushing away the wet. He didn't want us to go, I knew, but we had no choice, so I put on a brave face to please him.

I dragged myself out of bed. I had not slept well that night on my horse-hair mattress, not so much because of the lumps but because it was the night before Hans-Erik and I were to start school in Omaruru. I was seven-and-a-half. My brother was not yet nine. Having seen the hostel before, where children from the district had to live while attending school, I was not at all looking forward to going there. Exchanging home for such a drab place was a difficult and dreadful prospect.

Although I did not want to go to school, my dad had insisted. "You have to go or else I will be in trouble," he explained. "Your mother can no longer teach you. The government will allow only trained teachers to teach children, and she isn't trained." Until now, Hans-Erik and I had been lucky. Children in the area had to start school at age six, but our mother had taught us both at home. She taught my brother first, but since he was my playmate more so than my younger siblings, I spent the hours with him at the small white table where she tutored him in the three R's. By the time I was five I could read and write and have fun with numbers without realizing how much I had been learning. She taught us until I was half through Substandard B, the second year at school. Later on, when my grandma came to stay with us, my cousins Sieghart and Manfred came to live with us so my grandma taught them the way my mom had taught us.

"The law says you must attend school, and I don't want government officials to come around to investigate," Dad continued. "Besides, you have to get an education. This school is all we have. Everyone from the other farms is going. You are going. That's how it will be!" Black children, like Paul's, they were ever so lucky, I thought. They did not have to go to school at all, especially not to boarding school. They could simply go on playing outside. I envied them intensely.

At least there is still the ride with Dad for twenty miles through my much-loved bush. The thought cheered me a little as I dressed. So did the knowledge that we would return home every third weekend during the term, from Friday afternoon to early Monday morning, a return that would remain a heartfelt relief from our barren hostel life. From this day on, every time on coming back from school, I realized how much I missed my parents and my siblings, even Hans-Erik, as I rarely saw him at school. Boys and girls were strictly separated. With every homecoming the love for everything—for my mother, her potted plants, her tasty food, trips to the farmlands with my dad, even for the sand in the yard underfoot—was firmly renewed. My brother and I were simply happy to be back in the lap of the family, if only for two in twenty-one days over the next six years or so. School definitely turned into my "them." The adults and most teachers were authoritarian, hard and harsh, members of the Dutch Reformed church, rooted in Calvinist theology, people that were to be feared rather than liked. Many children were cruel, especially the Afrikaans-speaking boys. I also thought them to be really stupid and not interested in learning anything. The big Afrikaner boys liked to beat up the little ones. Hans-Erik could tell a story about that, only years later on. "They really got us to hate them," he said decades after leaving the place. Yet we rarely complained about our difficulties, and when once we did so, our parents were deeply shocked. "Why on earth did you not tell us?" they wanted to know. We felt it would have changed nothing. Hostel-life was a time that in many ways established for me that we as German-speaking children were different from other white children who spoke a different language, who disliked school the same we did, but who didn't like learning anything at all, who only wanted to get married as soon as possible, and run a farm. As if that would have made life better.

This morning Mom had prepared creamy porridge for us, a last taste of home for some time to come. Hans-Erik and I sat at the kitchen table, slowly eating our big helping of oats with lovely farm milk and crunchy golden sugar. Mom also gave us each a brown paper bag filled with oatmeal cookies she had made especially for us two, and many slices of freshly baked and buttered bread for the first break at eleven. I could not tell if she was sad also. Her face was calm and she kept herself busy, fussing over us until the moment came for a good-bye kiss.

My brother and I each carried a small suitcase filled with fresh clean clothes, all washed and ironed by Alwine. I quickly slid into the Chevy truck's cabin to sit in the middle, between Dad and my brother, leaving him to open all the gates. Opening gates always led to a tussle between us, regarded by us as a chore to be avoided. Dad took his place behind the steering wheel. He sat there for a few moments in heavy silence before turning on the engine and the lights. Off we went, out at the front gate, dipping through the little river just outside the yard, heading west down the tracks along the winding Omaruru River. It was a narrow, unpaved and bumpy road, twisting and turning through the bush that hemmed it in on both sides, with many gates to open and drive through on the farms we had to pass on the way.

An hour or so later he stopped the truck at the entrance to the hostel. My part of it was an L-shaped building, consisting of two large dorms, two smaller rooms for the teenage girls, and one large bathroom. Dry toilets were outside, a hundred yards up a hill. Each dorm housed about fifteen girls. There were also two apartments, each for a teacher, one of whom would look after us. Some years later another large dorm and smaller rooms were added to increase the accommodation. Along the inside of the L-shape ran a wide *stoep* (veranda) that provided shade. The dining room and kitchen separated the boys' and girls' quarters. On a large lot adjacent to the boys' quarters stood the U-shaped school building, an administrative area in the low curve of the

U, with four or five classrooms on each side. We girls rarely saw the boys, only those in our class, and otherwise at a distant table during a meal. I don't even recall what the boys' part of the hostel looked like, or whether I ever saw its inside – probably not.

Dad walked me over to my dorm, carrying my suitcase. Back at the truck, he gave me a big hug, saying, "See you Friday!" when he would come to pick up mail and goods for the farm and bring a food package from home. I squeezed him tightly, eyes shut equally tightly. Through my tears I watched him hug my brother, then get into the truck and drive away. We stood there with heavy hearts, lost in clouds of dust kicked up by the vehicle, clutching our brown paper bags with the bread and the cookies, straws from home. Finally Hans-Erik said, "We better go now. It doesn't help just standing here."

I dragged myself over to the classrooms, my heart thumping, not know-ing what awaited me. Little did I know that I would be teased: "China girl" because of my small eyes, *Bunte Kuh* (cow with different color patches) because my skin lacked pigment on my knees and my ankles. My parents had worried a great deal about them, and had taken me to many doctors to see if I'd get patches all over my body. No, they told us, probably not, most likely they'll even eventually vanish, which they did, almost, over many years.) Because of these visible markers I was treated differently. I don't recall giving the other children lip for their teasing. I simply disdained them for doing so. This first day went by in a fog. My body may have been in class but my mind was filled with yearning for home. I hardly noticed the other children. I simply lived in the world of dreams.

Early the next day I surfaced abruptly from a deep sleep. Someone was shaking my right shoulder vigorously and most annoyingly, a voice calling, "Helge, Helge! Wake up!"

"Stop this!" I grumbled, turning away, shutting my eyes tightly in an effort to stay in dreamland. Here in the hostel, my dreams and memories of home would become home. Was it only yesterday that I had woken up on the farm? Unbelievable! Only yesterday! That single day felt like absolute eternity, with an endless string of days ahead that surely would turn into years of day-mares.

"You've got to get up!" the voice urgently whispered. "Wake up! Get dressed! Otherwise you'll be in trouble!" The word "trouble" penetrated my consciousness like the stab of a knife. I had not known much of it before, though I soon came to realize that from now on there would always be something we were supposed to be doing, or not supposed to be doing, that led to trouble. To me it was never quite clear which. Trouble was lurking every day, all the time. Rubbing my eyes, I realized the voice belonged to Maria, one of the girls in my new class who was now standing next to my bed.

"Didn't you hear the bell?" she asked. I shook my still blurry head. *Why would I hear bells if I did not wish to be here?*

I was lucky that Maria was helping me out. She had been there for the first half of the year and knew the ropes. She became my first school friend, even though later she would sometimes annoy me by swiping cutout dresses of my paper dolls, insisting they were hers. She had black curly hair and a milky chocolate skin. There were rumors that she had "mixed" blood. I wasn't exactly sure then what that meant. It was clear to me that her skin was darker than that of most kids, but having grown up with dark-skinned people who were kind and helpful, I couldn't care less. And Maria happened to be just one of these!

Sitting up in my pajamas under the sheets, still feeling fuzzy with sleep, I put my arms on top of the blanket but had to pull them back quickly. The brown-black Karakul wool was so hard, so incredibly scratchy, so unlike the soft warmth of the pelts of the lambs, so very unlike my blanket at home. I vaguely thought about the difficulties my dad had in trying to sell his wool after shearing. Not much could be made from it because of its short, wiry quality. Surely they could have made something other than blankets with it, I thought with a grimace. My brothers complained about bedbugs - fleas? lice? But I don't remember us having had any. Even without them, this hostel felt just as scratchy as these blankets from day one.

Half awake, I scanned the room. There were fifteen beds with steel frames, each with a lumpy mattress on sagging springs. Mine reminded me a little of my horsehair mattress at home. It was just as lumpy, although its hollows were not shaped to suit my body. This mattress here, well, I hoped it would not be mine for long.

The walls looked shabby. It must have been many years since they had been painted. Nobody seemed to care. My bed faced the door to the stoep. Looking through one of the three windows on that side, past the beige curtains with their faded blue stripes, I could see only dust in the yard, inches deep. One enormous ancient Camelthorn, with hefty long white thorns and many large velvety crescent gray pods, was the only live plant thriving there. *Can't walk barefoot there!* At that moment I imagined the tree all covered with tiny yellow flowers as if it were spring in July. I could almost smell their wonderful scent that sweetened the air for several days each year, letting me forget the dust, the sting of its thorns, and the uncaring surroundings of people and dust and thorns.

Later I often wished my bed were on the other side of our dorm. The view from there was so much more pleasing. My eyes would rest on the thick, shiny green leaves of the lemon trees that grew at the back of our building. I could see the creamy, satiny petals of their fleshy flowers, or later, in May, their rough-skinned golden fruit glowing in the dark green foliage. Their hue of yellow suggested when the forbidden fruits were ripe, hanging there patiently, waiting to be wrenched secretly from their stems, their thieves remaining undetected. Nothing else flourished back there in the dense loamy soil except the hardy privet hedge by the fence along the dusty street, the visible yet insurmountable barrier to our freedom, always beckoning us to escape beyond its limits into a more exciting life.

On this early Tuesday morning I saw that the other fourteen German-speaking girls, ages six to thirteen, who were sharing this large room with me were already up, dressed, washed, and combed, their beds made neatly. I definitely had to hurry. Tugging on the clothes set out previously, I shoved my feet into my sandals to avoid the splinters of the rough wooden floorboards, grabbed my towel off the peg on the door of my narrow dreary khaki steel cupboard, and dashed next door to our bathroom.

Several white porcelain basins lined the wall on the side of the yard. On the other side there was one bath, which stood within a wooden partition with a door, and two showers, each with a plastic curtain for privacy. Usually there was not much privacy with so many girls all jostling to get washed, but in time we got used to seeing each other's skinny bodies. Some girls, though, were not quite that skinny. We were not supposed to look at budding breasts and tufts of hair in weird places. Looking at nakedness was thought indecent after the age of four or five. But it was compelling. We looked furtively, trying hard not to stare.

Now I was alone in the bathroom, the wet and slippery red-painted cement floor prickling cold underfoot. The water from the tap was also cold, especially so at six-forty in the morning. Hot water was just a weekend pleasure, and then only when you had a designated bath. It was heated in a "donkey," a forty-four-gallon metal barrel once used to transport petrol, now hoisted onto a metal frame outside at the back of the washroom, filled with water, and heated from below by a wood fire. No wonder my mom had to soak us for hours when Hans-Erik and I, and later when all of us children came home from school, scrubbing us vigorously to remove a three-week crust of dirt that clung to us, especially to our feet. The Friday bath was fun, with my mom playing the record of Beethoven's sixth symphony or other pieces of music while we children slid in and out of the tub or along the well-soaped cement floor before getting the final scrub down.

At this early hour, however, I simply splashed my face once or twice with the cold tap water, startling myself into stark sobriety. Making my hair took a while longer. I brushed and plaited my two braids in a hurry, then rushed back, made my bed, and stood attentively at its foot for the awaited inspection at six-fifty. Just then the bell rang again. I was lucky and relieved to be on time. Punishment for being late, so I had been told, was usually a few painful raps with a ruler on the knuckles, or some kind of deprivation.

Miss Le Roux, a young Afrikaans-speaking teacher, stepped into the room on the dot of the minute. Her black hair curled neatly around her tanned face. Her dark eyes, lipstick-red lips, and peachy powdered cheeks gave her a doll-like appearance. I peeked at her hands and her unbelievably long red finger-nails. My own were cropped short. "That way you can keep them clean more easily," my mother claimed. Were Miss Le Roux's nails clean underneath all that red? She might look like a doll, but she certainly wasn't one, as I assessed her, taking in her presence.

Miss Le Roux wore a skirt with a colorful floral print, gathered snugly at her waist, its hem reaching to mid-calf, while a white blouse clung tightly to her ample bosom. She wore a pair of red pumps with high spiky heels. How could one walk in those? I puzzled, staring at them. My mother would not at all have approved of her appearance—not of her lipstick, nor her painted nails, and especially not of her shoes. Even I could tell that this kind of footwear would be impractical on the farm. We children were usually barefoot. At most we wore a pair of sandals, real shoes only on Sundays, with or without socks, depending on the season. My mom wore lace-ups even for fancy occasions. But pumps? Miss Le Roux was surely the epitome of decadence! Amazingly, the older schoolgirls could not wait to be still older so they could also walk around on such spiky heels. I quickly discovered that they couldn't wait either to turn sixteen, not only to be rid of school but also to have babies, come hell or high water.

As Miss Le Roux stood there at this early hour, both stern and intimidating, she cast her eagle eye around the dorm, assessing the state of beds made and girls dressed.

"Go on now, *meisies* (girls), line up! Let's go to breakfast," she told us in a martial tone. We all quietly followed her out, along the veranda, across the dusty yard, and then lined up in two rows at the door of the hostel's dining room.

"All right," she continued. "Now hands out!"

We held out our hands — first nails up, then palms up — so she could see if all were clean enough for eating. Here was something else that was not tolerated: plain old dirt! Only after her approval were we allowed to enter the dining room. Without it, we had to return to the bathroom to scrub away the last invisible specks of this evil.

Inside the dining room we sat on benches lining both sides of a long table. This day we had oatmeal porridge for breakfast. Sometimes the porridge was made with *mielie* meal (cornmeal), sometimes with brown maltabella (malted grain). Whatever ingredient was used, it usually contained little white maggots and little black beetles. Every day we fished them out of the gruel, lining up the cooked creatures along the rim of the plate to be counted. We always knew exactly how many we found for we competitively compared numbers. High numbers brought high status and much admiration.

Before I came to the hostel, my mom had asked Annemarie, a neighbor's daughter five years my senior, to take care of me until I had settled into this new life. Her idea of caring proved vastly different from my mother's. Annemarie had the knack of squashing the barest greening of independence and individuality in others, especially in me, no doubt having been severely squashed her-self. Whatever in my appearance (comb your hair properly; wash your face when it was the middle of the day; wash your hands again; tuck your blouse in!) and in my behavior deviated from her established standards found her disapproval (don't talk so loudly; stand up straight; stop talking!)

During those first months Annemarie did not allow me to sit with my friends at mealtime. I had to sit between her and her friend Hilde, Maria's beautiful, blonde oldest sister. I often wondered how two sisters could have such different color skins and hair. Sitting there put me into a bad mood right away.

"Look at your hair, these strands that are still hanging into your face," Annemarie nagged me immediately, roughly pushing them back, lifting her nostrils in disgust. "For that you can't have sugar on your porridge! And for heaven's sake, wipe your snot nose!"

I liked porridge, especially with brown sugar and milk. And now I was not to have sugar! *Old cow*, I thought, but I kept my lips shut tightly, knowing that saying this out loud would cause even further trouble. I quietly nudged Hilde on my left. She was sympathetic, my real caretaker. When Annemarie deprived me, Hilde would make up for it. She quickly and covertly sprinkled those lovely golden brown crystals on the *pap* (porridge), pouring milk over both. Silently she nudged me back. I briefly leaned my head against her shoulder, signaling my affectionate yet unspoken thanks. Having finished my porridge, I counted six dark brown beetles and ten maggots. Indeed a promising start of the day!

Annemarie's standards were high, certainly much higher than my own, even higher than my mother's. If I talked back, out came the hairbrush for a spanking. I became increasingly defiant, giving her lip. I was not about to simply obey her. But we rarely told our parents about how bad hostel life was for us. Nobody did. Parents would not be able to do anything about it anyway, and we would be in trouble for telling. We learnt early that some things in life could only be endured.

Eventually Annemarie made me write a letter to my mother. "Dear Mother," she dictated to me after I had been at school a few weeks. "Anne wants me to tell you that I don't listen to her. She wants me to tell you that I talk back a lot, that I am not being a good girl. With good wishes, your daughter, Helge." My mother was horrified on its receipt. "Why didn't you tell us?" she wanted to know. I remember that this letter ended the "care" Annemarie gave me. I felt self-assured. It was right to give lip, not to accept everything. My mother had vehemently supported and defended me. She always defended her children. "Don't listen to them," or "you're right," she'd say. She also did so in view of the teasing I so often had to endure. "Shrug it off!" Her support made me strong!

Mealtimes passed in silence. All of them. They were supposedly not for talking. Grownups were sometimes so hard to understand: there was always much to talk about, but they required silence above all else. Oma Dieta repeatedly and loudly said that children should be seen and not heard. It wasn't fair! How could children learn to speak, let alone think for themselves, when living with this imperative?

Once everyone had finished the milky *rooibos* (red bush) tea, we filed over to the school building. There was no time for fun or talking with anyone on the way through the boys' section. Before classes began we also had to hurry up the stony hill to the dry outdoor toilets. I never liked going there. There was only one lamp outside, high up on a tall pole. At night its light cast dark shadows everywhere, especially inside each separate toilet. Even during the day it was gloomy in there, just like in our outhouse at home. You could not see properly then and would not notice the creatures that tended to hide there—spiders, scorpions, bugs of all sorts, maybe even snakes! It had already happened a few times that someone had come across a snake in there. Using the toilets was a scary and risky business. Besides, a foul smell pervaded the building, despite many gallons of milky antiseptic poured into the murky depths below the seats. Using the endless supply of cut-up newspaper spiked onto a nail in the wall wasn't too inviting either, though at least one could read them for bits of old news while otherwise occupied.

The first dreaded ringing of the school bell for getting up started at ten minutes after six in summer, in winter half an hour later. There was a bell for breakfast and one for going over to the classrooms. All day long that bell rang—for meals, for signaling the beginning or end of lessons—and there were ten of them! Bells for breaks! Every time you heard one you had to stop doing, stop thinking, and immediately start something new. It was most confusing and annoying. The bell also signaled the end of school at one o'clock, when finally the time had come for a desperately longed-for lunch followed by a welcome nap. Life by the bell was an ordeal, so different from the quiet routines on the farm that were directed by the sun. At least the sun did not ring, I often thought with yearning. No bell ever rang for Paul's children. They were so lucky!

My first teacher, Mrs. Katharina H. called by us Frau Kati, was German-speaking. She was called "Frau" because, according to German tradition, all women over thirty had to be called *Frau* (Mrs.) whether or not they were married. Frau Kati was older, perhaps in her fifties, very much an old-fashioned spinster. She did not look a bit like Miss Le Roux. She did not cover her narrow lips with lipstick. She did not use powder nor did she deign to wear pumps. There was nothing deceitfully doll-like about her looks. Her hair was mottled gray, rolled into a chignon all around her head. She held her back stiffly straight as if she had swallowed a *dropper* (a wooden prop used in fences). And you could tell instantly that she was strict, even stricter than Miss Le Roux. Being taught at home had been good. Being taught in class by Frau Kati I soon found to be a different experience altogether.

On this second day at school, as the only new student in the class, Frau Kati called me to the front of the room. "Tell us something about the farm," she said, beckoning me toward her, inviting me to participate.

Slowly I shifted out of my desk and inched forward. I dreaded going to the front of the room. I felt exposed, shy, overwhelmed. So I stood there mute, looking at my feet while everyone was looking at me. I was unable to think of what to say. Never before had I endured that much attention. Seconds gathered into eons of silence. Then Frau Kati said, in an effort to encourage me, "Well, say something now!" Yet she had no idea why I was unable to talk. Everything was so new to me, the people all strangers. I remembered later how my mom told us that she and her siblings all went into hiding when strangers came by. I couldn't run away except into silence.

Nailed by her gaze, I managed to squeeze out a whisper. "I know a nursery rhyme." That felt much safer than just talking.

"Louder, my dear, speak louder. I can't hear you. Nobody can hear you. And look up! Don't look at the floor!"

I collected myself. I raised my eyes toward the ceiling to avoid having to look at the children, and once more tried to gather my courage to speak.

"Why are you now looking at the ceiling? I don't think there are any angels around up there," she said, smiling coldly while some of the children laughed. I squirmed inwardly, feeling deeply humiliated, not knowing what was so funny about that comment.

"Sit down," she finally relented, exasperated. "I certainly hope you are going to learn something here."

I slid into my desk, planted my chin in my hands, elbows on the desktop, and stared at her defiantly and with venom. I already know, I thought. *I can read! I know my numbers! I can write! Nothing you know you will ever teach me! I could do all this since I was five and now I am a lot older.* I felt caged by her misunderstanding, her lack of empathy. Her unsympathetic way, the irate tone of her voice, and even more her remarks making fun of me made me dislike her intensely. I was silent in her class. Later that year, when she had her Christmas party for us, I hid inside the privet hedge. Nothing and nobody would ever persuade me to enter the apartment in our hostel building where she lived. A few girls came walking by, calling out to me to join them. I did not answer though I felt torn. Just the thought of her pale blue eyes, her bent nose and thin lips, her stern voice and her harsh manner put miles between us.

When the bell finally rang to announce lunchtime around one, we hurried over to the dining room. We were terribly hungry after such a long morning. I had eaten those brown bread slices with thick butter from home during our break the day before, so today I munched the cookies. But I was still hungry. We were always hungry. We shifted quickly into our seats across the benches, boys on one side of the room, girls on the other.

When grace had been said the food was passed around. The goat meat was roasted, brown and crispy, surprisingly yummy. For my part we could have it every day. Later on I did not care for the beef stews with bones and bits of fat and sinew floating in the gravy, always the same gravy. When the next dish was passed around I took some cabbage, all soggy and cooked to death. I wrinkled my nose. Next I took only one spoonful of what we called "horse teeth"—those big, white, tough mielie kernels as nature grew them. Sometimes they came shaped like rice and were called rice, but no matter what they were called, they still were mielies.

Looking at my plateful I had visions of the cabbage my mom served with browned butter. And her mashed potatoes! Her cooking was not very adventurous—Dr. Oetkers was her only cookbook—but her meals were always tasty. Here we rarely got potatoes or beets, green beans or carrots, just the usual white cabbage or pumpkin, and horse-teeth. Sometimes we were served sweet potatoes, which I disliked for their sweetness and their color. They were definitely not potatoes. Thank goodness we weren't served spinach, like the country pancakes I used to see on the ground around the water troughs after the cattle had eaten fresh green grass. No thanks! I knew greens were rare and therefore expensive. The matron decidedly wanted to save money, I concluded, not thinking that there were not many vegetables around, let alone greens, during those years through World War II and just after.

Food was the ever-important subject for us boarders. Wednesdays and Sundays were regular days for dessert. So on this Tuesday I dreamed of the next day. Would there be red or orange jelly? Or perhaps mixed dried fruit cooked? With custard for a surprise! We rarely received an orange or a mandarin from the school's orchard, carefully tended by the principal himself. The fruit were his pride. It became ours to steal them.

We were always hungry—hungry for variety, hungry for supplies from home, hungry for love. Every Friday morning my dad visited my brother and me briefly, later all four of us. Each time he brought wonderful things that he handed us over the fence of the school grounds during a ten-minute break at eleven o'clock. Parents of other children did so too. Sometimes they sent food in a parcel. Dad brought freshly baked bread, forever the taste of home, spread thickly with that delicious homemade butter. Sometimes he also brought crumbling caramel fudge, peanut brittle, *Zwieback* (rusks), honey bread, or "horse food," a yummy self-invented concoction of oats, raisins, and sugar with a bit of cocoa and peanuts, all mixed and packaged by Mom. Any food from home was crumbs of love.

After lunch we drifted over to the dorm. Miss Le Roux usually appeared fifteen minutes later to make sure every girl was on her bed. I spread my towel across the scratchy blanket before lying down. I was used to naps at home, from one till three in the afternoon. It was a welcome quiet time during the hottest part of the day when all activity ceased. Even the flies hid in the shadows and corners for their rest. The whole village subsided into midday silence. All four shops were closed. Not a car was to be heard. I dozed off quickly in the soothing quiet (no bells for a change!), broken only occasionally by a whispered conversation or the rustling of pages turned by those who preferred to read.

As we had no homework during these first years there was lots of time for play. At home, play and work melded into simply activity. There, we had designated trees for good climbing, the tree becoming the village, its branches the streets and buildings, a bakery, the post office, and more. We created other homes, outlining them with "walls" by using rocks and stones, roads leading from one house to another. We played in the river, building homes of sand, building bridges using sticks and rushes, our cars getting stuck when the ground was too wet. My sister and I played a great deal with our dolls. We had only one each, and we loved them dearly. We had one pram to share, painted blue with a stripe of daisies all around, to take our babies for a stroll round the house. Karen cooked. I made clothes. My brothers had a set of Meccano, more intricate than modern Lego, with metal bars and nuts and bolts to construct whatever you imagined. They also had wooden blocks made by Jakobus. Naturally I wondered what we would play with at the hostel, especially during endless weekends, when time simply was ours. Apart, of course, from mealtimes, we were allowed occasional visits to the river to play rounders (a game similar to baseball), to climb the reed, or the willows. Sundays we had to attend the service in the small mission church right next door. I liked singing the hymns, but not listening to pastor Kuhles' endless sermons. Maria once shocked us all into fear-filled wakefulness by simply fainting, falling over right in front of me in the pew where we stood. *That should teach him to say less* remained a thought never expressed.

"Well, what can we play today?" I asked my new friends, Maria and Irma, as we sat on the edge of the stoep outside our room after our siesta, legs stretched out front, feet bare and dusty.

"How about marbles?" Irmchen suggested.

"*Ja, ja! Machen wir das!*" Maria and I responded simultaneously. Let's do it.

It was surprising that we had agreed so easily. Perhaps that was because I was still new. Later, when we knew each other better, we often disagreed about what to do next, arguing and bargaining. Now Maria and Irma fetched their small sisal bags filled with marbles from their steel lockers, generously dividing them among the three of us. Then we headed to the lemon trees at the back.

"This is the best place for this game," Maria said. "The soil is nice and hard, and there's not much dust to stop the roll of a marble." They explained to me the rules and the importance of the ghoon, a large, heavy steel ball bearing: the most-prized marble to possess. If it was part of your collection, everyone knew that you were a good thrower. But I still had to prove that. Each marble was thrown toward the ghoon. If the marble touched it, it was yours, and should you miss it but touch any other marble, that one became yours instead.

I took the ghoon. "Now throw it!" Irmchen told me, while drawing the taw across the hard loam with a stick, the line no one was allowed to step across.

"Oh damn, that's too far!" Irmchen shouted after I had thrown it.

"Oh, shut up! That's quite all right," Maria told her. "Remember? You're not such a bad thrower yourself!"

Irmchen pulled a face. "All right! Then I'll go first!" she demanded.

Now the game really started, and when Maria finally captured the prize we returned to sit at the edge of the stoep. We looked at each other's marbles and did some swapping. Next time I'll get the ghoon back, I thought most determinedly. Once done, we watched a few girls skipping rope over near the Camelthorn to the rhyme of "Two Little Dickey Birds Sitting on a Wall." I joined them. When I was out after falling, we went inside, spending hours cutting out clothes and accessories for our paper dolls, exchanging them, having a grand time dressing them up for great occasions: life in fancy houses where weddings took place, birthdays were celebrated, fun parties held, and sumptuous dinners given.

Supper was at six. Usually we had sliced bread with watered-down tomato jam containing any amount of horrible skins. The mere thought of the jam still makes me shudder. Sometimes the slices came with local Cheddar cheese. And always we drank milky rooibos tea. During the last year of being here, I remember sharing the privilege of collecting the boiled milk from the cooler. It was a privilege because it allowed us to keep the creamy skins skimmed from the top of the milk to spread on our bread at dinner. Afterward we were allowed to play outside till dusk. But by eight we had to be inside, bodies washed, teeth brushed. At nine o'clock the bell rang for a last time. Then Miss Le Roux came around to check if we were in bed, to say goodnight before switching off the lights.

The hostel had any number of rules to be followed, not written in black and white, known only by word of mouth. "Do not step outside the school's or hostel's fence" was rule number one. Should anyone dare tread beyond an actual fence, expulsion was sure to follow. I don't recall such an event actually taking place, but the connected fear and shame it might incur were sufficient threats. Lesser trespasses, such as talking when silence was required, resulted in knuckle raps for the girls, raps on the calves for boys. The boys in general had a much harder time. My brothers and a cousin told us how the Afrikaner boys simply robbed them of their clothes, pilfered their food parcels, beating them whenever possible. The grape vine had it that some Afrikaner men shot the last rhinoceros seen in the district; and our headmaster, Mr. Terblanche, perhaps even Mr. Nel, used a *sjambok* (a kind of whip) made of its skin to beat the boys. Using a willow branch was bad, but a sjambok? That dreadful hard strap with such cutting edges! How could anyone be so unbelievably cruel! It should never have been allowed. These years at boarding school left the boys scarred in more than one way.

Instead of such beatings, girls were sometimes required to write endless lines in their best hand, on and on, no erasing permitted:

IwilldoasIamtold!IwilldoasIamtold!IwilldoasIamtold!
Iwillnotanswerback!Iwillnotanswerback!Iwillnotanswerback!

There were too many rules, all seemingly as serious as the Ten Commandments. "You shall not talk; you shall not lie; you shall not answer back; you shall always pay attention!" I often wondered what bad things Jesus must have done to be killed on the cross, blood dripping from his side and his hands, blood like that of the lambs when their throats were cut. I wasn't being crucified, nor was my throat being cut, but the scoldings following supposed transgressions, and all the other punishments were bad enough, sufficient to force anyone into submission, even me. Although physical escape was not really possible, I escaped with my mind. When I missed home, I "visited" my father and mother, the farmlands, Alwine and Paul, and Lena, Lendina and Gideon, comforting myself day and night with these images. My dreams became home while life in the hostel proved a harsh timeless eternity, deeply resented, yet one that simply had to be endured.

After my sister Karen joined me in the hostel, she cried often. I was mad at her about that and gave her a hard time. It was difficult not to cry, and I certainly did not want to be lured into crying all the time. I was angry with her because it was easier to be angry about everything rather than sad. No one had cared for me, so why should I care for her? It was better and certainly much easier to drift into dreams in order to escape the pain of being away from home. I never liked leaving home. Leaving was always a reminder of that time when my parents sneaked away with Hans-Erik from Lievenberg while I was napping at noon, leaving for Germany without me, leaving me behind with Grandma. She told me once how sad she had been to watch me search for them throughout the house for a very long time. I was angry for many years for having been left like this for six months, months of eternity. What did I know at fourteen months? It was as if they had died. No doubt the first six months at boarding school were the hardest for me, as they will have been for every child. Yet as the following five years passed, as I grew older and stronger, and as I got to know the hostel system and the children better, it became easier to survive because you simply accepted that this was what it was like, what had to be. We adapted. We knew whom we could trust and love, and whom not. In the end, I was glad about leaving the hostel and the school, looking forward to different times. And with that, my anger lessened.

All the same, I still realized that things were much worse for the boys than they were for us girls. They were subjected to cruelly humiliating orders, such as being told to eat green grape leaves when they were merely suspected of wanting to steal one grape, or were flogged with a willow switch. Being a girl was perhaps not such a bad thing after all. Being the girl I was, I planned to fly, to become a pilot, to rise into the sky, soar over the cottony cumuli, float above the flimsy cirrus, visit the stars and the moon and the sun and anything else beyond school that I desired. I would vanish into the blue and be home with my family, with Lena and Lendina, with Alwine, with Paul and his children, their kindness and caring, and life as I knew it in my much loved bush.

Junior School

MY SPELL IN Frau Kati's class ended in December 1945, after having endured her for a year and a half. Until this time most public junior schools had two tracks: one in which German was the medium of teaching, the other in which it was Afrikaans. But as Germany had lost the war, the South African government shut down all German medium tracks. From then on Afrikaans was the primary language for everyone. I don't ever recall learning Afrikaans; I simply seemed to know it. Switching to its use at school was the only change I remember as connected to the war. Was I aware about anyone talking about Germany and its Allies losing it? Did I realize what was happening? I doubt it. I was only eight. For me, life went on as before. Until 1948, that is, when the National Party won the elections in South Africa, an election that deeply affected everyone. But even of this I became fully aware only very much later.

Frau Kati stopped teaching when the language changed from German to Afrikaans, allowing me to hope for better times in class with kinder teachers. This was not to be, not at first. My new class, Standard Two, was assigned to a large rented room near the railway station, our school being in need of additional space. Each day we trudged the half-mile to class crocodile-style, two by two. None of us looked forward to it, knowing that Miss Le Roux was to be our next teacher, waiting for us with her own means for maintaining order: that knuckle-bruising ruler most of us had already felt. I knew by now that her looks were positively deceiving. Although she was also a bit of a drama-queen – she had a way of fainting at critical moments - she demanded our deepest respect and unquestioning obedience or else she'd dispense those knuckle raps. Everyone had better be good! And being good meant that you had to do as told. I learned that quickly and thoroughly.

During that year I found desktops much more interesting than lessons. I furtively carved my name with a razor blade among those already there, between cryptic phrases that abounded, such as "Zolla loves Auggie." Zolla was five years older than I, yet she was just one class ahead of me. She had frizzy blonde hair, freckles, and ample breasts. She was lively, always smiling and laughing. She was also the school's fastest runner despite her short legs and stocky build. Auggie's full name was Augustinus E. He was a handsome Afrikaans fellow in my brother's class. They were intense rivals for getting highest marks and being first. While carving my name into the desk, I thought of Zolla and her secret folded notes that others smuggled to Auggie for her, and her excited giggles while giving firm instructions to the messengers.

Besides the desktops, Gawie M, an Afrikaans boy much older than I, who sat in the desk in front of me, was another focus of my interest. Like Maria, he also had a milky chocolate skin and black hair. I found the fact that he had eighteen siblings totally intriguing. Imagine that—eighteen siblings! Having three was bad enough. My parents had to work hard to keep our family of six while also paying off the farmlands. So how did his parents manage with only a few acres and so many children?

His family of twenty-one lived south of the river, a mile or two outside Omaruru, next door to a dairy farm. Every time we passed their driveway I tried to make out what his home looked like. It was scarcely visible from the road, barely a blob of white through the bush. I'd ask my dad to drive down to their house, but he refused to take that uneven track. "They are poor whites," he used to say. And with that remark the subject was closed.

Gawie's clothes were shabby, torn, dirty, surely all hand-me-downs. He himself usually looked dusty, his feet covered with fascinating dark crusts. Perhaps his family did not have hot water, let alone a bathtub. I used to think that poor whites always spoke Afrikaans, and that all of them looked like Gawie, ragged and dirty, and were as stupid as he. We weren't rich either, but I never felt poor, despite all the many deprivations.

Surely he did not have to endure those hour-long soaks in hot water as we did when home for every third weekend. Our baths were followed by serious scrubbing until our skin had a heavy pink glow, which, after the bath, became enhanced by a thick layer of glycerine intended to deal with dry skin. Once applied, I'd lick my skin for a taste of the viscous, sweetly stuff.

One day Miss Le Roux handed out a few new inkpots. First she called out some names, handing these children each a shiny white ceramic pot. They fitted into a hole in the desks, preventing any ink from getting spilled. Gawie got a new one. I didn't. *It's not fair! Why should a dirty stupid boy like him get a pristine inkwell?* Mine was chipped, with many dark purple stains. Surely I also deserved one. So I exchanged ours. Secretly, of course! But it did not end there, this inkpot business. Gawie, foolishly, or so I thought, wanted me to give it back. It led to our constant fighting during lessons that day. We paid no attention to Miss Le Roux's sage words, being so entirely preoccupied with the importance of asserting ourselves.

"Give it back to me," Gawie whispered, turning around to look at me.

"Watch out! Le Roux will notice you if don't face the blackboard!" I hissed back.

"You took my inkwell. I want it back!"

"It's mine—you've got yours!"

Bang! A loud rap tore through the class. We turned into salt pillars of propriety and attention. It did not help. Miss Le Roux had detected our hissing and whispering.

"Stand up, you two!" she commanded. "Come here, right up here to the table." She impatiently tapped her desk, most assertively, omen of what was to come, glaring at us. We looked innocent, or tried to. "You!" she said, pointing with it at me. "You, Helge! What is going on?"

"He took my inkwell," I lied.

She turned to Gawie. "Is that so?"

"No, Miss, she took mine!" We repeated this several times. She lost patience.

"Hold out your hands!" she commanded angrily and rapped our knuckles. Gawie was lucky that this time she did not rap him over his calves. "Now go back to your seats, and Helge, give Gawie back that inkpot! You did not get one, did you now?" she suddenly recalled.

Growling and blaming each other for the raps received, we went back to our desks. It wasn't fair that I had to give up the new inkwell, I thought, convinced of the injustice I had been dealt. *Why should a dirty and stupid Afrikaner boy get a new one and not I?*

I don't remember much else about that year with Miss Le Roux, only the relief that the time with her, together with the long, hot, dusty walks to and from the classroom, was finally over. Yet this by no means meant that things would get any better when I advanced to Standard Three.

The new class was ruled over by "Long John Silver" Nel. Mr. Nel was a very mean and bad-tempered man, probably, I surmised, because he had lost his right leg below the knee in a car accident. He needed a crutch to get around. He leaned on it when standing, else it lay on the floor beside his chair. I sometimes imagined having just one leg, hopping around on my right foot. That proved difficult. Hopping on my left was even harder. But whichever leg I hopped on, I never got far. It took so much effort. Admittedly he managed to get around well because he had a crutch and years of practice. Still, I was sure it must have felt strange to miss part of your leg that you desperately needed.

Another reason for his bad temper, I thought, was that he was not particularly attractive. He was a chubby bachelor. His hamster-like cheeks disappeared into his double chin. Because of his beer belly he wore braces that held up his crumpled trousers. I often wondered who took care of his clothes. They certainly did not look properly washed or ironed. Our Alwine definitely did a much better job. He also plied his hair with Bryle Cream to make it oily and sleek, plastering it to his head so it looked like a pirate flag's skull.

Aside from his bad temper and neglected looks, my biggest trouble with Mr. Nel was that he had taught my brother the year before. Hans-Erik was just a class ahead of me, yet teachers expected me to be as good a student as he was.

"Stand up," Mr. Nel ordered when handing me back some work. "How come your marks are so low?"

Silence on my part.

"You know your brother got an A for this assignment last year," he told me. I shook my head and muttered that a B was also good.

"What did you say?" he demanded with a frown.

I dared to speak a little louder. "I think a B is also good."

"You do? You do? I think you can do a lot better than this," he went on, eyeing me as I stood at my desk.

"My father says I'm doing fine," I further dared to answer.

"Now, now! No cheekiness here! You have to try harder and do better. Sit down!"

On went the lesson. I retreated into my shell, steaming inside. *I don't care! I'm not my brother. You're being quite unfair. And I'm still going to be first in class!*

I was usually one of the top three students in my class. My buddies— Freda-Marie v.F, a girl from the village, and Irmchen L, who shared my dorm— and I had our own little competition going. Günther, Freda's brother, once vowed that he would eat a razor blade if he got better marks than I did. It was a safe bet on his part. He never had to eat one, quite a satisfaction for me.

Instead of applying myself to walk in Hans-Erik's footsteps, I struggled with the more challenging effort of learning how to knit. We had to knit socks in our needlework class. The first part was supposed to be ribbed: purl one, knit one. As I knitted, there appeared strange large holes in between the stitches, their number uncannily increasing with the growing length of the item. I had to unravel my efforts many a time, get everyone to explain over and again what one did with the yarn when knitting one, purling the next. It did not help. Everyone's sock got longer. Mine got longer too, but it also always became wider. It took me many lessons to solve the mystery of knitting one, purling the next.

In January 1948, at the beginning of the school year and when summer was in full swing, I found myself in Standard Four, a proud eleven years old. I knew this would be a better year—better because I was rid of Mr. Nel and his constant comparisons with my brother, and better, because I had a teacher, Mr. Slabbert, who had not taught him. He was the new teacher at our school, and came safely all the way from Port Elizabeth in South Africa.

Mr. Slabbert was the hero of every girl in my class. Tall and slim, he also had beautiful wavy black hair and blue eyes, dressing most elegantly in suit and tie, just like Gary Cooper. We thought he was the handsomest man we had yet set eyes upon. He was full of stories about his country, a country none of us had yet been to. South Africa might as well have been on the moon. He often told us about adventures he had had while driving from his hometown to our little village. When he was talking we forgot about bells. We forgot about regular lessons. We swooned and dissolved into rapture. We did our best to persuade him to tell us stories instead of teaching us. He sometimes obliged, though not nearly often enough for our liking.

One place he told us about was the Kruger National Park in South Africa, and its lions, elephants, and other multitudes of animals we had not yet seen either. That winter, in July, my family took a first trip to our own national park, the Etosha Pan. I was convinced that there we saw, in a small segment of the Pan, more lions and elephants and zebras and wildebeest than the entire Kruger Park had ever contained.

He described car factories in Port Elizabeth, as well as the glories of living on the coast by the warm Indian Ocean. This ocean, he claimed, was infested with sharks that might devour you while you were enjoying a float on the swell of the sea. There, big waves thundered onto beaches. Sailboats dotted the blue waters. In Swakopmund, our own seaside resort, the ocean was so cold that even in summer your toes curled and turned blue after spending a mere two minutes in it. "That is why here there are no sharks, because the water is so cold," Mr. Slabbert maintained. For us the undertow was the real danger, not sharks. No one dared go out very far for fear of drowning. Had that not happened to several people, to children as well as adults? Swimming in the Indian Ocean indeed sounded much more attractive and enticing despite the possibility of getting swallowed by a sea monster.

We hung on every word that came from our adored teacher's lips. Our marks became suspiciously high, no matter what the subject. He had no ruler.

He didn't raise his voice. He didn't get angry and rarely punished us. Once he caught us "smoking" under the Camelthorn in the far corner of the schoolyard on a cold winter's day, only to discover that we had fooled him. The "cigarettes" were merely empty Prosopis pods, the wisps of "smoke" we blew out of our mouths our own foggy breath condensing in the cold air. He didn't mind having been fooled. He just laughed and walked away. Being in his class was almost like spending time in paradise.

The year went by much too quickly. When it was over, he left to return to his hometown. We missed him sorely. I continued to dream of him. Even so, we had to move on to Standard Five and yet again a new teacher. Mr. Erich Otto Peter was short, with bushy brows and dandruff on the shoulder pads of his jacket. He also made us work without ever raising his voice. He had a special way of catching my eye with a knowing look as if to say, "I know what you are up to, and you better get on with what you are supposed to!" And I did.

He was a wizard at geography. He loved it. He always referred to the globe that stood on his desk, pointing out details. He opened the world to me still further than my grandma already had. I worked hard at making maps of the continents with all their countries, coloring them carefully and beautifully with crayons. I marked their capitals, knew all the names of rivers and mountains and lakes. I learned about the people who lived there, the things they crafted, the plants they grew there. Eagerly I discovered that our world was big, bigger than even than the Berlin of Uncle Wilhelm's boyhood.

Until now I had not been far from the farm. I had visited a few other farms in our district. I had been to Oma Dieta's Lievenberg some eighty miles away. I knew Omaruru, of course and the farms on the way, had visited Swakopmund. I had even been to the Etosha Pan. But this was the total extent of my travels up to age twelve. Until this time we had no television, and movies only once in two weeks that we could not attend for lack of money, devices that could have informed us more about the wider world.

Of course, I knew about Germany. After all, that was where my dad came from and where my mom had spent a few years. And Oma Dieta came from Emden. Although they talked about Germany from time to time, it was difficult to imagine what it was like. What were 'dark pinewoods' that my mother mentioned so often? What were large cities? We had no woods here. And we had only one city, our capital, Windhoek, tiny by comparison with Berlin. How high were the high mountains, all covered with snow?

Snow itself was especially intriguing. All these other things I had seen in pictures, but snow? None of us had seen even one flake of it. Pictures with it were simply white where it was supposed to be. So what was it? The grown-ups often talked about snow, as if it were the most wondrous thing under the sun. We sang Christmas songs about snow, sleigh bells jingling, while it was unbearably hot and usually dry in our part of the world. We dreamed of a green Christmas, not a white one. Perhaps one day I might actually experience a white one. Did we not have family in Germany? My dad's mother often sent letters. Maybe I would see snow one day if I visited her. That actually came about when at age eighteen I visited Germany for the first time.

In the year of standard five a new boy, Wolfgang S, joined the class. He came from Germany to live with his uncle and aunt Mr. and Mrs. Schubotz, who happened to be friends of my parents. Once, when they had invited all of us over for Sunday dinner, I had to eat weird food: pig's trotters with spinach. I had never tasted nor seen trotters before. Now the trotters or hoofs lay before me on my plate, a piece of leg still covered by its skin, with a layer of fat underneath. My stomach churned just looking at it. I pried off a bit of meat, but its taste was spoiled at sight. I left it untouched. My mom encouraged me to at least try some of the meat. I declined. I knew I'd now have to eat my spinach. But I hated it. I collected it in my napkin and discarded it secretly after the meal. Fortunately for me, no one noticed. Or if they did no one said a word. They were nice people, Mr. and Mrs. Schubotz, and Wolfgang, their grandchild, known to all as Wolfie, was my first heartthrob.

Wolfie was good-looking, a little taller than I, with soft, dark brown eyes. He combed his long, straight brown hair smoothly all the way back to his neck, kind of like Elvis did later. At the time he joined us he knew no Afrikaans, but soon he had top marks in class. So far I had been Mr. Peter's prized pupil in arithmetic. Now I had a tough competitor in him. I had to work hard to keep up with him.

During art lessons I sat behind him and his pal. It was easy to look over his shoulder and watch him draw instead of drawing anything myself. Once he created a circus. There was a tent with horses and elephants, the people looking very real. They wore clothes, had expressions on their faces. He was great at drawing, while I managed only stick people. Occasionally I caught Mr. Peter's knowing glance resting on me, but he never said a thing. How could he? Did my dad not often bring him a hefty kudu thigh for his pot, gallons of rich farm milk, or pounds of yellow farm butter?

The last year at Omaruru Junior School turned out to be my worst. The principal of the school Mr. Solomon Samuel Terblanche, taught this class. He was the meanest, most cruel teacher I have ever had or heard of. He too was a South-African. Most parents tried to make sure they were in his good books. They invited him out to their farms to hunt, or they brought him and his wife produce from their gardens. I remember him staying with us a few times over a weekend. It was a total trial for me, given how he treated us at school, especially in the year when he was my class teacher.

His wife was the matron of the whole hostel, as well as the "mother" for the girl boarders. She was twice as tall as Old Terry, as we liked to refer to him. And while he was slim and lithe, she was buxom. Very buxom! Maria and I often speculated about their love life.

"Oh my god," Maria would gasp, laughing and laughing. "Imagine them kissing!"

"Yeah," I would join in, "she'd sit on his lap and squash him!"

"No! No! She couldn't do that. Don't you see? He'd sit on hers!"

We both fell down in a heap, tummies hurting, knickers wet.

The couple was simply hilarious, a source of endless amusement when we thought of them kissing like that. And kissing, in those days, was as far as it went.

Old Terry had short, gray, frizzy hair and icy pale blue eyes behind silver-rimmed spectacles. He kept his thin, straight lips clenched, probably to avoid yelling too much. His large table was neatly arranged with the tools of his trade: a few piles of prescribed books, an inkwell, pencils, pens, and, most importantly, a willow switch. Many willow trees grew along the banks of the big Omaruru River, so his supply was guaranteed, absolutely. The switch was about three feet long and extremely supple. Whenever he pointed with it to what he had written on the blackboard, he flexed it playfully, reminding us, while pointing, of his total authority and power. At its sight all our daring vanished like *meerkatte* (African prairie dogs) into their burrows. We became silent, malleable like putty. We always said yes. When he deemed it necessary, the boys got their blows on the seat of their pants while the girls took the blows on their hands. It helped to be smart, though not always.

One day our homework had been to write a business letter in English. I had worked it out carefully before copying it in my best handwriting into my exercise book. I enjoyed the act of writing. Had I not won a number of calligraphic competitions held in schools across the country? When finished I noticed that, despite all my care, I had misspelled two words. "Bother!" I exclaimed, almost out loud. I picked up my eraser, gave it a little lick, and began working on the errors. First I rubbed over them gently. Not much happened. I gave the eraser another lick, applying more pressure. That worked a little better. So I repeated the action. Alas! The result was two holes in the precious page. Oh, well, I thought, holes are better than mistakes! And I happily forgot about them.

Then came the day when Old Terry handed back our work. He picked up each exercise book, checked the name on it, looked at the written work, and made his comments. I waited. Every time I hoped it would be my turn. Every time it wasn't. There were twenty of us. My anxiety escalated. What did I do wrong? Why did he not give me my book sooner? I had no idea. Finally he picked up that last book. Mine! He opened it, holding it with two fingers by the page my letter was written on as if it had a disease, the disease of holes he wanted everyone to see! I cursed silently.

"Stand up!" he commanded. I stood up.

He made some comment he no doubt thought was funny, about writing on paper and not on a sieve, then walked over to my desk, put the exercise book down, and demanded, "Hold out your hands!"

I was livid. I looked down at the page. There were no red marks, no mistakes, and now he wanted to beat me for a few holes? There was nothing I could do. Or was there? I held out my hands. I watched him out of the corner of my eyes. He raised the arm that held the switch. The instant it came whooshing down I pulled back my hands. Whack! The switch came down across the desk and my book. I stared at it. There, just look! A heavy brown line showed across it! Good, I thought defiantly, yet feeling tight as a guitar string. The class had subsided into tense silence. I no longer dared to breathe. Surely I was turning blue. The suspense was terrible. A question hovered in the air over all of us: What would Terry do next? How would he deal with such impudence on my part?

"*Nog eenkeer* (Once more)!" Old Terry commanded, staring at me with more than the violence of "How dare you, brat!" in his eyes. And this time I endured the whack, a statue of brave containment. After class I rushed to the tap in the yard to run cool water over my stinging hands. My friends followed to take a look at the red stripe.

"He's such a bastard!" Freda assured me. The others agreed. Daniel suggested planning a trick. "We should let the air out of his tires on Friday so he'll have to pump them up before he drives off to go hunting!" In those days there were only hand air pumps, though he'd probably command a black man to do the job. The thought that Old Terry would get some good exercise was what mattered more. Everyone grinned and nodded assent.

"I'll tell my dad never to invite him again," was my suggestion, although I wasn't sure I would be successful in persuading him.

"No!" Günther called out. "Let's go steal all of his oranges, absolutely all of them!" We knew that the little citrus orchard was Old Terry's prized possession. That would definitely get his goat. We were almost bursting with the desire for revenge.

"Yes!" Gawie called out, "let's do both!" Gawie, my ink pot classmate from Standard Two onward often had to endure the willow switch because he was not that smart. He had his own reasons for revenge.

Everyone agreed. There and then we plotted our retributions. We stole his oranges! We flattened his tires! He never found the perpetrators. All the same, he must have suspected something.

That year was my final year at the district junior school of about 180 kids in 1950. December was finally in sight. First we had to take the end-of-the-year examination. The marks were sent to the central Board of Education in Windhoek. When they came back all children and their parents gathered in one of the larger classrooms. We sang the school song. We tried to listen to Old Terry's sage words. Finally, we were handed our junior certificates. Mine was red, the color of a first-class pass! It was first class despite everything. It was as red as Hans-Erik's. So there, Mr. Nel! I felt strongly about having endured, pleased and proud with my achievements and self-assertion. I had made it. Made it my way! My father was proud of me also. My mother simply expected the result.

Together with my parents, Jürgen, and Karen, I walked through the school gates over to where my dad had parked the truck on the main road. I was as elated to turn my back forever on this school as Hans-Erik had been. But he had not yet returned from his high school in Stellenbosch, a city a thousand miles away in South Africa. My dad forded the dry river, drove past the dairy farm and the lot of the poor whites, back to our home under the palms, the Casoarinas, and the pepper trees beside the Omaruru River. We three children stood on the back of the old Chevy, singing all the nutty songs we had learned at school while Dad negotiated the bumpy road and its corrugated sands, including

Saai die waatlemoen / saai die waatlemoen,
saai die waatlemoen / saai die waatlemoen (Sow the watermelon)
My papa roei die skuitjie (My daddy rows the little boat)
My mama blaas die fluitjie (My mommy blows the little whistle)
My boetie draai die orreltjie (My brother turns the little organ)
Saai die waatlemoen!

Along the track the dust of our unforgiving land prevailed, just as it did in the schoolyard. It was, after all, December, and it had not yet rained. The veld looked bleak and dry. Camelthorn acacias and *omukaru* trees lined the banks of the small rivers while other acacias and wag-'n-bietjies were to be seen everywhere. Bush as usual. Now we would be home for six long weeks and, above all, for Christmas. What mattered most: the endless weeks of summer to come and spend at home.

Rustenburg High School for Girls

EFORE MAKING MY way over to find my classroom in this new school, I sneaked to the front of the hostel. This part of the grounds was off limits, but I wanted to take a good look at my new abode from this side. I walked over to the palm-lined driveway that led up to the entrance at the center of the two-storied building. Two impressive pillars and a number of large windows to its left and right framed it. Then I stepped onto the lawn. It was a strange feeling, that soft cushion of short-cut grass underfoot. The lawn was expansive, and it was green, as green as our bush back home after good rains. It stretched all the way up to the fence along the Campground Road on the edge of the Rondebosch Common with its umbrella shaped Cape Pines. The grass on the farm was rarely green for long, and turned to gold when the dry season began. Looking carefully at this thick cover, this carpet of broad dark-green blades, I could not remember ever seeing a lawn anywhere before, except on last year's quick visit here, and afterward in Stellenbosch. This green felt like a good omen. So was the red of callas flowering unabashedly in the heat of mid-summer's season. On the opposite side, at the back of the hostel, were two grass hockey fields, and beyond them the walled-in swimming pool, all lying south, with the large quadrangle of the two-storied school to my left. Although the contrast to Omaruru could not have been greater, and although what I saw was so pleasing, at this moment it was just another school, as yet unappreciated, the distance from home casting its own shadow of sorrow. It only slowly dawned on me, with increasing amazement, that my dad had chosen this school for Karen and myself. So far I liked what I saw. Yet my hope for a greener time than Omaruru ever vied strongly with the darkness of distance.

The time to leave home and continue school in 1951 came only too quickly, ending the precious days of the summer holiday at home. As my dad had insisted earlier about us having to go to school, he insisted now that we had to learn English. "If you want to get on in the world, you have to know English," was his new refrain. However, Hans-Erik ended up at Stellenbosch's Paul Roos Gymnasium, an Afrikaans school, as my dad had applied too late for him to get into Rustenburg's "brother" school, Rondebosch Boys' High. While Karen joined me two years later at Rustenburg, Jürgen eventually attended another Afrikaans school, Jan van Riebeeck, located in Cape Town itself, right on the slopes of Table Mountain. Unfortunately for my sister I remained as unhelpful towards her as I had been in Omaruru. Before she came, I had to fend for myself all alone. So, I asked angrily: why should I be helpful toward her? But once she settled in, our relationship changed. I remembered playing a piece for two pianos with her at some school concert. We each played our own part, but we played them together.

The year before, when Hans-Erik had to start at Paul Roos Gymnasium, we all traveled with him by pickup truck. The trip turned out to be a big adventure for everyone, just as going to the Etosha Pan had been three years before. My parents loaded our three quarter ton Chevy with everything we needed for camping, and, leaving just after New Year, we drove as the crow flies a thousand miles south for three weeks. It was a first visit to South Africa for all of us except for my mom who had worked in Paarl in the early thirties. It rained most unexpectedly during the first night we made camp near Kalkrand. The next morning we had to hang our bedding and clothes all over the bushes close by so they could dry. What a funny sight that was! Along the way we had several flat tires. We crossed the famous Orange River into South Africa – and it wasn't even orange. One night a thief caused a big commotion by trying to steal mom's wristwatch while we were camping near the town of George, my mom chasing him like a ghost in her white nightdress, vainly screaming and yelling after the thief. We visited the Oudtshoorn caves where my dad got stuck in the Devil's Chimney. It was hilarious to see him stuck, but he took it in good spirits: mom's worry about his love for potatoes and gravy had cause. We also went to one of the famous ostrich farms of the area, watching people trying to ride ostriches, a very funny sight, nothing like riding horses. In Cape-Town itself we took a brief look at Rustenburg High School, crouching at the foot of Devil's Peak, the school I was expected to attend, about which I remembered nothing. Finally we ended up in Stellenbosch, one of the oldest towns at the Cape where one of its first governors lived, where streets are lined with ancient oaks and cottonwoods, beyond which many equally ancient Cape Dutch style houses still stand. We left a sad Hans-Erik at his new school before returning home. Now, in 1951, only my dad came with me. And we went by train.

My mother spent much of the summer vacation preparing my uniform for the Rustenburg High School for Girls, that posh private school in Rondebosch, a suburb of Cape-Town. She placed a large trunk in our guestroom, and everything that I needed that was ready to go was put into it so that nothing was forgotten: for wear in the Cape's hot summers six pairs of white socks, four sky-blue dresses, two pairs of black lace-up shoes, tennis shoes, several white knickers, a white Sunday dress; for wet and cold winters four sky-blue blouses, two ties, a navy gym-dress, six pairs of black tights, several navy knickers, a navy skirt, a navy white-collared Sunday dress, a navy sweater, a navy blazer with a Rustenburg badge, and a navy coat. A tag with my name had to be sewn into all these items of the uniform. And, last but not least, two private dresses were added to the heap. My mom chose not only the fabric of both - blue, her favorite color, not mine - but also their dirndl style with short puffed sleeves. I liked neither. I never grew to like the uniform either. It turned me into one of many girls, with only the number missing. Subsequently, even fashion became mostly irrelevant to me, as I thought it too de-emphasized my individuality. This year pink was "in", next year white, another blue. I simply wanted to wear what I liked, what I thought suited me. My mom had taught me how to sew and embroider meticulously. If the seam did not turn out perfectly straight, she'd tell me "Undo it and then try again." So, slowly, instead of complaining and confronting her, I began to make my own clothes: my choice of style, my choice of fabric, for many years to come. My mom mostly liked things to be done her way. I'd listen to her, say nothing, and then do what I wanted. And somehow she let me. Maybe she did not notice or was not interested or too busy with her chores. She had her confrontations with the boys.

Only too soon the day for leaving was upon us. My dad and I had a basket of goodies from home: cold chicken, smoked meat, *biltong* (beef jerky), zwieback, lots of brown bread and butter, fruit, toffee, honey bread – everything that we would need for our three day train trip to Cape Town. We bought drinks, coffee, tea or beer and coke from the dining car. Later that year, in July, when traveling alone for a first time, the food basket was inadvertently left behind at Wilhelmstal in the commotion of all those boarding the train. I was extremely upset and distraught, despite the fact that other children readily shared their tuck with me. I had so suddenly found myself without any comforting crumbs from home.

The train trip itself was interesting. My dad and I shared a second-class half compartment with three bunk beds at the end of a long corridor close to the coach's exit and the washrooms. Most compartments had six bunks, and the train many coaches as it ferried about 300 children to the various schools in the Cape. Dad stored our luggage and the bedding the railway (SAR: South African Railway) supplied on the top bunk. I slept on the middle bunk, my dad on the lowest one. During the day my bunk was lowered, providing a back to the lowest one for a seat. A special treat was the cup of tea a waiter from the dining car served us at six each morning. After drinking it, I curled up again under my blankets to enjoy the *tok-tok* of the wheels as the train hurtled along the tracks over 1500 miles to its destination. We spent many hours just watching the scenery go by: the Auas Mountains just south of Windhoek, the *Swartrand* and the *Kalkrand*, the Karas Mountains near Keetmanshoop, crossing the Orange River. We bought watermelons in Upington, and passed through the oily and root-blackened rail yard in De Aar, an enormous hub for trains from all over South Africa. After stopping at De Aar the rails crossed the gray flats of the Karroo with it's low brush and Merinos, its many tabletop mountains, slowly climbed and descended the *Swartberge,* and finally rushed through the *Vlakte* (plain) toward the distant Table Mountain with Cape Town at it's foot. In summer it was hot in the compartments, sometimes so hot that we covered ourselves with wet towels to provide us with a little cooling, as at that time there was no air-conditioning. The engine's soot seeped in through the windows whether they were open or not. We just had to put up with its filth. In winter it was cold, the blankets supplied by SAR not warm enough, so we had to bring an additional one from home to be cozy. Dad and I chatted, and read many books. On later trips we children visited each other to catch up with holiday stories, about home or our travels, to play cards, tell jokes, or visit Hans-Erik who often entertained us playing his accordion. We'd sing along songs, or simply listened to his music, such as "The Chattanooga Train" and "Don't Fence me in." He liked to play jazz. We liked to listen.

I don't recall how we eventually got to the boarding house from the main station, or what happened on our arrival, or when my dad left. I simply shut the eyes of my soul, sad over being left, and feeling overwhelmed by so much that was new: not knowing anyone, or where to go, what to do, in fact, learning the complete daily routine, having to learn life here from scratch. As I hardly understood any English, I guess I just followed the flow of bells ringing, and drifted along to where others went. I was placed in a dorm on the north side of the building in a cubicle next to the prefect who probably helped me out, yet I don't remember any of it. There were six dorms altogether, each one housing fourteen girls, every girl in an individual cubicle. Although the walls of the cubicles did not reach up to the ceiling, they still created a space though not completely yet almost private, that was also closed off by only a curtain, not a door. They were Spartan quarters: no decorations allowed, no carpets anywhere. Each contained at most a bed, a closet and a bedside table and chair. There was one bathroom with a bath and washbasins for each dorm with enough hot water daily for washing, and one weekly bath in the fifteen minutes granted between 8 and 9.15 of an evening. Initiation was mild: new girls had to make the dorm prefects' bed every morning and polish her shoes every evening for three months. I did not mind such easy tasks.

From my geography classes I knew that Cape Town was a beautiful city. Mr. Peter had shown us pictures of Table Mountain with Devil's Peak and Lion's Head on either side, The Gardens and the governor's mansion at its foot. Now I had a view of Devil's Peak every day for four years, later for another four during my student years at the University of Cape Town that stood upon its slopes. I still remember part of our beautiful school song:

"On the slopes of Table Mountain, in the shade of Devil's Peak,
In the old Cape Gov'ners garden where the Liesbeek's winding creek,
In a field of arum lilies and a sky of azure blue,
With the golden sunshine round us, we shall sing one or two:
In the old Cape Gov'nor's garden, 'neath the oaks of van der Stel,
With its white stoep on the highway, let Rustenburg excel!"

However, being at Rustenburg and in Cape-Town slowly created in me an internal fault line. I came to see one more way of life, another culture very different from mine, with also a third language. What should I retain from the past, what acquire from the present? Those were my silent questions, trying to live with this dividedness as best as I could.

The school catered for 484 girls all dressing in this uniform of navy and sky blue. As I didn't much like wearing what everyone else was, I seemed to lose my sense of self in this sea of girls, yet at the same time felt different from them. We were eighty-four boarders. Some came from more distant locations in the Western Province in which Cape Town was located, some from other African countries, such as Northern or Southern Rhodesia, (now Zambia and Zimbabwe), a few even from Europe, from Holland and England. Meals were most memorable, especially the breakfasts, which were vastly different from the fare we had been given in Omaruru: toast with fried eggs and bacon, or scrambled eggs, or baked beans, or marmalade, sometimes porridge, and coffee or tea or milk to boot. No worms! No beetles! Most girls were on a diet so that I, always starving for food, had lots of butter at my disposal.

The school offered many subject choices in the first two years. Everyone had two languages: English and Afrikaans, with a choice of Latin, French, or German as the third. Everyone also took mathematics, history, geography, biology, and science (physics, astronomy and chemistry) and, possibly, home economics. In the third year I chose the combination of math, history and science, and took German instead of Latin. The only trouble was that I already knew German and had to have a private teacher so as not to get bored. This teacher was nice but uninspiring, not terribly imaginative, and, in the end, I was glad to be done with her. In addition each class had a weekly singing lesson, as well as a period for gymnastics. After school we could join a number of societies, such as a debating club, a science club, and others. All of us had to participate in sports: in field hockey, netball, tennis, and swimming. And, as we could pay for extra classes – thanks to my dad, I finally was able to have piano lessons! For some six months I had had lessons in Omaruru with a lovely teacher. Years later I met her when a grown-up. "Yes, I remember you! You had no sense of time and came wandering over at any time on a Friday afternoon when you were supposed to have your lesson. You were such a dreamer, but so sweet. And I always gave you some fruits from the garden afterward!" My heart melted that she remembered me so kindly.

At Rustenburg I loved my piano teacher, Desiree Taylor. She was a concert pianist, but as she had broken a little finger at some point in her career, she switched to singing while still teaching the art of playing the piano. I practiced daily for two hours and reached the sixth grade level in the fourth year. Other girls who had lessons with her always asked me what mood she was in. "Was she friendly? Or disgruntled?" I couldn't say. I had fun with her, while I think she appreciated my taking music seriously. Music was my life. It sustained me throughout the difficult times of high school.

Because my grandma knew French, I had joined the class that offered it as a choice instead of Latin. However, after four days being in this class, our headmistress, Miss Gwen Hazell – referred to by us as "Nutty" – appeared. She was a formidable woman, both physically and mentally. As I discovered very quickly, every girl was afraid of her. She was tall and buxom, with honey-red curly hair, and piercing blue eyes that nailed you. She had a sharp mind, and, as the school grape vine had it, she had regular conversations with the Latin teacher in – guess what? – Latin! Fortunately or not, she left at the end of 1951.

"What are you doing here, in this class, Helge?" Nutty boomed at me.

Quite petrified, I responded: "I want to learn French!"

"Oh, no! Your father wants you to learn Latin. So you are going to learn Latin. Collect your books. I myself will take you now to the appropriate class!"

I steamed while she marched me to the appropriate classroom. But what could I do? I told my dad that should I fail Latin he could consider it his own fault. I managed a D in the first year, while in the second I almost managed to fail it. *So there you are! I told you so!*

Miss Margaret Thomson, the new headmistress after Nutty left, was a math genius. The only math she failed to teach me was geometry. She would not have insisted on my complying with my dad's wishes, I liked to think, as she was young, at least a lot younger than Nutty. She was tall and slim, with very dark hair elegantly kept. She looked beautiful when wearing a wide-brimmed hat. She always wore stylish clothes that suited her. Besides, she also had a sense of humor and was not only strict. When teaching my class math for the last two years, she often chalked up a diagram on the blackboard as soon as she walked in. "Now girls. Which theorem are we dealing with here?" she'd ask, expecting an immediate response from us. My brain often drew a blank, obviously having trouble with integration of information. Until one day the quite unexpected happened. She had done her signature drawing on the board, and, as usual asked who knew the answer. Silence. "I can't believe this! Really, no one knows the answer? No one?" She looked around the class. I did as well. I could hardly believe I was the only one who thought she knew. *Our whizz-girl Rheina didn't, and Annemarie didn't either?* "Anyone?" she asked once more. I timidly raised my hand a little. "Helge? Well, how wonderful. Someone does have an answer. Tell us." I did. And I happened to have been right. I glowed, hoping that I was not quite so bad at integrating facts as I thought I was, even though this remained my only glorious moment in geometry.

During the first three weeks I hardly ever said a word. It was difficult for me follow daily conversations, even more difficult to follow lessons. For much of the first year I felt left out because of my inability to understand or express myself in this new, unknown world, and with no one to guide me. Not surprisingly I was lonely, sorely missing my family and the world I knew. But the girls were friendly. They kept encouraging me to speak. "You can't possibly remain silent!" They never laughed at my garbled efforts. Yet on the whole I remained quiet, always watching, and absorbing this world in which I felt so foreign.

Although my grades dropped precipitously in my first year, they resumed my usual level for the next three. My English run-of-the-mill teacher, Mrs. Wakeford, kept encouraging me. "If you keep on working hard like this, you'll manage well," she'd say. In the next year I received similar encouragement, and began to like and understand literature and poetry much better. Although I had lost my old friends, I found new ones. In particular there was a day student, Carla S. from Holland, with blonde hair, blue eyes, and a small perky nose that pointed to heaven. We spent four years in the same class. I sat in a desk behind her; it was easy to check on vocabulary at close quarters, reading the dictionary in an effort to improving our English, comparing notes, going over each other's homework. Carla was a language genius. Her dad was Russian, her mom Polish, and she mastered both tongues. They had fled to Holland during World War II, where she went to school in Leyden, where she had to learn Dutch, German and French, and English as well. Eventually English became my third tongue, almost replacing my German. Jumping into the deep end of waters was not my way of doing things, but now, here, I simply had to swim.

I had known life at this school would be a new experience. What I did not know was how different a world I had entered then, a world so far from home that I was able to return home only twice a year: for six weeks in December and January, for three in July, every time making that three-day trip by train.

Despite the many difficulties I discovered positives about boarding school. Had I not hoped for a better time? I liked the different environment: the friendlier nature, the friendlier climate, and the novelty of meeting girls from all over South Africa, even from outside it. One amazing novelty was that we all received a checkbook, were required to make out checks for what we bought, and as well present a quarterly financial report of expenses, which, of course for me, could not exceed my allowance of three pounds per quarter. Other girls received much more than this. Using a checkbook made me feel very grownup and efficient. Another novelty was the thriller experience at the end of most quarters of an organized midnight feast, using the kitchen – the only off-limits area in the building - as our venue. It wasn't easy to be very quiet when tiptoeing in the dark so as not to wake the three grand old ladies that acted as our housemothers. It was both spooky and exciting. The cheek, the nerve we had just to eat baked beans in the dark! A further new and very different experience from Omaruru was that we had to regulate our table manners ourselves. No one should have to ask for anything. You were expected to notice and pass to your neighbor what they needed. And above all, we were allowed to talk!

What was also new were the different ways of doing things— for example how you used knife and fork at table, where you kept your hands, how you spoke to others. My German table manners differed from those of the other girls. They teased me when I made an open sandwich, eating it with knife and a fork. "It's not a steak, you know!" they'd point out. All the same, life here remained as strict as it had been in Omaruru. Overstepping boundaries was punished harshly. Apparently girls who left the school grounds without permission had been expelled in the past.

We talked about much more than we ever did at home, especially about boys and girls and their bodies. Who had the most beautiful breasts? Audrey apparently did, though I had never seen them. "Sex" was discussed many times – involving having periods with or without cramps, and kissing and dating. Girls talked about boys all the time: who said what; who was handsome; who was smart and whom you had dated, had actually kissed. What was also new here, though, was that, unfortunately, there were no boys around. The only time we saw some was at the quarterly dance that was organized for us in conjunction with our "brother school." On those evenings the house-mothers, all three of them, sat on the stage of our school hall, their watchful eyes roaming hawk-like over the scene, a deterrent to any action that might be anything other than dancing, while watching us no doubt also stimulated their own desires. I learnt to dance in the fifteen minutes we were allowed into the gym after homework time at eight in the evening. One of the girls would play the piano there, and those that knew how to dance taught those who did not. I especially recall learning the Charleston, first finding my balance against a wall in order appropriately kick my heels. The Matric (last year at school) dance was an ordeal: with a blind date and wearing a plain pale blue taffeta dress of mom's choice. Do I hold his hand between dances? Do I allow him to put his arm around my waist? Do I actually kiss him goodbye? It was a most awkward evening of uncertainty about how to be with a boy that I didn't even know.

In Omaruru we had a pool to splash in and spent some afternoons doing athletics, running, long jump and high-jump. Here we were offered more than that, and I particularly enjoyed tennis with my friend Christine as a doubles team, and field hockey where the two of us chose to play back defense, she the right, I the left. She was one of my new friends, and came from the Copperbelt in what is now Zambia. We played well together, and both of us felt that the gym teacher, Miss Chamberlain, did not give us the team placement we considered our due because we excelled at both. "You're as good as the first backs, " she told us. But did she ever let us play first backs? Not in her lifetime! And although we even beat our first tennis doubles team she never let us play as first team. She definitely and most unfairly was a woman who had her favorites.

I had two other special friends. One was Pat from England, though unfortunately she returned back home after a year. And the other was Ute. Ute W. came from Grootfontein in South-West Africa. There were only four German-speaking girls at Rustenburg. She was one, and Anka V. the other, who came from Windhoek. Karen, when she also came here, and I were the other two. Ute's parents were the friends of a couple who owned a hotel in Claremont, a suburb not far from Rondebosch. Ute and I spent most weekends we had off to visit family or friends with them, staying at their hotel, which was probably the first hotel I had ever stayed in or had even entered, where I saw my first menu and had to choose to me hitherto unknown dishes. The first dish I chose happened to be *baboetie*, a Malaysian curry dish. I had simply ordered what Ute had, fully ignorant of what curry is, only to discover I was eating meat on fire. Besides novelties such as a menu that included other novel dishes like baboetie, I also had to come to terms with the vast amounts of cutlery arranged all around my plate. When to use which fork? Which knife? Which spoon? It was quite confusing. One of each was without question much simpler. And on top of all this I had to figure out how to deal with a waiter – there was indeed an endless number of new things I had to absorb. I often felt very ignorant and awkward. Learning through experience was definitely the hardest way to learn.

I did have a few teachers that I liked. One was my biology teacher, a small, bosomy, soft- spoken woman. Her knowledge inspired Christine and me to become her best students. On our required pre-breakfast walks crocodile style through the immediate environment of the hostel we collected leaves and flowers, later in the day testing her knowledge with our pickings in class. She knew the answers for all we knew, and took our pranks seriously, encouraging us to find new plants.

I even liked my strict science teacher, white-haired and pink-faced Miss Heath, and spent two years being her monitor, setting up the lab for our chemistry experiments. No one else liked the job – the other girls were scared of being told off by this fierce and demanding woman. I wasn't. Omaruru had made me tough.

Our very elderly Afrikaans teacher, Miss Dormehl, was the kindest of them all. She reminded me of my grandma, because she was almost blind and wore very thick spectacles that allowed her to see at least a little. She had a soft heart for teenagers, and many of us talked to her about our sorrows with parents and boyfriends, and she kindly organized blind dates for the end-of-school Matric dance, as she did for me. We all liked and respected her. No wonder I always had A's in Afrikaans. Miss Dose gave us singing lessons and led the choir; Miss Taylor, my piano teacher, finally helped me realize my dream of playing the piano. Both furthered my love for music, a love that my dad had already instilled in me with his piano playing and our endlessly singing folksongs on many an evening when at home.

Although this new life allowed me a richer view of the world, I felt I paid for these riches with more losses than I would have chosen. I missed my family. Attending Rustenburg was not an easy experience, yet one that gave me a new perspective on life at home, providing a wide array of new and very different experiences, expanding the horizons of my life. Everything was so different from what I had known so far, from what I had felt comfortable with. The contrast was often enormous. In Omaruru most children came from similar circumstances. We were all more or less poor. Attending this elite school opened a view on life that showed even greater varieties, also economic ones, explicit differences that all existed simultaneously. Somehow I stayed afloat on this ocean of a new life, graduated with 99 other girls and received a first class matriculation certificate as a stronger though still very quiet person.

After four years at Rustenburg nothing would ever be quite the same again. Certainly the cultural conflicts in our family escalated, between our parents and us children, more especially with my mother. She strongly resisted any signs of our independence and coming of age. To her, I think, our growing up was a loss. We changed too much for her liking, certainly more than she could tolerate. She did not like our new loves for clothing, especially not for shorts – might not men – and most especially not black men - see more of our legs than they should? But we were alive, and living meant we'd change. They had chosen to send us away, at least my dad did. And I don't know how he ever persuaded mom to let us go. She did not want any of us to ever marry someone other than a German-speaking person. It turned out that the boys complied with her wish, we girls did not. My father was much more easy-going than my mother. He usually gave us more trust and freedom than Mom did. On my first trip alone to Rustenburg I had left my watch in the bathroom after washing up. It had been a special gift for my confirmation. I felt terrible. What would my parents say? Scold me for being so forgetful? To my greatest amazement dad simply wrote: buy another at Garlick's – the department store where we could buy things occasionally on his account. No reprimands from him. That was typical of my dad!

After I had matriculated, he even gave me the choice of either going to university right away, or of visiting the family in Germany first, which no doubt also was to my mom's liking. I chose to visit, to see where my parents and brother had gone without me when I was little, this strange place that was so different from the land and the farm I knew, from our way of life in Africa.

The eight months of visiting family members proved special for me. I was always the center of attention. Everyone wanted to hear from me all about

Africa, a continent about which they knew not too much, mostly only from books, not from experience. Very few had been there themselves. Some knew someone who had lived there or had actually visited if they had had the means to travel in the difficult post-war years. Sometimes questions were stunning. "Can you tell "real" Africans apart? Don't they all look alike?" *Of course not!* Or even really stupid questions such as "What happens to the sand when it gets hot?" I hesitated before deciding to give an unrealistic answer. "Well. You surely know about atoms, yes? Well, sand behaves just the way atoms do. Grains move ever faster the hotter it gets. It's a strange feeling to walk on hot moving sand." Amazement - they did not know that. So I discovered how gullible people could be. This trip made me feel special because I could tell them about to them different experiences. But it also made me experience myself as being different, enhancing both my sense of coming from somewhere unusual and therefore special, of being an African, feeling at the same time more uncertain about where I belonged. I used to be a quiet child. Importantly, this trip released me from remaining so silent.

Dealing with these changes and losses of growing up was painful for all of us in the family. Life was becoming more complex, the question of identity more haunting. Where did we belong? Our coming of age as the fourth generation in a new country on a different continent established rifts with those who came before us. Undoubtedly I felt I belonged to Africa forever, the Africa of South-West, not to Europe, not to Cape-Town. Yet throughout my days of schooling I always wished I could have been closer to home, closer to the comfort of a past I thought I understood.

Choosing to Teach

J ust as Dad had decided that his children should learn English as a prerequisite for a career, he also insisted that we should attend university. He himself had received only a "red" school-leaving certificate at age seventeen. The German government had issued so-called red certificates to students not because they had actually completed their final school year, the Abitur, but because they were "deemed old enough" to be drafted into the country's depleted army that was losing the war: World War One. My dad was fortunate to have received his certificate too late for him to be sent to a German war front. However, because of the turmoil after the war, and without a proper school-leaving certificate, he did not attend university. For a while he rode with the Hussars of Kassel and worked on farms. His oldest brother, Erich, was an officer in the navy, and his second and older brother, Alfred, was able to study medicine despite the circumstances.

Dad was determined that his daughters as well as his sons should have a better academic deal than he had had, and so for three of us the University of Cape Town became our alma mater. Hans-Erik studied architecture, I history and German, and Karen received a degree as librarian. Jürgen was more practically minded; he did a four-year apprenticeship as a motor mechanic in Kiel, Germany.

My degree was generally known as the "marriage degree." Although I had vaguely thought of studying theology afterward, I had no particular goals in mind, not yet even the one of getting married young like the Afrikaans speaking sixteen-year old girls in Omaruru had. I hoped there were more choices of what to do with life. The possibilities seemed to abound like stars in the sky, but not one shone particularly brightly.

As far as the curriculum was concerned, my years of study at the UCT were remarkably similar to those at high school. Even there the content for every subject's annual course was determined from the very beginning. Although one might read more than was required, the basic list of books and articles prescribed, and the number of essays that had to be written were more than enough material to keep one working hard. Of course there were some significant differences between high school and college. For myself the most important realization from studying history was not accepting printed words for truth. Historians, and not only they, needed to discern sources, the circumstances of who, why, when and at what moment words were written or spoken, and with what possible intent, an insight further emphasized by my later three semesters studying theology. Another and very important difference was experiencing the struggle of students against the government's efforts to segregate us along "racial" lines. Interestingly enough, actually only very few "non-whites" attended the so-called "English" universities, such as UCT, Wits, Rhodes, Natal, and Fort Hare. It was not their numbers that were the issue at stake. It was the principle beyond it that really mattered.

Though the political scene of apartheid had been familiar and accepted before, it now gained a cutting edge. The players at UCT were not politicians. They were young, passionate students involved in the most political of confrontations, a confrontation that had begun with the very creation of the Cape settlement in 1652 as a refueling stop for Dutch ships, and that continued ever since then: the colonizers, who happened to be white against the natives who were not white. "They" were not "we." In the long run "we" wanted what "they" had.

I watched the process from the ranks of the Student Christian Association. In this association (SCA) I was also confronted with a great variety of questions others were asking, questions that had never before occurred to me, not only about politics but also about religion, and especially about social attitudes regarding dress, sexuality, relationships—questions that ruffled the smooth, unquestioning surfaces of my faith and the way of life I had simply accepted for so long. Looking back, I think, it needed many years for the experiences of those days to permeate me effectively, stuck as I had been between wanting to leave and wanting to stay, experiences I suspect that affected me, probably imperceptibly even from the very beginning. I watched carefully what was happening, listened intensely to the students who were protesting, and struggled to discard the habit of simply submitting to the expectations of my parents and others, merely being cagily obedient. I had to find my own feet first in order to assert myself, accept my personal difference before being political – or was that precisely being political?

Instead of joining in the protests I chose my friends myself, made my own decisions about how to style my hair, what to wear, how to spend my time and my money. Our choice of friends became a heated conflict for us children especially with my mother. English-speaking friends were not terribly welcome, especially not young men or women we might be interested in, because, she claimed she would not be able to talk to them. But she could speak English well. She had worked for an English-speaking family in Paarl for about two years before she married. Besides, we were but four German-speaking students at high school, and only a few more at university. Even in my German courses at UCT there was only one other native speaker of the tongue. What did my mom expect?

My mother also refused to allow me to travel to Zambia's Copperbelt to spend my first December holidays away from home with my twin friends, Robin and Wendy. I refused her demand and even asked for the money for the train fare. It was my dad who sent me the money for the trip, asking for a compromise on my part: to come home for at least half the holiday. That I did. My mom seemingly did not like any change, nor did she like her children to be independent, and especially not different from her own generation's customs. She confessed to spending many sleepless nights after I cut my hair without asking her permission, this having been the next act of my independence. Even worse was the effect of the photo I sent to inform my parents that I had cut my hair, which showed the stylish cut and my bare shoulders. Bare shoulders implied too much visible sexuality. The years at university most certainly provided the impetus for forging my own views and attitudes, establishing my own individuality.

After receiving my degree from the University of Cape Town in 1959, I spent almost three years in Germany. I wandered, like Wotan, in search of I did not know what. I lived in Hamburg, doing odd jobs to pay my way.

I cut out ads for newspapers and journals, in particular for the journal *Der Spiegel*. I got up at four in the morning to cut *Plattenkuchen* (flat cake baked on large trays) into sellable squares in a bakery. I sorted punch cards on Hollerith machines for insurance companies researching demographic information about their policyholders. I did similar work for the post office, although there it became more of a social event as six of us worked together around a table, talking and telling jokes all the while sorting cards. I picked up whatever work was available, no matter how boring or how repetitive. Though earning my keep, I was really looking for something much more challenging. I spent a semester for international students of theology at Chateau de Bossey in Switzerland. I was fascinated by the variety of students attending, the way I had been fascinated by the different people on Omburo. I met a Sotho pastor from Lesotho who had perhaps never yet sat at a table. I met Sewesi, an Abessynian we called "Sunshine" because of his constant smiling, a man who believed firmly that eating rice enhanced a woman's fertility. Another student, a Nigerian, had spent six years of study in Great Britain. An Indonesian student and I endlessly discussed his options with him: of staying in Britain, or of returning home. He did not wish to go back, arguing that nothing much had changed in Nigeria since it had obtained its independence. "The system," he claimed, "has remained the same. It's only the color of the players that has changed. Besides, I can't go back to the old ways there: they have fallen apart."

During my time off work I attended not only lectures about theology at the University of Hamburg but also others. Some were inspiring, like those by Professor Friedrich von Weizsaecker on relativity. He had such a clear mind, exposing complex ideas with extreme lucidity. Study physics, was my enthusiastically impulsive idea. It led nowhere. Other lectures were dumbfounding, like those about the German poet and writer Hoelderlin, ones that left me feeling: *I don't know any German! I don't understand a thing!* They impressed on me how obscure German could be, even to other students - "real" Germans- that took the course. Even while studying the language at UCT I often thought it a strange tongue, filled with to me unknown images such as of woods, and meadows in the morning mist and snow. For me it had grown on foreign soil, a soil different indeed from the African soil familiar to me.

When I began taking courses in theology, I had no particular goal in mind, though unwittingly I had wanted to explore this Lutheran Christian faith in which I was raised. My mind had grown in a society imbued with religion, with values and priorities that permeated life, all breathed in without thought, like the air. But my awareness grew as the questions that began raising their heads at UCT grew stronger in yet another new environment. Ultimately, however, I was unwilling to overcome the hurdles to pursue a degree in theology. Studying Latin for five years—a requirement for being a full-time theology student—was the final deterrent. I had detested the subject at high school. Asserting myself, I was almost successful in failing it. Besides, not knowing Latin was a good excuse to pursue something different. Although courses in Greek and Hebrew, in Old and New Testament hermeneutics and in comparative religion were captivating, ultimately they contributed to the further thinning of my faith into paler doubts. Religion, it seemed, was useful in several ways. The most important one I made out was that it removed the believer's fear of death, that there would be no ultimate separation from loved ones, no relegation into the abyss of non-existence, as if never even having lived. Religion gives meaning, it makes you feel safe, there's someone who cares about you even if no one else does, and often even takes the responsibility for what happens in this world.

The Bible is indeed a complex Book. The theology I was confronted with presented too many perspectives. "Orthodoxy", whichever one claimed, was simply to be accepted, never proven. Thoughts seemed to be based more on philosophical premises, on opinions, on beliefs supported by suitable parts picked from the Bible, and on faith itself. Assumptions often presented a narrowness of mind, saw blaming a requirement for salvation, ultimately being somehow self-supporting, circular, and rather intended for social control. I came to think that even though Karl Marx's claim that "religion is opium for the people" was many-faceted, one claim I concurred with was that religion often provided justifications for actions of the powerful. "It is god's will!" Another facet that I agreed with was that it tended to provide the hope for a better future for the oppressed and the poor. Except that this change for the better was to be in heaven, not on earth. Besides, no one had yet come back from heaven to tell us about it. It was pure belief.

The same Book called forth interpretations juxtaposed with other interpretations, spawning divisions, each belief system claiming to be the right one, often the only right one, the truth, the only truth. There was the time in Omaruru when Pastor Kuhles primed us to recite our Lutheran catechism before we could be confirmed, where I glimpsed the rigorousness of the

Calvinism of the Dutch Reformed Church. At Rustenburg I participated in the teachings of Episcopalians and at university became familiar with the Methodist view. Without being particularly aware of this, I began to realize that I was looking to escape from such frameworks of existence, from fragmentation and divisive fences, away from the pietistic tradition of my great-grandfather Johann Wilhelm's mission, of having to save others as well as one self. Could one save others? Why did we need to be saved, and from what?

Though I marveled at how much trust my Ur-Opa Redecker had in his God, I appreciated the more mystical and romantic aspects of his pietism. I myself wasn't sure if there were many gods, or even only one. There was no proof for or against the existence of either view. It came down to a question of belief—and, needless to say, belief is a strong source of motivation, as it is also a fountain of strength for endurance and persistence. Yet even though I neither kept his faith nor shared its proselytizing quest, I admit that many of the values by which Ur-Opa lived are to this day a part of who I am: be true to yourself; grant others the space to be true to themselves; pursue personal integrity, and care for your-self as well as for others. Above all, remain human as best you could!

In my search of what to do with my life, I recalled with envy those Matric classmates, who, even before leaving high school had known what they wished to pursue in life: to study math or science, or simply to get married. *Was there nothing I could do?* I wondered in desperation. While I was still in Hamburg, I happened to hear an inspiring lecture on education. Be a teacher! I told myself. After all, Oma Dieta had been a teacher. Why shouldn't I? There was something attractive about it: about being curious, pursuing knowledge, attempting to achieve an understanding of the world, being able to explain things, imparting this thirst to others, thereby gaining a more definite sense of self. Teaching allowed for visions of possibilities, of both certainty and uncertainty. It was a way of thinking about life in this world together with others who also wanted to learn and understand more.

So I traveled back to Namibia in 1963 and enrolled again at the University of Cape Town to earn my Senior Teaching Diploma. During that year I hung out with David B., a fellow history student whom I knew from my undergraduate years. We talked a great deal about the student struggles in the fifties, about segregation being imposed on higher educational facilities in South Africa in general, more specifically on our own alma mater, a struggle that early on was mostly one of words, though, as it wore on and tensions rose, became more tangibly vicious and dangerous. Students were imprisoned for their acts of protest. Later, both blacks and whites went into exile to avoid being killed. I remembered many discussions and conversations I had with individual supporters of segregation. It slowly dawned on me that talking rarely changed much. It was deeds that counted. When talking all that seemed to be happening was a fossilizing and polarization of already established beliefs that in reality I felt was actually a struggle for domination and power. Rifts of opinion became ever more firmly established. Gaps grew ever wider, often expressing deep-seated fears covered by the conviction that "I believe that what I believe is right."

Beliefs seemed unshakeable, as in religion, so in politics. Was it because beliefs were an inseparable part of identity? Could one actually distinguish between idea and person? In Bossey I found a few European students distinguishing between person and ideas. For the rest ideas and person were one. Was the desire for power the obstacle, a narcissistic attempt at making the world "according to my own world" because a different world could not be tolerated?

The most contentious belief expressed directly, more or less since 1948, was that the message from God to "His" people, especially the Boers, was that each "race" was separately ordained. Each "race" had a special place in God's creation, a place that was to be retained until whenever—best until eternity. There were, of course, those who added that, ostensibly according to the Bible, some people, especially black Africans, were seen as "them," identifying them as the water carriers for "us," namely for white Africans in power. The political camouflage used was "separate but equal." Or, put even more seductively, "we're all equal but separate." Calvin's teachings were deeply rooted and hard at work. But were we not equal and different at the same time, equal in our humanity but different in the details, not preordained, as Calvin thought, but ever changing? It seemed to me that this belief—that every human being had a preordained identity and therefore an established place in life—spelled security for those in power, quelling their fears of being outnumbered, while permitting the believers to retain control over society. It also salvaged any guilt they might experience. Was everything not simply the way it was supposed to be? No one was responsible. God was! He, suitably, had ordained it to be so. Beliefs were the scaffold for feeling safe in life.

The perceived threat of being outnumbered, especially in economically hard times, usually deepens already existing fears that allow prejudice to affirm divisions and differences. I doubt that we will ever live without prejudice. It seems to be a part of our human condition because of our concerns and fears over surviving, our feelings of envy, because of our concern over our so easily threatened identity. Besides, how else would you know who you really were without the scaffold of the belief of "equal and separate?" Did it not provide each individual with a firm identity? Skin color is an easy definer, a visible and useful criterion. Beyond and beneath this belief nagged the denied truth of the past in SA that new biological identities of "mixed blood" had come into being, sexually transmitted via genes over decades, appearances that raised doubts about belonging. Laws, based on beliefs, had to come to the rescue and categorize people visibly, and, therefore, ostensibly, securely, even if only on paper.

Fearing that the 1960 uprisings in Angola against the Portuguese might spread south across our border, the South African government spent a great deal of money on constructing macadamized roads in South-West Africa, from the Orange River in the south to the banks of the Kunene in the north, from the Kalahari in the east to the Atlantic Coast in the west. The government also built airports and expanded the harbor in Walvis Bay. All this was done with a view of being able to move troops rapidly northward to keep any possible conflict outside its own borders, hopefully also outside its buffering mandate. Until then SA had not invested much in this mandate, its "fifth province." At that time South Africa had been divided into four administrative provinces: the Cape and Natal with more liberal tendencies, while the Transvaal and Orange Free State represented the conservative views of the *Voortrekkers,* the Boers, who forever wished to escape the control of British governments. As a fifth province with a small population it was easier for South Africa to implement its policies in South-West Africa, using it as a buffer against outside threats of change instead of really improving the lot of its people. This new threat, emanating from Angola, proved to be an extraordinarily motivating force for action on South Africa's part.

In 1962 Frans Hendrik Odendaal, nick-named the "Fox", headed a commission to study SWA with a view to implementing Apartheid as in the creation of "homelands" recommended by Dr. F. R. Tomlinson in South Africa itself. Odendaal's report was published in 1964, requiring the staking out of special geographical areas for every "racial" subgroup. Nine new "Bantustans," alias homelands, were meant to "protect" the possession of land by different racial groups, while also establishing the idea of equal but separate in order to control.

In reality we had already been living separately before then. People here had lived separately from the beginning, from the moment the first traders and explorers entered South-West Africa, though perhaps not quite in the formal and legalistic sense that the Odendaal or Tomlinson plans had had in mind. Missionaries in South-West Africa, throughout the late nineteenth and early twentieth century, had themselves in fact made similar suggestions of setting up "reservations" like the "homelands" to prevent indigenous folks, in particular the Herero, from giving up and selling all their land, losing it to white colonists. Although people of the same culture and language like to congregate anyway, and while so many different tongues do present barriers, there also had been the unwritten, invisible social rules of segregation, fences that quietly reconfirmed identity and station of people. We had long since been imbued with nineteenth-century ideas of "race." South Africa's ideas were not new to us.

More apartheid, stricter than before, came to be established after 1948, especially in the field of education. Black African children were still not required by law to attend school, while white African children had to complete all standards or any they were able to attain by the age of sixteen. This assured whites a desirable economic edge. On the one hand, for blacks, obtaining an education was essentially a question of economics, of whether families could afford to let their children attend school. Often every member of a black family was needed to contribute to making a living or helping with chores at home. Perhaps some folks even kept children home to prevent their youngsters from becoming imbued with "fancy" and different ideas. On the other hand, it was also a question of whether schools were at all available, whether there were any teachers at all trained to do the teaching. Sometimes the teachers themselves had attended school for only six years, if that long. But then, of course, you had to start somewhere.

Another difficulty was the one of language: blacks were required to be taught in their mother tongue in the first four to six years as confirmation of their identity. After this, Afrikaans became the new medium of instruction. In practice, of course, so many different languages presented an almost insurmountable hurdle for a more modern education. In fact, most African countries had to deal with a plethora of tongues, countries such as Kenya or Tanzania, where hundreds of languages are spoken, many more than in South-West Africa.

During these years the people who disagreed with the main governmental policy were "liberals." Since South Africa had become a union within the British Commonwealth, there had always been a Liberal Party. Being a liberal was gradually understood as pejorative, politically negative. Liberals were seen as sitting on fences, spineless and soft, masochists who tended to turn the other cheek, who lacked power, or who were loathe to use it to set limits. It became worse when, because of opposition to the establishment, they were also designated as being "communists," though some actually were. All those opposing the establishment were increasingly haunted and hunted, arrested, jailed, and exiled. Soon, instead of being communists, they were decried by the government as terrorists or guerillas (as many actually were) while they saw themselves as "freedom fighters," as the legitimate voices of the majority of the people.

As any real negotiation for change was found to be out of the question, people on both sides of the divide increasingly resorted to force. Beliefs were too intransigent, the fear of gaining or losing not only power too great. Violence bred ever more violence. How you judged the situation depended on which side your beliefs were to be found, on where your advantages existed, and what you thought defined your identity. The "white" definition of reality and identity was not to be challenged.

All the above described the situation in which I found myself at this time. It was a great deal to digest, to understand, to inform my own stand in life.

That year at UCT, 1963, I found the classes not only boring, I felt treated like an infant. Lecturers liked to dictate notes, including commas and full stops, something both David and I rejected and were not used to. We tended to have our own whispered discussions. Rather than take notes of the professor's lecture on the history of education, I preferred to write down the many wise quotes pouring from his lips: "A lecture is the process by which the notes of the professor become the notes of the student without passing through the minds of either." "Language is a great way of concealing your thoughts." These sayings rang true to my ears in the setting of dictated notes. Did they not prevent the processes of thinking, of discussion, of communication?

The one exception—and it remained the most exciting and enduring one ever —turned out to be the classes of "Tinkie" Heyns, our professor of educational psychology. Tinkie proved to be a master teacher. "You can forget this date," he'd say, and you were sure to remember it. Tinkie had invented an exemplary pupil, McCullem, in order to demonstrate his ideas. "Well," he'd say, "what will you do when McCullempy comes up with something that upsets your beautifully crafted lesson plan?" We had to prove our ability to remain flexible, to adjust to any changes in class that would arise out of student behavior, and use the moment of digression for teaching the young to problem-solve. "Always remember," Tinkie continued to impress on us, "that some of your pupils will be a lot smarter than you. Students learn from you and you from them. They teach you! It is a two-way process. Education is when you live by everything that you were once taught but have forgotten."

A lecture was never a lecture with Tinkie; it was always a discussion. And our most intense discussions were about intelligence. In his view intelligence was not merely a question of remembering facts, though, of course, a good memory was helpful. To him, intelligence was the ability to make connections between facts, between thoughts. It was a question of seeing the "gap," as in rugby, the realization of its existence allowing for making a touchdown. Seeing "gaps" by connecting facts, often those outside "the box," that was insight. This was the creative moment of all intelligence, the ability to solve problems by thinking outside the box of acquired facts and experience, a creativity that reached beyond the limits of the known wherever you might be living on our globe! Tinkie's thinking and his methods were exciting. I tried to make them mine.

My attitude toward education was also influenced by my experience of practice teaching later that year at one of the "Ivy League" high schools for girls in the area. The class history teacher there began his lessons by saying, "Please take out your handbooks. Open your book on such-and-such a page." Then he read from the book, explained a few points, and commanded from time to time: "Underline!" At the end of the lesson he'd say, "For homework, learn the underlined material by heart." No discussion took place. At most he answered a few stray questions. I was distraught and disgusted. Apparently Tinkie's ideas did not necessarily prevail in schools generally. That changed only many years later. Or maybe not.

In addition to this rote spoon-feeding, the senior teacher of this school told me, "I hope you will not be offended, but I advise you to wear stockings with your sandals. And do wear tops with sleeves! Bare legs, and the bare arms of teachers make a bad and undesirable impression on young girls. Also, the headmistress might reproach you. That would be embarrassing not only for you but for all the staff." I shuddered inwardly. I thought back on Miss Le Roux and her red nails and high heels. Was I really being too sexy without stockings or sleeves? What did it actually mean: "to be sexy?"

Despite the intensity of the summer's heat, I put on stockings and wore dresses and tops with sleeves. After all, I did want my diploma. But I vowed not ever to apply for a job in this or any similar school. David assured me that other African countries would welcome me, without stockings (they couldn't afford them) and without sleeves (they didn't matter). I myself hoped I might find a school where I could implement Tinkie's ideas.

In December 1963, I earned my senior teaching diploma from UCT. I was planning to teach in Dar Es Salaam, Tanzania, but instead returned to Omburo for a year to help my mother care for my sick father and run the farm.

Three years prior to his death my dad began developing a small but persistent cough. He had been a very healthy man until then. Visit a doctor? Absolutely not! Yet the cough would not go away. My mom worried, and only after months of her nagging he finally went for a consultation. "Silicosis!" the doctor in Swakopmund declared. "It's a result of years of breathing daily dust, not much to worry about." The cough, however, continued. Our family doctor also worried. Tests for tuberculosis remained negative. She sent him to Windhoek. Still no indications of TB could be found. Those doctors also worried. They sent my dad to Cape Town, where the doctors finally made a diagnosis: he indeed had tuberculosis, also in his brain. Some months after his trip to Cape Town his right side was paralyzed. Perhaps he had a stroke – we were not sure. For a while he could still walk with a cane, but eventually he needed a wheelchair and assistance with his daily needs. His helplessness was the hardest of all to endure.

He died on July 3, 1964. He was sixty-three years old. It had been such a harrowing experience that I could cry for him only many years later.

PART THREE:
FENCES IN THE WORLD AT LARGE

The Sekondêre Skool

Secondary School Grounds

IN SEPTEMBER 1964 I drove to Karibib, a small town between Wind-
hoek and Swakopmund for an interview with the director of the *Sekondêre
Skool*. I had planned to teach in Dar Es Salaam, Tanzania, but my Aunt
Hildburg, my mother's third sister who ran a hostel for black children in

Otjimbingue, persuaded me to at least speak with this director. They need teachers, she told me.

The Rhenish Mission Society (RMS) had established the Sekondêre Skool in 1963 as a private high school for black students. The students, mostly young men, came from all over the country, members of all tribes. Few had attended school regularly, either because they were required to help support the family or because there was no opportunity. Their ages ranged between fifteen and twenty-six, and age did not matter. What really mattered here was the desire to learn and achieve.

Yet I wasn't at all sure about teaching in Karibib. There were also other schools in Karibib: a middle school for German children; two public junior schools, one for white, another for black children; a craft school for weaving. We often referred fondly, tongue-in-cheek, to Karibib as the educational center of South-West Africa. But teaching black people? What did I really know about them? Still, why not? By this time, that is 1965, the lives of the different "racial" groups of people had become even more separate. There were more separate entrances to public buildings; there still was absolute separation of schools, and, as before, separate living spaces, which were more rigorously controlled. Designated separate everything! Would I have to choose sides? Where would I belong? I also wasn't at all sure about living in this semi-desolate place on the edge of the desert. It did not look promising even with all the schools there, culturally or otherwise. But now, two months after my father's death, I felt free to move forward, so I had made the appointment.

I did not yet own a car, so I would need to use the farm's Chevy truck to get there. When I told my brother about it, Jürgen said, "Good! We'll go together. While you have your interview, I'll check out some other things." It meant that he'd be driving, too fast, of course, but he'd be company. Despite our diverging political views, (his happened to change over the years) I really liked Jürgen. He was very much down to earth and practical, was a smart mechanic and great problem-solver, with a mind of his own. Hans-Erik was the most intellectual and political one, the most business oriented one; Karen the most religious and socially caring, and I... I was yet to find my niche. We were such different siblings. Did we really have the same parents?

Forty miles westward beyond Omaruru we crossed the plains of Karibib. The village nestled at the foot of a chain of limestone hills that ran along the southern edge of the plain. I hadn't been there in a long time, merely remembered passing through it. Scanning the view ahead, I saw tufts of dry sun-bleached grass, low dusty gray shrub, acacia bushes, a scattering of taller thorn trees. The solid mass of the Erongo Mountain blocked the horizon. I breathed in the beauty of it all, the pastel colors, especially those of the mountain's shapes, its shades of blues and pinks.

Having crossed the rail tracks we skidded to a stop where the gravel road joined the tarmac highway that ran via Karibib to the coast, constructed by South Africa due to the political unrest in Angola in 1959/61, and not due to any interest in developing the area! The tawny plume of dust that had followed the truck all along the way now turned chalky white. It caught up with us. We waited a while for it to settle, for us to see and breathe again.

"Here we are, *sus*," Jürgen said as he turned right. He nodded toward the Mobil gas station opposite the stop. "At least there's petrol here in case you buy a car." His tone was edgy, provocative. Of course every village had a petrol station, I thought in exasperation. And of course everyone had to have a car to get around. I would have to buy one. Did he think I'd travel by ox wagon?

"There's the bakery. Their coffee is so-so, and their *Berliner*s (doughnuts) are excellent, but you'd better bake your own bread," he pointed out as we drove along. Naturally he'd like the doughnuts; he liked sweet things. But buy bread? Who on earth baked better bread than our mother? Not this bakery, I thought, looking at the building half-hidden by a scrawny Prosopis.

We passed a large empty space lined with buildings. "The village square," Jürgen commented deprecatingly. "The post office and your choice of banks: will it be the Standard or the Barclays for you? No sidewalk! Who for, anyway? Just limestone and more thorny Prosopis! You really want to live here?"

"Why ever not?" I responded defiantly, irritated because I felt uncertain about this as a possible first job, but also because he was right: the place indeed looked minimal. "You make it worse than it is. I haven't decided anything yet, so just lay off!" I snapped. As our political views diverged he obviously did not want me to work here, nor live in this place, and certainly not at a school for black Africans. How would I decide?

We drove by Hälbich's General Store, the only store for miles around. I remembered that long ago Ur-Opa Redecker had run a shop for the RMS in Otjimbingue with a member of the Hälbich family, a man who had been a carpenter and gun maker. In Karibib the trading post, once privatized, changed into Hälbich's General Store. My skin almost prickled at the thought of the pietism of those days, of that desire to "save and civilize savages." My mother was always trying to convert me to her point of view, her own brand of pietism, and I had no intentions of following her beliefs. Would my working at the Sekondêre Skool mean agreeing to my great-grandfather's 1860s view of life and the world, for that matter my mother's, a view of a blind faith from which I was trying to escape? How deeply were attitudes of my lifetime rooted in this past? Could I manage to be different?

I was convinced it was his guilt, his terror of the damning judgment, and the fear of not being reunited in heaven with his loved ones after death which had led to Ur-Opa's conversion. It took him many gospel-haunted years as a young man to own the realization of being a sinner, but, once converted, religion was his life. No doubt he had joined the RMS with a sense of salvation and the hope of doing good work. From then on he would do his best to support those who were in the business of converting, pacifying, and "civilizing heathens." Although he came to see this as his mission, I suspect it was also a move on his part to escape the tyranny of his foster father. His parents had died when he was eight. He knew that surviving on linen weaving and on the small piece of land he might inherit would be impossible. He and his younger brother had wanted to immigrate to America, the continent seen for centuries as the land of opportunity. His foster father told them: "No way!" Like me, he had wanted his independence, a new and better life, wanted to find a new identity, and the only way to avoid any opposition to fulfilling this desire was to join a mission society. His foster father could not possibly object to that. But I did not wish to take sides because I did not see that as being a choice I wanted to make.

While he was in Stellenbosch awaiting his assignment to Damaraland (central South-West Africa), Ur-Opa wrote of his wonderment at seeing people of many shades of brown and black and white, speaking different languages yet gathering together to receive the word of God. They were all children of God! The Christian faith emphasized this, and I'm sure he believed it. Ur-Opa also believed that by converting the indigenous peoples of Damaraland and Namaqualand, i.e. the central and southern South-West Africa, to the Christian faith, and by teaching them to work they would stop their warring and settle peacefully—that is, become "civilized." That they were fighting supported Ur-Opa's view of them as "barbarous savages," while he somehow quite overlooked the conflict he himself had escaped when leaving home: Prussia's war against the Austrian Empire in order to establish a new Germany. Were the people of Europe less barbarous? That the indigenous peoples worshipped under the same roof with him supported his view that they were all God's children, yet he wrote: "One is filled with not a pleasant feeling when contemplating that one should socialize with such people"- my literal translation—meaning that no one, not only he himself but everyone would feel uncomfortable socializing with black and brown heathens across a gulf of cultural differences. Was it at all possible to do?

Are we not all children of our own time? To be able to step out of our social bubble or to stay inside, that surely is the question. Was it at all possible to step out without giving it up? And how was stepping out accomplished? One thing I thought was certain: it took courage. It also needed the experience and awareness of being different from others. Taking that step outside the bubble is anxiety provoking, yet most important in furthering the realization that differences actually exist, actually co-existed, that there was more than one way of living and being.

Further along the highway and beyond the Post Office Square we passed a private home. Proudly purple bougainvillea graced the entrance gate, pink and white oleander bloomed along the fence, and a few pepper trees shaded the two buildings in the yard. "See that? See those flowers, those trees?" I said edgily. "It's not as bad as you make it out to be!"

"Yeah, right," he growled as we crossed back over the railroad tracks to the other side. I noticed that we had left the village behind us. The tracks divided the place in two, one side for whites, the other for blacks. Why would I be surprised? Wasn't this the way we had been living all along?

My brother dropped me in front of an L-shaped building and drove off. The school's director and his family lived on one side, the mission's printing press operated in the other. A lone Prosopis growing near the crook of the L provided a little precious green and some shade in the barren yard. A handful of dust-covered cacti, a few geraniums and a struggling oleander bush were all attempts at a garden in the dust inside a chicken-wire fence close to the house. Though the distant setting was beautiful, the details close by were basic and bleak. Comfort, though desirable, was not affordable. The only extravagance supplied was learning. Education was ever to be the first step toward a different and, one hoped, a better future.

As I walked through the gate, Ortwin Jung came out, expectantly extending his right hand to greet me. He was middle-aged, his hair salt-and-pepper gray, eyes smiling blue. He had been appointed the year before, the second director of the school.

Photographer: Mr. H Born

We shook hands. *"Kommen Sie herein, kommen Sie herein,"* he said, inviting me inside with his warm, mellow voice, his accent typical for anyone from Westfalen in Germany. We stepped into the coolness of his study to talk.

The RMS established the Sekondêre Skool one hundred years after it had opened the Augustineum, a similar school, in Otjimbingue in 1863. The Augustineum had been the idea of missionary Hugo Hahn, who proposed to educate indigenous tribal leaders, acculturating them so they might be converted more easily, letting them set examples for the younger generations, training them as evangelists and catechists so that gradually all people would be assimilated into the new culture.

However, once the area was declared a colony of Germany, and once government became more institutionalized thereby increasingly asserting its power, the missionaries had to rely more and more on government contributions to further their work. Rather than focus on their religious goals they were obliged ever more so to accommodate government requirements—to teach the German language, instill discipline, obedience to authority, and in general educate students to be useful to the colonial society primarily as a workforce.

The missionaries' reliance on government support inevitably led to a conflict of interests. Many were fence sitters, and the people they had set out to convert increasingly wondered whose interests they were really serving. Which side of the fence were they on: on theirs, or on that of the government? As time went by the indigenous people trusted missionaries less and less, resenting the intruders more and more, until feelings erupted in the rebellion and warfare of 1904 to 1907. Even the hunter Erik Andersson saw many years earlier that such a conflict would probably come about, mentioning it in his diaries.

The Augustineum had to be closed twice, first in 1901 because of lack of resources. Once the resistance of the indigenous population was snuffed the school was reopened in 1911, only to be closed again in 1914 because of World War I. After Germany lost the war and its colony, the school was reopened under its old name in the early twenties by the South African government as a public school in Okahandja, still with the silently underlying idea of educating a useful workforce.

By the mid-sixties, the educational system in South-West Africa was completely fragmented. There were eleven different educational authorities, one for each group of languages: Tswanas, Damaras, Coloreds, Namas, Rehobothans (also known as Basters), Hereros, Whites, Caprivians, Kavangos, and Ovambos, as well as a national authority, all run along the lines of "equal but separate." Each system lacked concerted plans, qualified teachers, and reasonable goals and funds. Around 1965 the number of those who had started school decreased rapidly after the first three years; only about 40 percent of all six-year-olds began school at all. Most teachers themselves had not completed a high school education, let alone achieved a level of training that qualified them for formal teaching. As far as funding was concerned, the annual spread per capita for black children was approximately R1 (the rand being the South African currency) and R200 for white children. This lack of funding together with the fragmentation into groups, the implementation of the idea of "equal but separate" left little hope for real learning, never mind a prosperous future. Not surprisingly, only a few black students had graduated from high school at this time. Hendrik French Verwoerd, prime minister of South Africa from 1958 to 1966, who is generally seen as the builder of apartheid and the establisher of the South African Republic as independent from the Commonwealth, had set the objective for native education early in the fifties, implementing a system for the Bantu "that did not show him the green pastures of European society in which he was not allowed to graze."

In addition, the syllabus in all public schools was overwhelmingly Euro-centric, just as it was for white children. Subjects regularly offered to high school forms were English, Afrikaans, German, mathematics, sciences (biology, physics, and chemistry), history, and geography. Some schools, including the Augustineum, also offered classes in practical skills such as carpentry, metal work, office skills, and home economics.

By 1965 no colleges or universities had been established in South-West Africa. At that time there were only ten or so black Africans in the country who had completed high school, and who had also gained a university degree abroad. Altogether too much had been left undeveloped and dormant in all the decades South Africa had been designated to take care of its mandated territory. Obviously the education provided for black Africans lagged far behind what was offered to whites, leaving blacks at a disadvantage, both economically and politically. No knowledge! No money! No power!

By opening the Sekondêre Skool in 1963, the RMS offered students the option for higher education in a church school, an education aimed to be a little different from what the government was providing, hopefully less authoritarian. By 1965, six hundred black students attended the Augustineum. Döbra, the high school run by the Catholic Mission, had three hundred students, the Sekondêre Skool a mere seventy-five. By the time I left in 1970 125 students attended. Ages here ranged from fifteen to twenty-six. Only five were young women first enrolled in the year of the school's inception. It filled our students with great pride to eventually possess the best soccer team of all the schools thanks to colleague G. Tötemeyer. In their first year they lost their first match one to six goals against the best team from the Augustineum. After five years, they managed to beat them!

Mr. Jung's ideas about education at the Sekondêre Skool attracted me. They suited my own: furthering independent thinkers, encouraging initiative, making learning a meaningful activity instead of simply having individuals defer to a teacher's views, repeating any instructions by rote, repeating the teacher's opinions, or merely implementing a curriculum. In Germany the fundamental idea of education, as I had come across it, had been to raise independent and thinking individuals as well. However, even there the situation in the classroom often deviated from this ideal. Many teachers did not like their students to voice disagreement, let alone question their opinions. Generating secondary motivation was difficult and energy eating. I much preferred students who themselves were eager to learn.

It did not take me long to decide to take the job in Karibib instead of going to Tanzania. The work sounded both interesting and challenging, especially with students who chose to attend school and who, therefore, were probably eager to learn. Besides, it was close to home! Mr. Jung told me about an apartment available for rent. Where would it be but behind that bougainvillea-framed gate and the oleander-lined fence? It was the home of a friendly couple, Mr. and Mrs. Pieper, he a printer working for the press of the RMS. Thus, in April 1965, after subbing for the first quarter for a German teacher at the Junior School in Omaruru, I moved into my new apartment and began to teach at the Sekondêre Skool. I joined three already appointed teachers: Gottfried Töte-meyer, born and raised locally, instructor of history and Afrikaans, who had studied history and German at the University of Stellenbosch, the same subjects I had majored in at the University of Cape Town, Mr. Ortwin Jung who taught German, Mr. Hoebeb mathematics, my own subjects being English and geography. Later on two teachers joined us from Germany: Mr. Friedrich Blanke came to teach religion and Mrs. Christel Nordsieck music, and lastly Mr. Reneé Schaad joined us from Switzerland as our instructor of sciences.

Standing left to right; Joshua Hoebeb, Renee Schaad, Friedrich Blanke, Gottfried Tötemeyer;
Seated left to right; Christel Nordsieck, Helge Staby, Hannelowre Blanke

I wondered if taking this job would ever have any political effect. Some of my fellow students at UCT had been imprisoned for their protests against segregation. But that was ten or so years ago, and that was in South Africa. This was South-West Africa. I was not exactly protesting, so why should I be imprisoned for teaching there? I did not have any clear political intentions, though I certainly had educational ones. However, could not educational ones be political at the same time? I didn't belong to a political party, so how political could I be? What did it mean to be political anyway? Was it not simply by taking action in the community, the way anti-apartheid archbishop Trevor Huddleston did in the Johannesburg suburb of Sophia Town? Indeed, how political was anyone who was not involved in party-politics, who was unquestioningly "main-stream," who did not speak out in daily life while letting others take action? Were not silence and inaction also action, a way of validating the status quo?

Perhaps, sometimes, simply by being human, you might just be most political.

Teaching in Karibib

MY FIRST CLASS, Form One, was the entry class for black students to their high schools, the finishing class being Form V. They therefore attended one more year at high school than white students did, a year that was intended to even out the disparities that arose during the junior years. Besides, forms IV and V would be created as students passed Form III. With thirty students Form I was the largest class.

On the first day of teaching everyone in class rose as I entered the room. I took my place by the teacher's table in front of a large blackboard. "Please sit!" They sat down. Thirty pairs of dark eyes in more or less dark faces gazed at me questioningly. I studied them as they studied me. I felt tense yet curious. How would I manage this first and still for me somewhat unusual assignment?

I saw that one fellow in the front row was fairly light-skinned. Who of these was a Nama? Who a Herero? Who an Ovambo? Who a Colored? Who else was here? In my mind I checked through the generally employed subcategories of race. It was impossible to tell tribal or "racial" affiliations simply by sight. Each individual was different: in height, in color, in general appearance; each face was window to different thoughts and moods, to a different persona. I felt ignorant and challenged. Learning through experience was definitely hard.

Indeed, it would take me a while to make the connection between faces and names, even longer to become familiar with their personal stories, that is, if I ever did. I did not know any of their idioms, which added to my difficulty. Some of the students, however, spoke five, even six languages: the three official ones of Afrikaans, German, and English, as well as Herero, Nama, Ovambo, or Kuanyama.

It crossed my mind then how on my first visit to Europe people had asked me if one could possibly distinguish between the various peoples of Africa. Did they not all look alike? After all, were not all black? Did they all not have the same kind of hair, the same kind of facial features? How could you ever tell one from another? This question incensed me, obviously posed out of immense ignorance covered by preconceived imaginings. On the other hand, I couldn't distinguish Asian faces; I had hardly ever seen any, and to me they also all looked alike. Without question, you needed to know people to discern all the subtle differences.

"*Goeie môre, Juffrou* (Good morning, Miss)!" the students called out in unison once they were standing.

"*Goeie môre*, everyone. Please sit down." We continued to look at each other in silence. How would we get along? I wondered. What were they thinking? Definitely thinking something, but what? Maybe their thoughts ran along the same lines as mine. Or perhaps more likely, "What the hell is she doing here?" As the students waited silently, I felt I needed to speak.

"I'm Miss Staby, your new teacher," I began, "and I will be teaching you English and, of course, geography. But first I'd like you to introduce yourselves to me."

I looked at the list of names the director had handed me as one by one they dutifully stood up to tell me their name, their age, the place they came from, where they had attended school, and anything else they wanted me to know. When everyone had had a say, a fellow at the back of the class raised his hand.

"Yes? Please remind me of your name."

"Miss, I'm Milner. Milner Thlabanello. I'm a Tswana from Gobabis. Tell us, please, where you are from."

"I'm from Omaruru. My family has a farm in the district where I grew up. I also attended the junior school there."

A long "ohhhh" sounded from their lips. Heads nodded, eyes lighting up knowingly. Some of them obviously knew about me, not surprisingly, given my family's history in this area of which Karibib had been the center for much of public life, an area also from which several of the students came. Besides, Mr. Jung must have informed them.

Suddenly I felt uncomfortable. The gap between where I stood in my white skin, and where they sat, more or less black-skinned, was immense. What formed the gap? Was there a bridge across it? What, if anything, did we have in common? Although maybe we had more in common than I imagined at present. Perhaps we just did not know each other. To overcome my uncertainty and strangeness I took action through my role and set the class their first task. I let them know I was in charge.

"Take out your exercise books. You will now pen a short dictation so I can see what your English is like and what we need to do to improve it. I'd appreciate your asking questions at all times. Always look for explanations. Ask any questions you like—in English, of course. I'll try to answer them. If I can't, I'll try to find answers, or get you to find them."

Once they completed the dictation, the exercise books were collected and now lay on my table.

"Does anyone want to ask me anything right now?" My question felt clumsy, not exactly the best way of starting a conversation. Prolonged silence was my answer. Finally the fellow who had voiced the first question raised his hand again. Good! At least Milner is curious, and active. My assessment would prove to be correct. Five years later he was one of the first five students to go on to a university in South Africa. On coming home after the first semester at Fort Hare, he paid the staff at the Sekondêre Skool the greatest compliment I ever heard. "You know," he told me, "I thought I was going to a university. Instead, I found I was coming from one." But I am getting ahead of myself.

"Yes, Milner?"

He stood up. "Miss, why are you teaching here?"

I was not so much surprised by the question as much as it having been posed so soon.

"Well, I like to teach," I said somewhat evasively. "And I thought this school might be a good opportunity for me to do good teaching. May I ask why you are here?"

"Miss, it's because we want to learn," he replied, seemingly as spokesperson for the group. Agreement rumbled through the class.

"If that is so, if you like to learn and I like to teach, we should make a good team. Perhaps we can even proceed to think together. I had actually intended to go to Dar Es Salaam—you know, Dar in Tanganyika?" Most heads bobbed with informed agreement. "But my aunt suggested I look at this school instead, and then Mr. Jung persuaded me to stay here. I like his views on education, one of them being 'teach to reach.' So, I thought, why go far away if you find what you want on your doorstep? Well, here I am! And I hope we shall have a fruitful time together."

My answer merely skimmed the surface. There was so much more to be said, perhaps later on, but first and foremost I was here to teach. I believed in the power of knowledge, of thought, of being informed, in providing a space for students to find themselves.

The school year began in January and ended in December, but even here in quiet old Karibib time passed quickly. The seventy male students lived in small asbestos houses located just beyond the church and school rooms; and five young women who boarded in a rented house on the "*lokasie.*" Each night they were locked in.

Every weekday classes began at eight after an early breakfast and a brief morning service in the mission church. The church was the most impressive building of the school, built in 1912, a sturdy structure of bricks arranged in intricate designs, its steeple rising high up like a finger pointing to where the real and better life supposedly awaited us all. When it was my turn to lead morning prayers, I used the day's thoughts of Prof. Helmut Thielicke, a renowned German theologian whose thoughts were acceptable to me as being most in touch with the realities of living. The church's acoustics were excellent. The clicks of the Nama language, unfamiliar to me, the language many used in their prayers or songs, reverberated resoundingly in it, filling the enormous space. It took me a good deal of practice to produce the four clicks myself. I was proud to be able to eventually count up to ten: |*gui,* |*gam,* !*nona, haga, goro,* !*nani, hu,* ‖*khaisa, khoise, disi.* I often envied my mother for being able to speak it so fluently. My grandfather even spoke both Nama and Herero. They had been both lucky to grow up playing with children who spoke these languages. At home there had been only Alwine, Lena, Lendina, and Gideon. They had not been my playmates. As well, no curriculum at any of the schools I had attended made room for learning these languages.

Throughout the first months I established routines in my classes, insisting at all times that the students meticulously expand their English vocabulary, vocabulary, and ever more vocabulary! I insisted also that they learn the conjugation of verbs and spell correctly all words new to them. We read books, prescribed or not; we read newspapers; we had heated political discussions such as about the Odendaal Report, learned songs and poems, and performed one-act plays for the rest of the school community. They loved learning English. They loved acting. But in class they asked few questions, despite my consistent encouragement to do so. And they never used my name, calling me only "Miss," inhabiting distance.

"How come you don't like asking questions?" I challenged them one day. "Explain that to me if you don't mind."

The mood changed instantly. The silence turned tense.

"Come on," I encouraged them. "Please tell me. I want to know. It would help me understand why you don't. What are you thinking? Why don't you?"

It was again Milner who eventually raised his hand hesitatingly.

"Well, Miss, you know, we're not used to talking to a white person like this."

For the first time the issue of the social construct of "race" was raised, the gap between us made starkly visible, our established separation addressed directly. "Like this" obviously meant "like equals." I had hoped for such a moment of truth, though it stunned me into silence. What should I say? How can this be the real way? My mind was racing. I grasped for a straw.

"What do you mean with 'like this'? What is 'this'?" I asked evasively.

"Well, like we were on one level," he suggested carefully.

I stood there wordlessly. Equals. Yes, this was what he meant: equals! But he didn't quite say it. This was a big moment. This is what they desired in our world of separation: to be seen for who they were: human beings, the same as everyone else. It scared me to know that this was what was happening in class against the odds of the society that we lived in, to be as equal as students and teachers could be. Searching for words to calm myself, my mind went back to UCT, to the students and staff who both figuratively and literally stood in the line of fire by clamoring and demanding change, memories that now supported me.

"We can try the same level and see how that works," I eventually said, without any idea of what the implications might be. Some students nodded their heads. Some remained silent. None of us were yet to fathom the implications. We simply had to wait and see what would happen. We had to get to know each other, be respectful of each other, whatever our differences. That obviously needed more than nine short months.

Much later I noted in this class, that, although the young men now occasionally asked questions, the women did not. They never said much. "We're not supposed to talk when men are around," they told me, opening another can of worms, the can about gender roles.

Hendrik, sitting in the front row, spoke up. "Well, I think women should keep a house clean. They have to wash my clothes, and cook for me, and take care of me." I could hardly believe what I had just heard. The thought that he meant 'mothers' skimmed through my mind. He smiled widely. "What else should they do?"

The women laughed, as if what he had said was not new, yet they did not counter his opinion.

"If that is what you men really think," I said, "I certainly would not marry a single one of you."

Hendrik smiled while shaking his head. Others voiced disbelief. How could I possibly challenge this expectation? Were men not above doing chores? African men—in fact, many men, I was learning—felt unquestionably entitled to their women folk's service. The women were supposed to keep homes clean, fetch water, grow crops, cook food, sew on buttons, give birth to and raise children, the same as had been expected of Ur-Opa's wives, Caroline and Anna Maria, and, of course, my mother. Probably this was the expectation the world over: women do the work, keep covered from head to toe and raise children, while men hunt, play boule, drink wine in the plaza, talk, hunt... whatever. My horizon was indeed expanding. Our world here was becoming very personal. The students gradually disclosed some of their ideas, daring to speak up, to disagree, and slowly we began to discover what we thought and believed to be the way of life.

At another time Hendrik again shocked us with his opinion. I had once asked the class to talk about what they might be doing in future. Eager to inform us, Hendrik called out, "I'm going to be a teacher!"

"A teacher?" My question expressed my surprise. "How come a teacher?"

"Well, Miss," he enlightened us, "I want to be a teacher so I can beat the kids."

A gasp went through the class. "Beat the children? Why?"

"Because the teachers beat me before and now I can give some back!"

Hendrik was convinced of the legitimacy of his desire for revenge, avenging both the physical and psychological insults and humiliations he had suffered. How easily an act of hatred and/or violence, experienced passively can become one passed on actively! It made it impossible to separate the person from the task, making it clear that teaching was not merely teaching. I thought of Tinkie Heyns and his many smart ideas about educating others. He had once said that if you had the kids on your side, you would have already completed half their education. On another occasion he thought that as parent you could educate kids as much as you liked, and still they'd mostly turn out like yourself. In other words, the person educating was as important as the information and the understanding that was being imparted. I definitely expected myself to do a better job than Hendrik had in mind.

The discussion continued, with pros and cons fervently expressed, demonstrating how humiliation and anger were remembered, leading to revenge. I told them about myself having been rapped with a ruler and even with a switch. Even my dad once gave me a good spanking for not listening to my mom, a vague experience I rather left forgotten, feeling anger and outrage because I did not sprint immediately to wash my hands for lunch when Mom had called us. Some teachers were known to use a belt rather than a switch. From time to time one of our teachers beat students when he lost his patience and his temper with them. He himself thought nothing of it. This form of discipline wasn't new; in fact, it was widespread. At least we began to address the issue by talking about it as something that was generally viewed as appropriate by attempting to understand the process, creating awareness and disagreement.

On Friday afternoons students could leave the premises to go shopping or do as they pleased. The young women left every day anyway as they lived on the *lokasie,* a part of town away from where whites lived.

On such a Friday afternoon one of the girls, Mickal, returned from the village, visibly upset. She had gone to shop at Hälbich's. Our paths crossed at the rails.

"What's the matter? What happened?" I asked her on seeing her so upset.

Catching her breath, she said, "Miss, first I was the only one in Hälbich's Store, but when a white woman came in they served her immediately. They just let me stand and wait instead of her. 'Wait a minute!' I objected. 'I was here first. You should serve me first!' But then they insisted I leave without being served. It's not right! It's not fair! I am also a person!"

"I'm glad you spoke up," I said, "but it's not easy." We talked for a long time then, and many more times after that. I knew that many local Germans were what we called "brown," the color of Hitler's SA's uniform, representing their Nazi way of thinking. In fact, for many years South-West Africa had the largest and most active Nazi population in the world outside Germany. Many did not believe that the Holocaust had ever happened. My father had not been a Nazi, one reason, perhaps, why he had not been sent to Andalusia like my Uncle Wilhelm.

As the years went by, I realized that white people regarded the Sekondêre Skool with distrust. Its students increasingly spoke out on seemingly small occasions of differentiating treatment that they experienced as demeaning and demoting. Whites thought them "cheeky." "They don't know their place!"

A neighbor and friend of my dad's, Helmut R, once came through Karibib on his way to Swakopmund. He happened to drive by as I was walking over to the school and stopped to greet me. As we talked, my Damara colleague, Mr. Hoebeb, came along on his way to the village.

"Oh, here comes my colleague, that fellow walking toward us. See him?" I asked, slyly adding, "I'll introduce you."

"Do I have to shake his hand?" he whispered.

"Of course you should," I whispered back, knowing full well that he probably had never shaken a black person's hand in greeting. As I introduced them, they shook hands the German way, with one firm shake, not the African way, which added a second shake after hands had also clasped around the thumbs, the three of us exchanging a few polite words. The incident was never mentioned again, as if it hadn't ever occurred. The years in Karibib were filled with moments like this.

Except for this Damara colleague, Mr. Hoebeb, the other locally raised German-speaking colleague, Mr. Tötemeyer, and I, all our additional teachers came from Germany. Many at the German school also came from abroad. The local whites saw these foreigners as "outsiders," as people who knew nothing about this country and life here, yet thought they knew what was best for it, especially politically. What could anyone expect from people from afar who talked easily, about local life and customs with which they were unfamiliar, no sacrifice or commitment necessary? Although I liked these outsiders, our realities were indeed different from theirs, more complex because of the emotional involvement of preconceived ideas, arousing fears and anxieties and resistances to any change, their talk easy because they were only peripherally involved over a short time. I agreed with some arguments: there was no equality, not legally, and not in power sharing. But then, are people ever really equal? Was I just shilly-shallying? But I knew that for me people were just people, human beings like me, some of whom you liked, some not, some of whom were admirable, some who were not. That depended on something other than just the color of the skin, on the language you spoke, or the culture you lived in.

Teaching at the Sekondêre Skool was difficult. One reason was because I sometimes felt I was leading two lives, a private one and a professional one, two lives that were far apart. Probably in a homogenous society this feeling of being divided would not have arisen. I had befriended several teachers of the German middle school. We made music together. Occasionally we read plays; we always discussed books. I played volleyball with them or went on outings into the surrounding area, spent weekends away, and now and then drove to Windhoek to see a movie. We had meals together, often played Canasta into the small hours.

Teaching at the Sekondêre Skool was also difficult because of our lack of resources, or of no access to those that were available. All of us had to be constantly creative, constantly on the lookout for novelties that would aid our teaching and open the world at large through experience, a world far beyond the students' local horizons. Mr. Blanke was able to get hold of movies—about John F. Kennedy's assassination, about Martin Luther King Jr., about the Roman emperor Caligula, and many others. The music teacher, Mrs. Nordsieck, introduced instruments, orchestras, classical composers, and had students listen to the music they discussed. We had slide shows and tasted new foods. "Disgusting! Too bitter!" they exclaimed after eating canned olives I had brought into cloass. "Delicious! So sweet!" they said in praise of canned mangoes. We teachers shared postcards from our personal travels. We bought books. We went on trips with the students to learn about the local geology, to peer through a farmer's telescope at the moon and the stars. We read newspapers, and heatedly discussed the Odendaal Report. The staff walked a fine line between providing for departmental requirements and following our own ideas about education.

One of the books prescribed for English in Form III was about the French-British skirmishes and battles around Lake Champlain on the North American continent, including a chapter on the battle at Ticonderoga. The protagonist in the story was a young Irish fellow, sent away as the black sheep that had embarrassed his family. They hoped he might regain their lost prestige through his accomplishments of bravery away from home. Suffering from hunger and cold and dirt and illness, this fellow contemplated the insanity of war.

The story brought us in class to focus on the conflicts occurring on our own northern border along the Angolan border. The rush to independence that had begun in the mid- fifties in West Africa continued to wash over the continent south of the Sahara. Now, in the sixties, it had reached our border, unleashing the demons of dislocation close to home. Would the fighting in the far north of South-West Africa spread farther south? Would we become involved in this violence? The conflict in Angola was over more than merely independence and resources. It involved the American resistance to the spread of Communism and their support of Angolan's who themselves were for or against it. But really, I always thought, it was over power. Discussions in class were heated and self-concerned. At some point I raised the question of what would happen to me as a white person—what would happen to every one of us, white or black—should it be that the conflict might reach across the border.

"We don't know for sure what will happen, but the fighting may well end up on our own doorsteps. What would you do then? What would I do?"

"Oh, Miss, we'll protect you!" Philippus T shouted out with assurance.

"Of course! Of course we will do that!" others joined in.

"You might wish to do that because you know me. But I don't think you will be able to. Your comrades might not let you. They will have never seen me. They'll take one look at me and probably think *another bloody white person*! Take aim! And that would be the end of me. Besides, none of us here have experienced any fighting. It's pretty scary, you know. You might have to kill people. You might actually get killed yourself!"

"Why would we not fight? Of course we'll fight! We will protect you."

"But you know me," I reiterated. "I know you. We know each other as individuals. That makes all the difference. The guerillas up north don't know me. They don't know who I am and what I do or how I live, what I think. They will see my white skin. And I'll instantly be the enemy, like all the other white people I'll be a welcome target. They will just shoot me—and maybe you also if you don't join them!" I said, thinking that this was quite realistic.

"No! No! You are wrong. It will not happen!" they claimed vehemently and with bravado. Again and again this topic came up. And the question remained: how would we survive together? How would we live together? It still is and always will be the main question: how will we live together?

It was clear that change was in the making. The students, their families, their people wanted to be seen and treated as equals, not as third-class laborers who did the hard and dirty work, who were merely "water carriers" making it easy for the whites. But change would not come about easily. Thoughts of change instilled fear in those who were in power. The government had power, especially military and economic power. It also possessed power through laws, through knowledge and skills, through the threat of prison, and, above all, through the threat of death. Power is never given up easily. Change would have to be bought dearly. Blood would flow—mostly black people's blood, as far as some people, including the government, were concerned. Black people were never thought to be ready *now* for personal responsibility. Maybe tomorrow, next year, or in ten or twenty years, but never now! Change was for tomorrow, never today. Tomorrow would remain the answer of those in power for a long time to come, which, if possible, really meant never.

A change toward greater equality also meant that black people would have to change, integrate the concepts of work and time, not perform work as merely labor of the moment, but labor that could sustain a future. They needed to understand that getting things done usually required hard work and much effort and timely performance. In my student days I ran up against the idea that we from South-West Africa had no sense of work as a concept. I resented that. I knew all about work from my parents, from our day-to-day life on the farm. I grew up in the tradition of work, work that proved your success and your good faith in God, work that gained you a place in heaven. But what was work, really? Was work the only value in life?

In the north of the country the people of the Ovambo, Kuanyamas, Kavangos, all those tribes that lived near the Okavango River, were settled farmers and fishers. They also had cattle. They knew something about work, especially the women, about planting and harvesting. But the rest of the people had been nomadic. They had adjusted to the geography and the climate. They did in the moment what was necessary to stay alive. There were chores to be done, like milking the cows, getting hold of meat, searching for *veldkos*, pounding edible roots, making leather and clothes, cooking food and building huts. But that work, as in most of Africa, was usually women's work. Still, the idea of work as Europeans knew it—work that provided a daily structure of life according to a structure of time, a structure that provided the day's organization and who would be doing that which provided a means for making a living, a means that aimed at achievements that increased self-worth—this idea was totally different in Africa. Black Africans had their own ways of structuring society and regulating life, of relationships and family life very different from those in the West, ways that posed their own obstacles to economical improvement.

The idea of work once produced a serious conflict with me in Form V, as I saw it a conflict between reality and expectations. For students homework was, not surprisingly, often just a chore. As a necessity, most did it meticulously. Petrus S, a twenty-one-year-old Ovambo, was one of a few who avoided this activity with great determination. At the same time he was politically outspoken, expecting the world to change instantly the way he saw it. None of my encouraging suggestions to get him to perform the nitty-gritty of work that brought success made an impact until, on one day, I finally lost my patience, grounding him after he had not done his homework for the umpteenth time. Lazy so-and-so! I thought, swearing inwardly. I'll teach you!

"You will stay in today," I fumed at him. "Instead of going out you will stay in class and catch up with all the work you have missed this week! At three in the afternoon you will be here in your classroom, and you will do all your homework. I will come and check up on you!"

He said yes with a little smile, a yes that meant nothing to me while the smile meant everything: insolence and hubris. At half-past three that day I walked into his classroom. The blackboard, the teacher's table and chair, the students' tables and chairs, everything was present as usual. Noticeably absent was the man called Petrus.

I stormed out over the rough limestone yard to where the new and minimalist asbestos huts of the students stood. On my arrival, Petrus stepped out of his hut, yawning and combing his hair as if nothing else in the world mattered more than his siesta and the slick tidiness of his head.

"What do you think you are doing here? Why are you not in the classroom doing your work?" I angrily asked him.

"I guess I overslept," he answered nonchalantly while continuing to pull the comb through his hair. He seemed to be thinking *why should a young macho Ovambo like me listen to any woman, even or perhaps especially a white one?* This assumption of mine raised the level of my anger by several notches. I resorted to sarcasm.

"So!" I yelled at him. "So! You want this country to be an independent one! You want to vote! You want to be a politician! You even want to be the president of this country! You want to have a cabinet and run this country and you don't even know your English! You'll request a meeting with your cabinet and you'll turn up late, three hours late, and you'll walk in, yawn, comb your hair, and say, 'Sorry, comrades, I overslept!'" I was simply bursting with indignation.

"Now get moving!" I shouted. "And you better have everything done by six and present it to me or else . . . " I did not finish the threat. I stomped off to the director's office, explained to him what had just happened, and said that there would probably be some kind of fallout. However, that day Petrus did his work.

The following Monday Petrus' class had a double period for geography. The director mentioned to me early on that there had been lots of talking over the weekend. "Expect trouble," he told me, a knowing twinkle in his eyes.

I was ready for it, for the challenge of it. As I came into the room, the air almost crackled. Lightning is about to strike, I thought as I walked to the teacher's table to sit on its edge.

"Good morning, everyone."

"Good morning, Miss Staby," came their response. It surprised me. Still polite!

I looked at the sixteen faces. There was Henog K. His mates had nicknamed him "kapokhaantjie" - a small but belligerent type of rooster. Quite apt, as far as the fighting was concerned, but as for working? No. He was simply lazy. Behind him sat Petrus S, his mien serious, defiant and sullen. No wonder, as I had challenged his self-perception. He talked a lot, especially politics, imaging the future, and, as far as I was concerned, his personal views were mostly windmills. At the back sat Zacharias H, erect, alert, hardworking, had a sense of humor, certainly believed things had to change, and emanated a silent strength, a strong wish to succeed on a personal as well as a national level. He was definitely a man of a new future. In front sat Stephanus

B. He worked hard and was reliable, but lacked enthusiasm and imagination in class, though he certainly demonstrated them on the soccer field! The rest were hunkering down in silence.

"Well, now," I began. "I don't think we'll have the scheduled lessons today. I think we need to talk. And you may start. Anyone who feels he has something to say is welcome to have his say. Whatever you have on your minds we'll talk about, or rather you will talk and I will listen." I specified nothing, as I thought much more than just the little episode on Friday would surface. For the rest of that double period I listened with amazement to all my crimes and misdemeanors, quite unaware of how many I had committed.

Henog K was the first one to speak up. "You always have a funny smile when you talk to me."

"I do? Why do you think?"

"I don't know, Miss. Because I'm an Ovambo."

"Really? You really think that?"

"Yes, Miss, I do."

Oh god! When I smiled at Henog it was because I expected he'd confess, even before he actually did and even before I had put the question that he had not done his homework. The list of my transgressions was endless, most of them about why I had said or done this or that in a particular way. It was never the real reason that I knew for myself, not at all because they had said or not said, done or not done something, and all of it always connected to their tribal affiliation. In my mind responsibility was never a question of color or tribe but one of personality. To me they were individuals with particular habits and qualities. I rarely thought of them as Ovambo or Kuanyama or Nama. My assumed prejudice their excuse! This was truly an eye-opener!

It dawned on me how ingrained racism was in everyone, in white as well as in black Africans. It made me realize how personal qualities or appearances could be portrayed as expressions of racism. "He is lazy," not because Henog was Henog, but because he was an Ovambo. In my view he was simply a lazy student, thinking big but usually doing not much! He used being an Ovambo simply as his excuse, blaming me. I knew other Ovambos who worked hard. The attitude on the part of whites was often "they are dirty," not because they had no water or because it was far to fetch, but because they did not care to wash. "She smiles funny at me," not because she knows I didn't do my homework, but because I am black and she is white.

During my five years in Karibib I received a couple of letters, their white writers accusing me of loving black people more than white ones. I didn't. I liked some whites and some blacks, and disliked others. Were people not simply who they were? Did we not like some individuals and dislike others for personal reasons? Did color matter that much? Did this difference not serve as a target for projection of one's own psychic clutter? "I lost my job because you took it," a white person lacking the level of education might say to a black one with a higher one, resentment and envy smoldering. "You took my job" could actually be a matter of envy concerning ability and education and opportunity, expressed in terms of skin color. Would this problem ever be resolved?

I also heard rumors that I drove around with black men in my president gray VW Beetle, the insinuation being, I guess, that I had sex with them somewhere out in the bush. The reality was that I often gave three of them a ride to Omaruru when I took a weekend off to visit my mother. Omaruru happened to be their hometown. They had little money. The train-ride cost more money than they possessed, besides, it took forever. I had a car. So why would I not offer them a ride? Of course I knew about the Immorality Act of 1948, expanded in 1951, which barred not only marriage but also sexual intercourse between whites and blacks. There had been an earlier one in South Africa in 1927, and even one in South-West Africa in 1934. Sex was simply taboo all round, *the* taboo. Was sex not a threat to a clear and pure biological identity, perhaps even more so because that clear and pure identity was not what it was believed to be? Transgressions of sexual intercourse were punished severely. You needed only to read Athol Fugard's play "Statements after an Arrest under the Immorality Act." You needed only to see the 1960s movie "The Candidate," which explored the "purity" of blood in South African white society at large. Those who disregarded the taboo and the laws about having sexual intercourse were jailed, even worse, ostracized from society. Calvin seemed to think of sexuality as the ultimate sinfulness. So did the Pietists. It was its epitome, meant only for bearing offspring. I was not ostracized socially, but I sensed the insinuations, the subcutaneous hostilities that were never clearly expressed. It would be difficult to have a relationship across the "races".

Past ideas and confrontations concerning issues of "race" extended their influence far beyond their own time to affect all of us in the present, in particular all of us at the Sekondêre Skool. How could this ever change? How could we learn to look to the personal rather than the surface phenomena?

How could we stop assuming answers about others from different cultures? Could you – could I - sit on both sides of the fence? Did you have to be on one side only? Were there actually "sides"?

Long after I wrestled with such questions as a new teacher, I found myself asking them again as I read my great-grandfather Kaufmann's diaries, particularly his story of the "stolen" ostrich eggs.

The Business of the Ostrich Eggs

I N RECENT CENTURIES so many people left Europe because of changes that industrialization brought about, because of wars, intended to establish national entities, because of a desire for religious freedom, and for a better, less restricted life elsewhere on the globe where more opportunities, even unforeseen ones, beckoned. Yet once they arrived in strange new places, they asserted their own ways over those who already lived there. Usually intolerant of different and unfamiliar cultures and their peoples, Europeans tended to treat native peoples the way they themselves had been treated, pushing them aside to possess whatever resources and riches they found, enslaving or killing to survive. Though the details may have varied, colonial history seemed to read much the same way the world over: newcomers generally implemented what they escaped from, claiming as theirs what belonged to others.

My great-grandfather Kaufmann's story of fourteen ostrich eggs that had "vanished" in the bush was but one illustration of this aspect of colonial history. It exposed the clash of cultures, the different veins of entitlement and deprivation, of oppression and oppressing. This is the story in my words and is my understanding of what happened then.

On Sunday, December 8, 1913, as on most Sundays, my Opa Fritz Redecker and Oma Dieta and their children—my mother, Anna, her sisters Ruth and Renate, and her brother Wilhelm—had a happy day with Ur-Opa Kaufmann.

He was enjoying a long overdue visit with his daughter Diederieke, a visit that World War I would extend to early 1916. After a late breakfast and several hymns, Opa Fritz read verses from the Bible, following them up with a good evangelical sermon to succor their souls. The morning's ritual strengthened their willingness and determination to continue in their struggle to survive, deeply encouraged that their way of life in German South-West Africa had meaning through their faith in God, whom they served so well.

When they were through with the morning's ceremony it was already past noon, too hot for an outing that day. "We'll plan something else, a special trip," Opa Fritz said on seeing his children's disappointment. "Theodor, the cattle herdsman, told me a week or so ago about a nest with fourteen ostrich eggs. I asked him to keep an eye on it so that the eggs remain safe. We'll walk over to see them."

"I'd love to see an ostrich nest with eggs!" Ur-Opa Kaufmann chipped in excitedly. "I haven't seen one here yet."

"I have never seen one either," Opa Fritz replied. "With so few people around, they are rarely found, mostly only by chance."

"We could take a picnic along," Oma Dieta suggested.

"A picnic! A picnic!" the children shouted, dancing around. Picnics happened rarely in their lives, usually only when they took a trip by ox wagon. Most days their parents were dedicated to hard work that made life possible and, one hoped, more comfortable.

"Well," Fritz suggested, seeing the children's eagerness, "we'll go on Tuesday."

On Monday afternoon, however, Theodor, the herdsman, turned up unexpectedly at the homestead, panting and sweating and worried. He could barely get the words out when Mister Fritz asked him what was wrong. "The eggs are gone!" he said, fidgeting with his hat, afraid his Mister would be angry for not having done his duty.

"What do you mean the eggs are gone?" Fritz asked. "When last did you see them?"

"Early last week. They were lying in the nest. I saw them."

"Oh no, oh dear!" Fritz exclaimed with disappointment. "They are really gone?"

"Yes, definitely. Today the nest is empty," Theodor repeated.

Fritz's face grew dark with annoyance.

"Who could have done that, do you think?" he asked.

"Well," Theodor replied, glancing away sideways and down. "Well, I did see some tracks."

"Whose tracks were they? Do you know?"

Theodor hesitated before continuing.

"Hannibaub, the son of tall Johannes, he told me that he had seen three Nama women in that area: Lea, Regina and Sanna. The boy Karirub from the garden was with them." Theodor was torn between his duty to his Mister and loyalty to his folks, even though he was a proud Herero man and they, in his view, merely sly Nama women.

Fritz smoldered as he listened to Theodor. Those thieving women! He gave Theodor extra food rations for his efforts. He stormed into the house to tell Dieta what he had heard.

"These women took those eggs! They probably ate them!" he shouted at his wife in his anger. "They don't think about their value except as food. Just imagine! All fourteen eggs! They could have been fourteen ostriches. And each one of them would have been worth one hundred marks!"

"Calm down, Fritz. I'm sure they meant no harm," Dieta said. "They probably don't realize what they did. Besides, their diet is not exactly varied. And I imagine they were hungry."

"Don't you understand? They simply can't go about doing as they please! They should know better! And they have spoiled our pleasure. Never mind that now these eggs won't hatch. No money, no outing, no photos, no fun! Damn them!" He ranted. "They will have to admit that they took the eggs. But these Nama, they don't stick to the truth easily. They are so sly and evasive. They say they are Christians, yet they just tell you whatever to get away with things."

"First wait and hear what they have to say," she cautioned him.

"Oh, they probably won't know a thing. They will lie! I'll go to their pondoks in the morning, early, very early, and take Lea to the nest. If she owns up, perhaps the others will admit to her story. The boy Karirub will have to tell the truth also, even if I have to beat him. I don't like doing that, but if I have to, I will. The truth must be told at all cost. Besides, this is my land! These are my eggs!"

"You're right. They should tell the truth. But you don't have to beat them for it," she told him.

"How else will they learn?" he asked testily. "Of course, if they tell the truth, I will do nothing. I'll take a strap along, just in case." Dieta shook her head. Of course they should not have taken the eggs. But was that such a terrible thing?

On Friday morning, two days before Opa Fritz was talking about the family outing, Regina had woken as usual. As she lay on her bed of skins, the hard mud-and-dung floor beneath her, she looked out through the low door of her pondok. She thoughtfully scanned the day ahead. *We don't have much left to eat and so many people to feed. There is little water here. We'll have to fetch some from the well at the river. We also need to find some roots and berries if we can. But it's so dry. We probably won't find much.*

She stepped out into the deep dust that surrounded several clusters of huts in this area, where about twenty or so Nama and Herero workers and their families lived not far from Mister Fritz's farmhouse on Lievenberg. She brewed her morning coffee, afterward exchanging the customary extensive morning greetings with other women.

"I think we need to look for *veldkos* today—for berries, roots, bulbs, anything we can eat," she said to a few of the women. "I'm tired of mielie porridge and sour milk. I wish the Mister would give us some meat again. It's been too many days since we've had any. Will you come with me?"

"Yes, I will," Sanna, one of the women, agreed. "We don't have much food left. But it is so dry. Still, maybe we'll find something." Lea agreed to join them.

"It's a good thing Mister Fritz takes care of us, otherwise we might starve," Sanna said.

"He's good because he's from the mission," Lea emphasized. "At least he gives us food like milk and meat and mielie meal. And he hardly ever beats us."

"That is true. I've heard that other whites do beat people." Regina shuddered.

"We easily get the sjambok. Some Misters even kill a man when he doesn't listen," Lea continued.

"Yes," Sanna added. "Remember the one Nama who got shot when he tried to stop his white Mister beating him with that deadly sjambok? That white man was jailed for only a year." The sjambok was a long leather strip, very hard, with edges that cut easily. To get "twenty-five" left the person lacerated and cut, in terrible pain.

For a while they sat in silent agreement and pondered the changes and injustices. They used to move around with the rains. There was grazing and water for the cattle, so they had milk. They could hunt for game. The land had been theirs when they used it for grazing and water. They often fought battles with the Herero about it. Life had certainly not been easy then. But now they had nothing. No land! No cattle! Now they had to carry that disdained piece of metal with a number and their name, ask for special permission if they wanted to go anywhere. Now they depended on the good will of the whites. True, there was no more fighting. But had they not lost all? Now it was even harder to survive in this harsh land that was no longer theirs.

They sat around the fire for a long time, finishing their coffee, brooding about their changed life. Then Lea interrupted their thoughts. "We still have to go find food, don't we?" The other two nodded. The three of them set out carrying a pot, a pail, and a kettle. It was slow going, but then they had all day. Although it was still early they soon felt the heat prickling on their skin. They walked to the well in the river, drank water, filled the kettle, and set out with the garden boy Karirub to the place across the river on *Okandu-kaseibe*, additional land that my great-grandfather Redecker had bought in 1907 from Zacharias Zeraua, where they thought they might harvest some veldkos.

"I wonder where Theodor is," Sanna said to the other women. "He should be looking after the cattle over here." The four of them saw no one in the silent and barren landscape. When they finally reached the small plain they had had in mind, they rested in whatever shade they could find. Only after a good rest did they begin the search for food, digging, picking, and chattering away. Suddenly Sanna shouted, "Oooooh! Look over here! Come see this!" Regina and Lea continued their search. Only Karirub, more curious than they, went over to find out what Sanna was so excited about.

"Oh my, it's a whole big nest full of ostrich eggs!" the boy called out, hopping up and down with excitement. "I've never seen so many!"

Once they heard "eggs," Regina and Lea hastened over. They all stood around the nest, gaping at this great meal, this fortune, this find of finds.

"We better pick up the eggs fast before the big birds return and try to chase us off," Regina said.

"Do you really think we can just take them?" Lea wanted to know.

"Of course we can. We found them!" Regina said indignantly.

"Won't Mister Fritz be upset if we take them because he thinks they are his?" Lea went on.

"We found them, so they are ours," Regina asserted. "What is in the veld is ours, is anyone's. That's how it used to be. It still is. And if anyone says we emptied the nest, we will say we haven't been here at all. What do you think?"

Lea was afraid. "Mister Fritz will beat us," she said.

"No, he won't," Regina said. "He doesn't beat women. And even if he did, I'd still say I wasn't here," she insisted defiantly.

Eventually Lea and Sanna and even Karirub agreed with Regina. They felt these eggs were theirs, as everything had been before the whites' coming. And nothing would convince them otherwise. They would have their way and their say. So they carried the eggs back to their huts and everyone had a delicious feast that lucky Friday evening.

On Tuesday, at four in the morning, Opa Fritz set out to the huts as he said he would, clutching a leather strap. There he knocked loudly and firmly on the door of Lea's pondok, walked over to the garden with her to get Karirub, and made Hannibaub join them on the way to the site of the nest.

"So where are the eggs?" he asked Lea, standing at the edge of the empty hollow. "You came here on Friday and took the eggs, did you not?" accusing her directly of the misdeed as he saw it.

"No," Lea denied. "I spent all day long at my pondok."

"Don't tell me no," Fritz replied sternly. "Karirub, this boy here, he went with you. He was with you, was he not?"

"No, Mister, no," the boy said fearfully. "No, I was never here. I did not take any eggs."

"But you did!" Fritz exclaimed, instantly exasperated. "You were here, with Lea and Regina and Sanna. You helped them instead of looking after the donkeys. You helped them carry the eggs. And you probably helped eat them also!"

"No, Mister, I was all day long with the donkeys. I didn't eat anything!"

Fritz's anger flared given such stubbornness. "You're not telling the truth! Tell me the truth! This boy here, Hannibaub, he saw you on Friday. Did you not?" he said to the other boy, restraining his voice with difficulty. Hannibaub nodded a yes, too scared to speak.

"No," Karibub kept insisting. "No, I wasn't here. I did not see any women."

"You're not telling the truth!" Fritz yelled at him. "No shells are to be seen around here, which means that no jackal or hyena or any other animal has taken or eaten them." He took a firm grip on the leather strap, grabbed the boy by his neck, and whipped him over his buttocks. "No, no!" Karirub cried out. "Please, Mister, I did not do it!"

The lying drove Fritz to madness. He beat the boy. And beat him. The truth had to be out! "You were here! Say you were here!" Finally Karirub broke down under the weight of his pain.

"Yes, yes," he sobbed. "Yes, I was here, Mister. Please, please stop."

The crying brought Fritz to his senses. He caught himself. *Why am I doing this? They are just poor people. My wife is right. But there is a law. It should be kept. And I am the boss. This is my property. Besides, the truth should be told, always,* he thought, attempting to reassure him-self.

When he had calmed down, he confronted Lea.

"No, Mister," she persevered with her story. "No, I wasn't here, and I never saw any eggs, I never carried them away, and I never ate them. Never! All day long I sat by my pondok." Her face was sullen and determined, closed down. She vaguely admitted to having been there but to nothing more.

When he came back to the huts, no one was home, so Fritz broke the locks and entered them, and found pieces of ostrich eggshell. *These liars!* Later that afternoon he sent for Regina and Sanna and interviewed them in the storage room. Great-grandpa Kaufmann and Oma Dieta were already seated there as witnesses, waiting and curious.

"So you went over to Okandukaseibe on Friday," Fritz said to the women.

"No," Sanna replied, "I never went there."

He turned to Regina. "And you?"

"No, I stayed home all day," she replied. "I don't know what you're talking about."

Their impertinent answers annoyed him, but he curbed his feelings. He told the women what Karirub and Hannibaub had confessed.

"No, these boys, they are mistaken," Sanna said. "I was never there. They must have seen someone else."

Regina supported her. "She is right. I saw her at home all that day."

Fritz's irritation grew. He now sent for Lea.

"If you don't admit to taking the eggs," he threatened her, "the sergeant will come over tomorrow and send you to jail!"

This frightened her. That sergeant is a bad one, she thought. He is hard and beats people terribly. What would happen to my little one if I were to go to jail? On top of this I'll get only bread and water there. I'll starve. She began to cry and confessed.

"I was scared, really scared of the other women, Mister. That is why I did not say anything. They would make life very difficult for me."

"All right, all right," Mister Fritz said calmingly, her tears and her truthfulness softening him a little. Besides, he thought, God loves these people also. *The Bible tells us He loves everyone. I shouldn't really be so hard on them. But I had to threaten her; otherwise she would not have owned up to the truth. And the truth had to be out.* So he sent for the sergeant to come over the next day to deal with this serious matter of insolence and lawlessness.

The sergeant arrived at the homestead on horseback in full uniform. He was a man who thrived on keeping law and order. This seemed an important occasion to implement colonial law. He greeted Fritz and together they walked over to the storage room where the previous meeting had taken place. After the sergeant had seated himself he called the women up one by one. But despite his stern presence, enhanced by his uniform, and despite her fear of going to jail, Lea retracted her second statement and avowed what she had said first, that she had never been even near the nest. The sergeant became quickly and visibly impatient.

Next he called on Regina. "You realize, of course, that your denial does not change the fact that you took the eggs!" he said with a strong voice. "It won't make a difference because it is quite clear what you have done."

The weight of his presence did equally little to impress her. She remained stubborn. "I never went to the nest. I was home all day."

The sergeant lost his composure at so much insolence and disrespect for the law. As its representative he felt personally stung by the attitude. He stood up, stepped over to her, and slapped her hard in the face. The blow caught Regina by surprise. Her head almost turned backward and she saw stars and many colors. He can slap me all he wants, she thought through her pain. I will never say what he wants to hear. The officer relentlessly slapped her over and over again. Regina saw many more stars. Her cheek went numb. Though she kept her eyes tightly shut, tears ran down her face.

Finally the sergeant caught himself. He stopped slapping her and instead shouted at her and no one in particular. "You are liars, all of you! You need to be taught a lesson once and for all. We cannot allow this kind of behavior. You have to submit to the law. Without our law there will not be peace!" He was almost out of breath with the effort of his slapping and shouting. "Damn you women! Damn you Nama!"

The sergeant fell back heavily onto his chair. He pulled a handkerchief from a jacket pocket, wiped his brow, and, looking at Fritz, shook his head in despair. A long, uneasy silence ensued. He tried to regain his composure.

Once more he turned to Regina, still irritated. "What do you have to say now?"

By this time Regina had also composed herself. "Other people must have stolen the eggs," she answered. "I myself have done no such thing." The sergeant's eyes now sparked with a dangerous fury. He turned to Sanna, who repeated the statement, adding, "I swear to God! I never took any eggs."

On hearing this, he jumped up from his seat in exasperation and slapped her several times as well.

"But you have stolen the eggs! You have eaten them!" he repeated harshly.

"No!" she cried out. "No, I didn't! I ate nothing. I'm not lying, I'm not lying!" He slapped her again, but she stuck to her story.

"I will send you all to jail, all of you!" he yelled at them.

Lea then admitted again to taking the eggs, while the other two allowed the details of the events of that Friday morning to be extracted like bad teeth, slowly and one by one. At long last the officer heaved a sigh of relief and sat down again, satisfied with his achievement. But no sooner had he sat down than Sanna and Regina retracted their confession.

The sergeant rose from his chair to his full imposing height. "The pain of slapping did not make you stick to the truth!" he roared. "You keep avoiding it. But you are not, I repeat not, going to make a fool of me! I stand for law and order in this country. I represent its power. And you people will be subdued." He glared at them. "You will now walk to Otjimbingue, all twenty kilometers, and stay in jail for however long it takes you to admit your guilt!"

He fetched a long rope from his saddlebag and tied it around each of their necks to prevent them from escaping on the way. He mounted his horse, riding along behind them. By then the sun stood high above their heads. It had drained the sky of the last vestiges of blue. Cicadas were shrieking their indelible sound. The women walked slowly and silently, trudging over the patient sands and rocks along the track to Otjimbingue. They were thirsty, but there was no water, the sergeant allowing them only brief rests along the way. Eventually they reached the jail, where they remained for two weeks. But as soon as they had been released having admitted to eating the eggs, they once more denied that they had ever done so. As a result, they were imprisoned once more, this time for another two days.

I am sure that the missionaries and missionary colonists, as individuals, had the best of intentions according to their Christian beliefs, beliefs they accepted without question. Their personal mores and values, both as Christians and as Germans, were further nourished by the expectations of both the RMS and the government—expectations that the Nama and other indigenous people must be subdued, become acculturated and converted. Many other colonists, who were not missionaries, simply came to improve their own lot. With their more advanced technical know-how they saw themselves as superior to the native peoples. As a result, the newcomers neither allowed the Nama to be who they were, nor learned from them. There was much the colonizers did not see or understand about the Nama, yet much they expected from them: acculturation and conversion away from their world, applying different standards and judgments about time, about work, about possession.

Not surprisingly, the Nama, like the Herero and other subdued peoples, eventually resented their subjugation. They had lost their land, their cattle, their way of life and identity. They were not prepared to give up anything easily. For the Nama women who ate the ostrich eggs, words had been their only weapons, and lying had been their last means to deny the new reality of those who had subdued them. Words allowed them to avoid not only the experience of helplessness and submission, but to reject and defy those who subjected them, come what may.

History has shown that those who are subjected to the will of others usually find a way, even centuries later, to reclaim what they have lost. Here in Karibib, in this small place on the edge of the desert, almost sixty years after the ostrich eggs incident, a new generation of indigenous peoples had an opportunity to gain a new language, new skills to regain their esteem and agency. Only by this time the latest generations of colonizers also saw themselves not as colonizers but as indigenous, increasing the complexity of the situation.

Unless individuals live in a social group, they will not be human. If they remain in their own social bubble, excluding the experience of others living in another, they will tend to think of their own ways as the only ways, and see only one road to Rome - or to heaven. They are different, not we. They have a bias, not we. They threaten us, not we them. To survive we need to be more powerful than they are. Is this the only way?

And so it was that on the third day of their second imprisonment, still denying what they had done, the three Nama women were allowed to step out from their prison walls of mud bricks, allowing them to return to the powerlessness in their new yet unacceptable life. They walked back into the familiar landscape of plains, of mountains, of acacias and scarce rain, a space that at the same time had become one of new and different confinements, a space filled with more invisible fences.

The Oryx

IT WAS LATE in the month of July. July could be a cold month in the highlands of Damaraland, and it was cold now, glassy cold and bone dry. A wind had started up from the east singing its own brittle song. One could hear it bearing down the dry riverbed of the Omaruru, rustling low through the thorny acacias on its banks, swirling the dry soil against the golden-white grass, finding forgotten bits of paper in the yard, tossing them around in a wild, bleak dance.

When the wind and cold came together, all of us knew that winter was here and that it had come to stay. Although the sun was warm at noon, at night a thin layer of ice formed on the water in the chicken coop, and in the mornings the tap in the yard proudly wore an icy tooth. Each day the sun rose into a bleary blue sky, melting the ice. And then, at noon, always, the wind rose, blowing endlessly. Winter brought its own stark reality, with its gnawing hunger for colors and yearning for the relish of life.

It was during one of these July nights that I slept restlessly. Though my blankets were a cozy cover, I felt heavy, uncomfortable, my head blurry. Once I woke, with a vague recollection of dreaming about barking dogs. There seemed to have been a note of excitement in their tone, a touch also of raucous desperation that shook me out of my torpor. I shut out this uneasiness, pulled the blanket more tightly around myself, and dozed off again. But as the barking gradually and tenaciously seeped back into my consciousness I slowly realized that I had not been dreaming. I frowned. There must be several dogs involved, I thought. Judging by the sound they seemed to be somewhere far to the east. I looked at my watch. It was only four o'clock.

I puzzled as I listened. Several dogs barking this frantically could only mean that they had cornered a quarry. During the winter dogs could be such a nuisance with their pack hunting, killing duikers, pursuing even kudus that at times thought our yard a refuge. All of our neighbors had dogs. Workers on the farm had several. Throughout the years we ourselves had had many.

These scruffy four-footers were usually skinny, their coats dull and patchy. Only a few actually died of old age, like our Foxy. Some died of snakebite, some after terrible fights, like our Pascha. Some got lost in the bush and starved, or they died of thirst. Others were poisoned. Sometimes they simply disappeared. These dogs were never well trained, but we needed them to alert us to dangers, real or imagined. The nights were long and dark in winter. You could not know what might be lurking beyond the fence wanting to enter the yard, like the kudus, or the springhares, leopards, hyenas, jackals, snakes, or other visitors, unwanted and two-legged.

It was scary to think of a pack of dogs hunting. It meant their killer instinct had taken over and that for a while no one controlled them. The smell of blood and sweat sent them into a frenzy that ended only with death. I shivered, tucked myself more tightly into my blanket, but still listened intently. Even at this distance the barking sounded agitated and hoarse, now louder, now quieter, like the swell of the sea, rising and falling in the night.

All along the dogs' barking had been drifting over from the same spot. I followed the sound in my mind, sound that traveled more easily at night; for lack of other noises the barking was clearer and hence seemed closer. I thought the dogs might be somewhere near the spring and its water. During some years it flowed strongly, in others it was almost dry. Its water was hot, almost at boiling point. I loved to sit at the edge of the main pool and watch the bubbles rise. I liked to trace the colors of the slimy algae: hot blues and deep greens running into cooler russets and yellows. There was always some water there that attracted the animals. Yes, I was sure that was where something was happening, whatever that was.

As I lay listening I wondered what the dogs might have cornered—perhaps a leopard? Could they be keeping it up a tree? The thought sent shivers down my spine. In that case someone would have to go and find it; it was too dangerous altogether to have it around. For the moment I preferred to stay in bed and let events take their course. I turned over again.

Suddenly I heard my door creak. "Helge . . . Helge . . . Are you awake? Do you hear the dogs?" my mother whispered in the dark. "We have to go and see what's happening. You should go fetch the gun. We may need it. They have been barking for too long. I want to know what's going on."

She had already dressed. Her hair was still untidy from sleep, her face pinched with worry. Huddling in a warm jacket, she slipped out into the early morning darkness. I heard her steps crunching on the sand, their sound slowly fading as she moved toward the houses of the workmen. I sighed and sat up. Instantly my skin bunched into goose pimples as I felt the cold air. The shock spurred me to move fast, to pull on jeans, a sweater, and a jacket.

Still shivering, I shuffled stiffly into the dark, cold kitchen where the stove was not yet burning. I lit an oil lamp, started the Primus stove, filled the kettle, and put it on. I poured coffee beans into the white ceramic grinder on the wall behind the door and began to turn its handle. Like through a fog I listened to the fierce crushing of the beans while watching the flickering oil lamp send black smoke into the darkness above. I liked the smell of burning paraffin, the sight of the yellow flame twitching. I liked listening to the soft hissing of the Primus, the simmering of the water. These early morning experiences enveloped me with comfort because they were familiar to me. When the kettle finally boiled I put the ground beans into our old aluminum coffeepot, clear silver on the outside, thick layers of darkness inside, a rich coffee brown. I poured the water onto the grounds in a slow, thin stream, catching every dry island, watching them swell and froth and explode into that delicious, invigorating smell.

Soon my mother and the workmen came stomping in to huddle in the kitchen, warming their hands around the full hot mugs. Most importantly, there was Paul, our Herero herdsman. He knew the veld. I felt more comfortable when he was around. There was also his son Jan, tall, handsome, smooth-skinned, and Johannes and Kutimba, the migrant workers. All their faces were shining with smiles. This was the stuff of life they liked: excitement. This was going to be a good day, a great day, hot with hunting.

As soon as I had my coffee I went to my father's office to pick up the .303 Lee Enfield. It stood in the far corner of the room, away from the door. It always stood in that same corner, the shiny gray metal barrel on russet wood.

When I was ten and wanted to learn how to shoot, Dad used to warn me about its use. He told me it had a kickback that would make a blue mark on my shoulder. At first I simply watched, observing how he took aim and pulled the trigger. When he eventually let me hold it, I would look along the swaying barrel in my hand and wonder how one could hit anything with it. Surely it was only a question of luck, though later I once actually and surprisingly brought a kudu home for the pot. Now that Dad had died, someone else had to do the shooting.

I had liked hunting with my father, feeling the excitement of searching the bush for antelope that would provide us with meat. But it had been he who released the trigger; sometimes it was one of my brothers, never my mother and rarely I. Now, in the office, with Dad no longer there to go on a hunt, to take charge, to solve problems, I took on the task. Poised on the verge between past and present, all memories of childhood thrill over hunting dissipated into trepidation. I quickly shut down my thoughts and feelings and grabbed a few bullets from the box. They were large, about three brassy inches long, with shiny coppery heads and a bit of lead at the tips. I held them only briefly, my warm hand stinging with their deadly cold so that I quickly dropped them into my jacket pocket. I once more gazed at the gun, at this strangely innocuous-looking gadget that imparted power over life and death. I hesitated before forcing myself to take its wooden butt with my right hand, the cold barrel with my left. I turned as if fleeing the thought, stepping back into the yard and the dawning morning. Everyone was silently waiting for me on the truck. Having buried my feelings, I hopped behind the steering wheel, placed the gun to my left, turned the ignition key.

The beams of the truck's lights sliced through the early morning graying darkness onto the rough road that led out of our yard through a few small, dry riverbeds, taking course up and down several hills. After about a mile I turned off to the left down another bumpier track next to a fence that kept the cattle out of the wide riverbed. Still farther along the color of the earth changed abruptly from cream to red. Dark, rusty-shaded dolomite stones covered the surface of the soil where washed-out ruts dipped down toward the river next to the dolomite koppie with its chiseled drawings of old.

By now we could easily locate the barking deep in the bush. I stopped the truck. Everyone jumped off and followed Paul African-style, one behind the other. No one spoke as we stepped around bushes and boulders. Every now and then Paul raised his hand as a signal for us to stop. We stood motionless, like statues in the cold of the early morning, straining our ears, redirecting our steps toward the frenetic barking once he dropped his hand.

On having stopped once more this way I held my breath. All I could hear was the pounding of my heart. The silence itself began to pound even more loudly. A sudden crashing through the bush startled us into pillars of anxiety. For a moment we stood, frozen, relieved to see just a few panting dogs cutting a circle around us, only to disappear again ahead into the bush.

We followed them slowly, soon reaching a small clearing where we stopped to peer through the last branches of *wag-'n-bietjie* (wait-a-bit) acacias that formed a wall around it. In the middle of this space rose an enormous anthill. At its base it measured perhaps six feet, rising to a narrow top eight feet high. A dead tree trunk reached out of the hill at an angle, and there, in front of both, stood an oryx, its head low to the ground, facing us, protected from behind by the hill.

The oryx is a beautiful antelope, a streamlined animal peering through a startling black and white mask. Pinkish gray on the back, one black stripe down its spine, another along each side, white belly, black tail, large ears, and two straight three-foot horns that rise from its head like ribbed corkscrews. It is a hardy creature, able to go for weeks without water while withstanding scorching heat. Usually oryx roam in a group. Only occasionally you will come across a single animal, like this one.

We stood there for some time observing this oryx. It looked our way briefly, its dark, liquid eyes watching us through its memorable mask. It was fending off the darting and attacking dogs with sweeping motions of its head, forcing them to rush out of the dangerous orbit of its horns. One dog had already been injured and was lying low under a bush, licking its wound. The others were panting, their tongues lolling and frothing. From time to time one of them would take a break and, once rested, would rejoin the frenzied attack.

The back and forth sweeping of the animal's head was slow. It must have been exhausted. I noticed how scrawny it looked. I could almost count its ribs. And then, all at once, I saw it! I saw the one hoof, the left back hoof. The animal had lifted it in pain. It was festering, crusted with sand and puss and blood. I wondered how it had been injured. Did it get caught in a fence when trying to scramble under it, the hoof getting tangled in one of the wires? How long had it been stuck like that? The injury was bad. I squirmed just looking at it. The animal must have been heading for the water, every step piercing agony. Perhaps it was taking a rest before struggling over the last bit of the stony, arid way when the dogs pounded on it. There was no longer time to reach the spring and live another day. A bullet would surely make a kind quick end of its misery.

I stepped forward. I lifted the gun, its weight heavy in my hand. It was difficult to find my target in the constantly moving melee of dogs. I wanted to use only one shot. There was nothing worse than wounding an antelope and then having to track it through the bush endlessly.

A brief lull in the commotion allowed me to focus and pull the trigger. I shut my eyes as I squeezed it, hoping that I would both hit and miss. The gun kicked back ferociously, as if flinging itself against death. For a moment the explosion drowned all other noises, the bullet spreading its acrid, prickling smell. The dogs yelped and scattered. The oryx broke away with a crash head-on into the bush where it was at its densest. Then all was silent. For a while we all stood there, dumb and startled, paralyzed by the event, I with the gun still heavy in my hands.

After some moments the dogs idled up to us, then moving in the direction the oryx had taken. They allowed us to surface into the awareness of our own sense of being, reminding us that we were still alive. Paul was the first to move. He waved us on. Once we had crossed the clearing he motioned me to go ahead. Unwillingly I took the lead. I ducked under branches, and though I looked down to avoid tripping over stones and the brush cover, my every sense was alert and directed ahead.

Where did the animal go? Was it dead? Was it waiting close by to charge? If it were close, there would be little chance of taking another shot. I took a few tense steps, stood still, listened. I could hear nothing, not even the dogs. I took a few more steps around some low, thick bushes. And there, in another clearing some twenty feet away, lay the oryx. The dogs were sniffing it all over. That meant it had to be dead, though it still looked very much alive. Slowly I walked up to it. I noticed hardly any blood on the scrawny yet beautiful body. My heart was still pounding. I breathed deeply to calm myself.

For a long time I gazed at it, without moving, caught in a deep stillness. My mind was filled with another image that I had seen not long before, when I had stopped to look at a dead kudu that lay by the roadside. At first it seemed to have been killed recently, but, on taking a closer look, I could see that the animal, though dead, was yet alive, alive with millions of squirming maggots. Death of one was life for another. Nature was a brutal struggle for survival. It was beautiful only without thought for this, only when the mind had erased its brutality and uncaring. It frightened me. Could we, as human beings and ourselves a part of nature, could we be less brutal, more caring?

I turned away abruptly and walked back to the truck. By then the sun stood higher over the Otjikoko Mountain. Though the air was now a little warmer I felt chilled. The wind was starting up again, reminding me that it was still July and the dead of winter. The veld looked so bleak and dry. I wondered if it would ever rain again.

Oma Dieta's Death

I N 1970, AFTER six years of teaching at the Sekondêre Skool, I was ready
to move on. The first students had graduated the year before and gone
off to South African universities. That year, because of the government's
homeland policy, the school was forced to move to new premises on the
boundary of Damaraland near Okombahe, one of the recently designated
homelands. The director and his family returned to Germany. Mr. Tötemeyer, with whose methods of disciplining students I disagreed, became the
new director. As a woman I had been paid less than male teachers, despite
having the same level of education. I minded. I left South-West Africa and

moved to Berlin, where I had signed up for training in counseling, as I had gradually developed a deeper interest in problems of communication.

I visited Namibia in August 1973 before moving to London to expand my counseling experience by training as child psychoanalyst. My grandmother had recently been hospitalized in Usakos with a broken femur. By now Oma Dieta was ninety-one, and I saw her death written all over the walls of my mind.

The trip to Usakos from Ondekaremba, the airport serving Windhoek, was long and tiring. Winter had ended early that year and now the heat was terrible, dry and suffocating. While the car was eating the miles through the bush, my thoughts were eating me, reviving my past encounters with death, reminding me of life's fragility. I felt threatened, fearful that my own life at this moment along its journey might fragment, that I myself might lose my heartbeat, my breath, functions that represent most visibly the mystery of life.

There is no warning, ever, no knowing when that moment might strike, like a venomous snake, making this breath the last one to flow, this heartbeat the last to pulse, life fading into nothingness. Only five years earlier my mother had survived a cobra attack on Omburo while a friend of Oma Dieta's was visiting us from Germany, and I could still feel the hysteria that had welled within me when I thought my mother might die.

We had been sitting under a Prosopis tree at dusk, Mom, my brother Jürgen, and our visitor, Mrs. Dreekman. With our legs stretched out comfortably, we were sipping a cool Windhoek Lager. Foxy and our two sausage dogs had been barking away for some time near the trees by the workbench, making Mrs. Dreekman more and more nervous. Having never been to Africa, she had claimed to be looking forward to adventure, but now, as darkness fell, her brave talk gave way to fear of the dangers that might lurk beyond sight.

Suddenly, she leaped from her chair, determined to put an end to the noise. "If you are not going to see to those dogs, I will!" she said.

I tried to pacify her. "No, no! Please sit! Don't get upset. I'm sure the dogs are fussing over nothing, but I'll go look. Those sausage dogs usually bark at everything, even just shadows moving." I found a torch and walked over to where the dogs were so restless. I moved the beam of light around and found the cause of their unrest. "They have found a snake!" I shouted.

My mother came rushing over. "Oh dear," she exclaimed. "It's a cobra, a spitting cobra! We had better kill it."

I tried to persuade her to leave the snake alone, to let the dogs deal with it, but she quickly grabbed a spade from nearby and, lunging at it, tried to sever its head, as if in revenge for having been bitten once before. But the snake was faster. In a flash my mother was wailing, "Oh my God, it spat me in the eyes! Oh God!"

We were shocked and confused. This had never happened before, a snake spitting in someone's eye. No one could think of how to deal with this. Someone called out to phone a doctor. I sprinted to the telephone, my heart racing with anxiety. I frantically turned the handle of the old brown box in the corner of the entrance hall to the left of the back door to get the operator. After what seemed a few years she finally answered. No, Dr. West was away on vacation. No, Dr. Simon had gone out for the day to a farm and could not be reached.

"But what do we do?" I screamed. "We don't know what to do. My mother can die!"

"Calm down, will you now," the operator scolded me. "I'll try to find the nurse. I know she is visiting her sister at the Epako railway station. I'll ring them there." Trust her to know where everyone was, I thought critically. But right now that was really useful.

I waited anxiously. Soon I heard the nurse's voice and her calm words of advice.

"Rinse the eyes, first with water, or with milk, give her a few aspirins for pain. That should do the trick."

"Is that all?" I asked, not believing that the remedy could be so simple.

"Sure," she said, "and she should lie down and rest. And keep her warm."

Mrs. Dreekman obviously had overheard me on the telephone and had taken over. She had already helped Mom rinse her eyes with water. Then she packed her down on the sofa in the sitting room under a blanket, and seated herself next to Mom, a basin of milk on her lap, a pipette in hand. Milk supposedly neutralized the poison. There was nothing she would allow me to do.

I wandered about, pestering Jürgen with my anxiety. Would Mom die? It was on the farm Otjua that another cobra had bitten her, at night, when Hans-Erik and I were little. After applying the known first aid, it took eight hours or more for my dad to drive her to the hospital in Windhoek, where she remained for six weeks. It had been touch and go. Later she often showed us the spot on her left thumb where the snake had bitten her. And now this calm evening had erupted into crisis, stretching endlessly and frighteningly before us.

Over the next three days Mom's eyes swelled to look like Ping-Pong balls. She felt feverish and nauseated. But the symptoms gradually subsided and soon she was well again. Possibly the bite years back had immunized her a little.

Death had been part of life on the farm, always. As a child I had not known it to be otherwise. Sometimes, near the woodpile, Uibeb chopped off the heads of chickens meant for the pot. My eyes widened on seeing a head fly off to one side, while the body, blood spurting from its neck, frantically flailed about as if still alive. *The chicken is supposed to be dead, isn't it? How can it be alive without its head?* Yet once the chicken was plucked and browned in the oven, I forgot about the life that had drained out of its body. I still liked to eat chicken even if I did not like live chickens.

When I was four or five, I often used to watch these birds in their coop on my grandmother's farm. But the fancy red Rhode Islanders and the super-white Leghorns all just gawked and squawked. "Who are you? Are you a chicken? Also going to lay an egg?" they seemed to ask, eyeing me suspiciously, their heads cocked sideways, red combs flipping over. But nothing ever happened. They did not lay even one egg while I was watching them! And I had so wanted to know how they laid eggs. Stupid, boring creatures! How could I care if they were killed?

Slaughtering the lambs was different. They charmed me. They were lovable, soft, and small. I thought it terrible that they should die.

As I drove along toward Usakos and Oma Dieta, I recalled the first time I minded death most deeply, and the loss it brought. It happened when I was about five, when our first dog, Pascha, died. Our farmhand Petrus and his family kept a fair number of dogs that had to seek their own sustenance. It was these dogs that ended up killing Pascha.

Pascha betrayed his origins by his wolfish looks, his shaggy hair and penetrating gaze. Though strangers were afraid of his ferocious bark, fearful fangs, and gleaming amber eyes, we loved him. Whether we pulled his tail or his ears, sat upon him or tickled his paws, he never minded. Although he was ever playful with us, he often had fierce fights with other dogs, usually coming away the victor. He loved to travel on the back of our truck, front paws placed on the side, intently watching everything that went by alongside the road.

One day, early on in the afternoon, as we drove home past the huts where Petrus and his family lived, Pascha saw some of their dogs and jumped off to join them. When he did not return to the house many hours later, we began to worry. Finally at dusk he came back, dragging his feet. We cried out when we saw him, covered in wounds all over. The fight of many against one must have been fierce!

My mom filled the old baby bath with tepid water and disinfectant, placed it in the workroom, somehow got him to stand in the bath, and gently cleaned his wounds. We silently watched her, aching to see him in such pain, yet not uttering a sound. He couldn't even lie down. "He won't survive," Mom said. "There's a hole in his throat, right in the windpipe. He can't breathe properly." She tried to feed him a little milk laced with aspirin but he took nothing. He simply stood there, a heap of pain. We all cried for him, unwilling to leave him. The next morning he was still standing the way we had left him, his life visibly draining away. Later in the day he died. Oh, Pascha! Our Pascha! We gave our beloved dog the burial he deserved, under the Camelthorn on the riverbank behind the well, marking his grave with a wooden cross. Although a few years later the river felled the tree and washed away the grave, his death remained etched into my soul.

Now, thirty years later, driving through the endless, monotonous bush, the distant memories of Pascha's death allowed the more recent death of my dad in 1964 to resurface even more vividly and painfully. During his last weeks, he and my mother had been desperate, hoping for a miraculous cure for the tuberculosis that had gone misdiagnosed until it was too late. On a farm nearby a woman had been advertising her eastern healing skills, skills she declared to be connected with yin and yang, supposedly balancing forces of life. When nothing heals, you will surely try anything, grab at any straw. My parents decided that Dad should try her cure. I stayed with him for about ten days on that farm as my mother felt she had more experience than I to run it. I disagreed, absolutely, but she did not budge. So I went. Yet all he wanted was go home. He felt terrible, his diabetes being exacerbated by the diet he had to maintain according to the healer's cure. I called my mom. "No, you have to stay," she insisted. I called our family doctor. "Take him home!" she said. I told my mother, "I'm bringing Dad home."

A few days after his return he developed pneumonia and a high fever. I knew without doubt this meant the end. He soon slipped into a coma. He no longer saw us. He no longer talked. When our family doctor came out to see him, she said, loudly and clearly for my mother's benefit, "I fear he will die soon," though my mom was unable to hear this. For her, Dad's death was unacceptable, unthinkable, just like her father's death had been years before.

Karen was in New Zealand, Jürgen in Germany. Hans-Erik came from Windhoek. He and Mom and I spent two days hovering around Dad. His body was there, silent, still alive, but his soul had already passed on. Words were lost between us when so many feelings neded to be expressed, so much more to be said to him. Instead, Hans-Erik paced in agony. I sat on the floor at the foot of his bed, Mom on a chair by his side. I don't remember us eating or sleeping. We played the "German Requiem" by Brahms over and over, Brahms being Dad's favorite composer next to Chopin. The music was unforgettable: *"Denn alles Fleisch es ist wie Gras und alle Herrlichkeit des Menschen wie des Grases Blumen. Das Gras ist verdorret und die Blume abgefallen."* The words can be found in 1 Peter, verses 1 - 24. (All flesh is like grass and the glory of man as the flowers of grass. The grass has withered and the flower fallen off).

I listened to the music, aware that my dad was now the *Mensch* destined to turn into dust just like Pascha, like we all would one day. This Mensch, still alive, not just any man, but my dad! During the early hours of July 3, 1964, his last breath escaped, forever. We buried him close to our house on Omburo.

As I drove, every detail came to mind as if it had happened just yesterday. All those years melted into now, welded into one moment in my soul today. The mystery of life merged with the mystery of death. No breath? No heartbeat? No warmth? Flesh returning to dust, was that it? No! There was more: eyes no longer to get lost in, voice no longer to be heard, ties to the heart severed, a loss forever.

I stopped the memories, the thoughts and feelings, the questions, steeling myself against more sorrow as soon as I arrived in Usakos. In its heyday the city had been an important rail depot, a dirty, black, coal-dust-coated spot sitting deep in a valley at the foot of the Erongo massif. Large Ana Acacias and Camelthorns lined the banks of the Khan River that passed the village on its way to the sea. Sweet-smelling white and pink oleander lined the Main Street, signs of plentiful water and better days. I had often passed through this place on the edge of the desert, never stopping because it had seemed so dismal.

I drove up to the Railway Hotel and asked for directions to the hospital. The small, cream-colored building with its red corrugated steel roof was easy to find. I parked in the meager shade of a white thorn acacia, took a few steps up to the veranda, and found the office at the entrance to a short corridor. The dark gray concrete floor was polished like a mirror, my steps leaving a dusty trail as I walked to the room the nurse had indicated.

The glaring hot afternoon sun came in through the window. The bed's white enameled frame, a cream-colored blanket, the white walls—all contributed to the room's brightness. For a moment my vision was blurred. I narrowed my eyes. The mattress had been raised under her head. Only the face of Oma Dieta was visible from under the blankets. She was sleeping.

My mom, who knew I was coming, had waited for me and now greeted me in a whisper. We hugged. She told me that Grandma had developed pneumonia, not a good sign for a person her age with a broken leg. I sat on the chair by the bed while Mom took a break to walk, to have a cup of coffee, to chat with a nurse. She welcomed small changes from the routine during the days she spent in the hospital with her mother.

Looking at Grandma's pale face, I marveled at her many wrinkles. Some crossed her brow as if in worry, some fanned out from her eyes, suggesting smiles. Others, forming deep furrows around her mouth, exuding strictness. My dad's face had been smooth and pale in his last days, its fading color reflecting his end. Those furrows on her brow reminded me of my many visits to her as a child to borrow items I always seemed to need so desperately.

"Grandma, do you have scissors I can borrow? I can't find Mom's."

"Yes, but be sure to bring them back!"

Later I'd ask, "Grandma, do you have some string for me?"

"Well, where are my scissors, my dear? Did you bring them back?"

"No," I had to admit, hanging my head. "No, I forgot."

"Well, go and find them. Maybe then I'll have some string for you." And I had to go off to find her scissors. She was a neat and orderly person, more so even than my mother. She was strict about being tidy, being responsible, respecting other people's things, about keeping your word.

Usually her eyes were enormous pools of light blue behind her glasses. When she was going blind a decade or more before, two operations and thick glasses allowed her to see again. It was such a blessing. Now, lying in the hospital bed without her glasses, her eyes sunk into the depths behind the lids. Without dentures her lips vanished between her gums. She looked so frail, the essence of memories distilled from a long, long life, so ready to leave us.

Would she wake? Would she still recognize me? Would she still be able to talk to me?

I don't know how long I sat there, perhaps half an hour, when I noticed her gaze upon me. She asked for her glasses, put them on, and smiled.

"You are here!" she whispered, breathing joy. She pulled her right hand out from under the blanket and took mine into hers with the soft touch of old age. "You!" she repeated.

"Yes," I said simply. "Yes, it's me."

"You know," she said softly after a long pause. "You know that I always thought of you as a special person." She patted my hand. "You, and also Renate." Renate was my aunt, my grandma's fourth child and third daughter. "Yes, Renate also was special. God has special things in mind for you." She nodded slightly, keeping her gaze upon me.

My grandma and I had not ever talked much about God, even though she had lived with my family for nineteen years before she moved back to Lievenberg to be with her youngest son, Hans-Dieter, and his wife, Erika. God was simply always around, like the air we breathed. At breakfast, when my dad read the page of the calendar with its daily verse from the Bible, expanded upon by some theologian or preacher; at night, when we said our prayers; on Sundays, when Dad read a sermon from a book of sermons and we sang hymns while he accompanied us on the piano, or when we made the trip to church in the village. My grandmother took God's existence very much for granted. She believed firmly in him, and that her whole life—indeed, the whole world—was in his hands. That was all that mattered to her. These were not discussible issues. They were such a certainty that she never pressed me to have the same faith. I was simply a part of this, her world, unquestionably so.

I did not ask her that day in Usakos what she thought God had in mind for me. It was enough for me to know that she had said it. A warm feeling of having been recognized spread through me. For a moment it undid the pain that knotted my heart on finding her there. The unspoken thought of death briefly hovered in my mind, but quickly vanished. At this moment I simply wanted to enjoy being special, being with her. She barely seemed to breathe. She closed her eyes again for a while as if in sleep. Unexpectedly she went on.

"I have so much time here to think. There is one thing, though, I have never understood." She fell silent once more.

"And what is that?" I asked quietly. She did not answer me for a long time, but finally spoke her mind.

"Why did my mother have to die when I was only four years old?" she asked abruptly.

I gasped. All her life she had seldom spoken about her mother, though I knew about her death. Most often she had talked about her dad. How would I know the answer? Why did she think of this now? I kept looking at her, struggling to reply to her perplexing question. After a long silence I said, "I don't know, Grandma. These things happen. We don't know when we will die, or why."

"I don't think it was fair of God to let that happen," she said querulously. "I was too young. It has bothered me all my life. And I could never get on with my stepmother!"

I could not find an answer. Was there one? After so many years she still suffered the loss! I could barely grasp this fact. She was silent again, shutting out her pain, as I did mine. I was aware how much it must have cost her to think and talk about this, a rare moment of frankness about her innermost thoughts and feelings.

"I guess it is up to God, even if I have found that difficult to accept," she eventually added, submissively. She was still holding my hand, squeezing it softly. "I'll soon be with him. And I want you to know that I've had a good life. He has always known best," she said with a few little clicks with her tongue. Ts, ts! I had to smile at this habit of hers through all the tears welling up in me. Then she said, "It will be good to be with him," hesitating for a moment before adding, "and to be also with your grandfather." "My beloved" was what she really meant.

She took off her glasses, handing them to me to put back on the bedside table. She kept holding my hand, and holding it she went back to sleep. I stayed there for I don't know how long, my head and heart in turmoil. Eventually my mother came back into the room. I softly kissed my grandma on her forehead, tears rolling, my heart filled with pain. I knew this was a last goodbye. I hugged my mom. She walked with me to the car, said a brief farewell, we did not know until when. I could think only about Grandma. I was sure I'd see my mom again.

I had to leave, drive the long way back to Windhoek, fly to Berlin, pack up, and move to London to begin my training there as child psychoanalyst. My mind stood still. I could not think clearly, just did what I had to do.

Two weeks later and before I left Berlin in order to go London, my mom called to tell me that Grandma had died. It was only long after her death that I could think of her more clearly, once the first tumultuous waves of grief had washed over me and slowly subsided into gentler lapping waves of loving memories. For me, she was a rock I could cling to. She still is. She was always present in her faithfulness, her endurance, her constancy of belief, her everlasting interest in others, qualities much more important than her stern appearance and her insistence on order and obedience. Her love for her Fritz, as his for his Diederike, gave them strength and courage to survive hard times and solve life's many problems. In the end, theirs was a good life as far as they lived it within the parameters of their beliefs, in spite of its course, perhaps even because of it.

Once more I envisioned my home on Omburo, surrounded by the many different trees, saw the spring and the animals and all the people. I am Africa, this Africa, I thought. I do not know what is to come or who I will be, but I know I am what had been for me. I am the people I grew up with, the animals that shared our land. I am the space, the distant horizons, the barely blue of the sky, the violet of the mountains, the blinding brightness of the light, and the heat of the sun. I am the drought and the terror and the pain. I am the yearning for rain, always more rain, for the sight of hesitant green and the everlasting, enduring hope of life.

Epilogue

O F COURSE LIFE continued after 1973. I completed my studies at the Hampstead Clinic, married Angus Deaton, a professor of econometrics in Bristol, U.K; raised my stepchildren Rebecca and Adam, and moved with my family to Princeton in the US in 1983. Throughout the years of married life I worked part time as child psychotherapist. Before the move to the US my family and I visited Namibia in 1983, and then again in 1991. I became a US citizen in 1996, and divorced later that same year. It was at this point in time that I began to write.

On re-reading my manuscript for a last time, still changing a word here or there for a better one, clarifying sequences of ideas, I felt that something was still missing. I am amazed that I actually finished this work, beginning with only a single story, that of the Oryx. It was followed by more stories that eventually were combined into this book that ended with my departure from Namibia in 1970, and the story of my last visit to my grandmother in 1973. 1970 was definitely a year in which my life started on a different and quite unforeseen trajectory, a path that took me further along the road of understanding the past, its history, the people that mattered, myself, the subtext that had remained inaccessible to me throughout those years. I know now that should I write these pages now, fifteen years later, the story line would remain the same, but expressed very differently, weaving together different threads of what was important. But I also am convinced that only by writing all these pages the way I did allowed me to access what I might write now in 2011. Because writing the story changed me. In fact, the act of exploring the past realities of life was affirming it's very transience, that the exploration in itself was perhaps even an act of defiance and insubordination in the face of that past.

I realized only once the work was complete that my urge to write began in the anguished months of my divorce, a divorce that I had not wanted and that unrelentingly forced to me to look back to reassess my personal origins. I desperately needed to know my roots and cling to them. Friends told me in those days that they wouldn't have survived the way I had, that they would not have had the strength to do so. I know my writing was not only a way of grieving for what had passed or for dreams that never came to be. It was also a way of remembering the gains of all my experiences. I came to see the different threads of life, not because I had forgotten them, but because at the time of writing they were not relevant or not accessible. I not only gained a whole new understanding of what kind of life I had until 1973, but could also see more clearly what happened to me in the years that followed, when I had to figure out what I still wanted to do in years to come. I was able to put much behind me, as best as one ever can, accepting that this was my life so far, allowing me to see those opportunities that may have presented themselves previously but which I had not wanted to see and grab hold of. I also ask again: is writing about forgetting rather than about remembering? I think not. I found that at different times different feelings emerged, each calling forth their own string of remembrances, ones not mentioned before, ones that seemed to have been unknowable yet had not been forgotten. Life is surely ever green!

My sister Karen first married a New Zealander, Paddy Benstead, with whom she had two children, Michael and Shirine. She worked as librarian in Auckland where they lived. Within ten years she got divorced and later married her student sweetheart Jim Boyd. They lived in Fiji for four years, after which they moved to Brisbane in Australia where they still live now. She read the manuscript when she and her husband came for a visit in the summer of 2009. When she'd finished it she told me that she could never have written this – it would have been emotionally too difficult. When I apologized to her during those days for having been so mean to her at boarding school, she simply said: "But we were just children then!" Indeed, we had grown up. We each have, in our own different way, come to terms with our past and made peace with each other. Her words touched me deeply.

Brother Jürgen and his wife Christel still live on the farm in Namibia. He married her in 1969 and they have two children, Silke and Anke. After completing his training as motor mechanic in Germany in 1966, he ran the farm, first with my mother and from 1976 on on his own with his wife. After farming for forty years he recently sold it to another but younger Namibian, but kept some thirty acres to live on in their retirement. In my view he, with the help of his practical and creative wife Christel has been a successful farmer. He was always an active member and leader of the farming community of the district of Omaruru, even beyond. He was the one to inherit Omburo because he loved the way of life and always was – and still is – attached to the land, its animals and its people.

Recently, in November 2009, brother Hans-Erik died most unexpectedly, a deep loss suffered not only by his family, but also by the whole country. He married Erika Kassbaum in 1961. They have four sons: Sven Erik, Thorsten, Joern and Arved. He had been engaged on many levels in Namibian life: throughout his working years as a successful architect; politically as a member of the group that wrote Namibia's new constitution; as a member of the new parliament in 1990; as chairperson of many sport clubs, be it tennis, cricket or rugby, and as well always as an active leader of the German community. I miss him very much and am saddened that he did not see the outcome of the book that he supported so extensively with intense interest in all its detailed facets. I am truly indebted to him and miss him deeply.

My mother also passed away though much earlier, in July 2000, at the ripe age of 92, dying on the same day my dad had died thirty-six years before, and the day her parents had been married, uncannily declaring her bonds of love. I had become closer to her during the years prior to her death, and was glad I was able to be present in that dark moment of hers even though I had to travel in a hurry all the way from the US. Many others mentioned in my stories have also passed away: aunt Amanda, uncle Wilhelm, uncle Hans-Dieter, Hermine Enslin, teachers both in Omaruru and at Rustenburg High School, a number of school class mates, and some I had taught at the Sekondêre Skool, such as Milner Thlabanello and Daniel Tjongarero, and others I don't know about.

There have also been joyous times, like weddings, especially those of my stepchildren Rebecca (in 2000) and Adam (in 2006). I now have three grandchildren, have many friends right here, and an extended family of nephews and nieces, and their offspring, albeit spread all over Europe, Australia and Namibia. It's not easy to keep in touch with them all – but I try.

Several ex-students of the Sekondêre Skool obtained posts in the new government of 1990. Mr. Hoebeb went on to New York, representing Namibia at the United Nations for a while, and after his retirement farmed near Otavi in the northern part of Namibia. Zephanja K became the speaker of the house for ten years! Being a pastor by profession, he was later on appointed bishop of the Evangelical Lutheran Church. The Sekondêre Skool, on moving to Okombahe in 1970 because of homeland laws, was renamed Martin Luther High School. Here in the US I am a member of the Namibian Community in the Americas (NCA) that includes several of former students of the MLHS. I have been an NCA president for two years and still try to remain in touch as far as the busy life we all lead will allow.

With Hans-Erik's death much has changed. He had been so much the focus of our family life. One of his favorite songs was one Louis Armstrong often featured in his programs. " *I see trees of green, red roses too, I see them bloom for me and for you, and I think to myself 'what a wonderful world! I see skies of blue and clouds of white, the bright blessed day , the dark sacred night, and I think to myself 'What a wonderful world!' The colors of the rainbow so pretty in the sky are also on the faces of people going by, I see friends shaking hands, sayin', 'How do you do?' They're really sayin' I love you! I hear babies cry, I watch them grow, they'll learn much more than I'll ever know, and I think to myself 'What a wonderful world!' Yes, I think to myself:*

What a wonderful world!"

Who will follow in his footsteps to become another abiding focus? Only time will tell!

Acknowledgments

MY JOURNEY INTO writing began with the encouragement and support of a dear friend, Madeline Wise. Although she loved the first draft of my story "The Oryx," she also saw that there was much I needed to learn about the craft of writing. Fortunately, for me, she turned out to be a great mentor and teacher, with an eye for detail and precision, for tension and emotion, for showing instead of telling. Madeline, I still appreciate the many hours you spent in your busy life looking at each word, each sentence, and every thought that I wrote and sent to you to read. You helped me understand that every word has to be right, not just correct. You pointed out when often there were too many of them—less is more—and when they appeared in the wrong order, when thoughts were unclear and garbled. I am so grateful to you for also seeing beyond the detail and believed that I had something worthwhile to say, and for eventually even finding a publisher for that first story of the oryx. I feel eternally indebted to you.

Thank you also to Ellen Shull and Bob Richmond, editors of the Palo Alto Review, who not only published my first story but also encouraged me to write more, publishing three further stories, thereby allowing me to believe in what Madeline had already told me.

My thanks to Hanna Fox and her writers' group, who sustained my growth and further writing efforts for many years, keeping me on my toes about showing rather than telling. My thanks also to University of St. Thomas English professor Lon Otto and his writers' workshop in Iowa City, not only for clarifying the many tools writers use, but for imbuing me with respect for other people's work as he had for mine and the rest of those in my class, and for recommending to me the best of editors, Michele Hodgson, who helped me, above all, with the seemingly impossible task of shaping my disparate stories into flowing wholeness.

Thanks also to my brother Hans-Erik for all of his interest and support and for supplying me with photos, sources, and comments that he considered of interest to me in writing the stories that eventually became this book; to Gunter von Schumann for his careful reading of the manuscript, adding information and correcting facts, for his help when I researched the state archives that he heads, and altogether for his interest in this work. A special word of thanks also to Dr. Mickal Kamuvaka who refined my oft forgotten Herero. I am grateful and glad for you all who have crossed my path in life. Thanks also to all of you who have read this document and made useful comments. You have enriched my life incredibly.

Thank you!

Appendix 1

A Brief History: From Damaraland and Namaqualand to Namibia

Before 1760

Up to this date different peoples lived in the areas of Great Namaqualand (southern), Damaraland (central) and Ovamboland (northern SWA), between the Orange River in the south and the Kunene and Okavango Rivers bordering on Angola. They constitute, more or less, what today is Namibia. Rock paintings and carvings indicate that unknown peoples lived there centuries before the Khoi San and the Damara, later the Oshivambo and Herero moved in from the African interior. Most peoples led a nomadic life of hunting and gathering. Some also herded cattle. Only in the far north was agriculture practiced relatively extensively along the Okavango River, an area with high precipitation and the constant flow of water in the river. Many smaller groups of Nama, comprising Oorlam and Basters, moved in from the Cape around and after the turn of the nineteenth century, their land having been appropriated by European settlers moving inland from Cape Town. They often battled over land, grazing and water, and efforts of establishing supremacy over each other.

1486–1805

During this period Portuguese sailors land at Cape Cross and Angra Pequena on the desert coastline, known as Skeleton Coast. The Cantino Chart, the earliest known map of the coastline, is dated 1502, and was constructed by the Portuguese. Very few hunters, explorers, and travelers crossed the Orange River from the south.

1805

The two Albrecht brothers, Abraham and Christian, Moravian missionaries under the auspices of the London Mission Society, establish the first mission station on the Hob River at Warmbad, just north of the Orange River. They leave after five years because of skirmishes between groups of Nama living in the area.

1828

Several small mission societies in Germany join to form the Rhenish Mission Society (RMS) with its headquarters in Barmen. After 1828, and in agreement with the London Mission Society, the RMS took over mission stations in Namaqualand, an area in the western Cape that stretched north as far as and across the Orange River. South of the Orange River were stations such as Pella, Koggamas, and others. In 1839 Jan Bam, and in 1840 Franz Heinrich Kleinschmidt, were the first missionaries sent by the RMS to Damaraland.

1842

Carl Hugo Hahn follows in 1842, and he and Jan Bam settle first in Windhoek, but later move to Gross-Barmen (Otjikango) in 1844 to avoid controversy with John Lewis, a missionary working for the LMS in Windhoek. Not long after this the LMS, in agreement with the RMS, withdrew its missionary activities from the area north of the Orange River. Obviously mission societies competed for their share of the "field." The enterprise of the RMS took place amid periods of much fighting between Nama and Herero about cattle and grazing, alternating with short periods of peace supported by the RMS.

1857

Dr. Friedrich Gotthard Karl Ernst Fabri is appointed third inspector of the RMS, a post he holds until 1884. He developed a special brand of mission work, its central tenet being that indigenous peoples had to be acculturated before it would be possible to convert them. This required the RMS to send out "missionary colonists" that would train potential converts in occupations and become, for example, carpenters, blacksmiths, and gardeners.

1864

The first missionary colonists are sent out, among them Eduard Hälbich who sets up a trading post in Otjimbingue for the RMS. By establishing such a post the RMS attempted to protect especially the Herero from selling their land and cattle in order to buy goods, especially guns and brandy. By this time Otjimbingue had become a central hub for mining, traveling, and trading in the area. However, the trading post was given up by the RMS in 1873 because it was economically not successful. The participating "colonial missionaries" then turned their trades into individual private enterprises.

1866

My great-grandfather Johann Wilhelm Redecker travels to Cape Town and is employed for eleven months on different mission stations in the Western Cape.

1867

J. W. Redecker finally settles in Otjimbingue, appointed as chief domestic economist of the RMS.

1873

Redecker takes over the trading post in Otjimbingue and Hälbich the branch in Karibib.

1879

Dr. Fabri publishes several pamphlets titled "Bedarf Deutschland der Kolonien?" It was later referred to as a book, titled in English Germany Needs Colonies. Dr. Fabri maintained connections with many businesses, furthering the cause of colonialism in general by fanning the competition between Germany and other European countries, especially Great Britain, in what has been called the "scramble for Africa."

1880

Skirmishes between Herero and Nama start up once more after ten years of quiet. Missionaries attempt to obtain protection from the Cape. As protection was not obtained, they turn to Imperial Chancellor Otto Von Bismarck to provide them with safety. Initially, he denied them protection.

1883

Merchant Heinrich Vogelsang buys land from Nama chief Joseph Fredericks in two treaties. Controversy arises around this acquisition. Vogelsang bought land by the mile, in his mind the German mile (7.4 kilometers), while Fredericks understood it to be an English mile (1.6 kilometers). Vogelsang thereby gained a much larger piece of land. He prematurely raised the German flag in Angra Pequena as a private individual. The act led to disputes with Great Britain, as they had already claimed three islands in the small bay. The German flag had to be taken down.

1884

After the controversy with Britain is settled (though not the one with Chief Fredericks), the merchant Adolf Lüderitz hoists the German flag once more on August 7, 1884. Chancellor Bismarck is now forced to declare the territory a German protectorate, called German South-West Africa.

1889

The first twenty-one German troops arrive.

1897–1902

Construction of a narrow gauge railway track from Swakopmund to Windhoek is carried out. Transportation from the coast inland required numerous oxen. Their supply was limited by the constant recurrence of the Rinderpest and drought, creating escalating costs and uncertainty, forcing the issue of finding alternative transportation.

1904–1907

Several battles take place in 1904 between Germans and Hereros, culminating in the battle at the Waterberg and in the shattering of the Herero tribe. They had fled with their families and cattle into the dry Omaheke to the east of the Waterberg. The German soldiers were ordered by General Lothar von Trotha, who was determined to quell any resistance once and for all, to pursue them and shoot everyone in sight, be it men, women or children, even those who had fled and were trying to return. Most of the fugitives died in the almost waterless Omaheke of thirst and hunger. Many of the few who managed to survive were gathered into camps by missionaries, but were later forced into labor by the government. Numerous leaders were first incarcerated on an island in Lüderitz Bay, subsequently expelled to Togo and/or Cameroon. Most of them succumbed to the climate and bad living conditions in these countries. The Herero lost approximately 80 percent of their population, and there is ongoing discussion about it as being the first instance of genocide in the twentieth century, although the concept was not yet operative at that time. The Nama, who had joined the Herero uprising, continued their resistance in guerilla fashion in the south of the country until 1907. They lost half their population during their resistance.

1907–1914

Germany expands its administration. Another rail track is built to the copper mines in the north near Otavi; a wooden jetty (known as the "bridge") is constructed in Swakopmund; telegraphic communications are established; Karakul sheep are imported from Russia; the Etosha Pan and other areas are proclaimed nature reserves; marble-works are opened in Karibib; more rail tracks are built from Windhoek to Keetmanshoop in the south and from there to Lüderitz Bay on the coast.

1908

Diamonds are discovered near Kolmans Kop, not far from Lüderitz Bay.

1914

World War I breaks out. The South African government sides with Britain and their troops invade German South-West Africa as they feared a local uprising.

1919

The Treaty of Versailles assigns German South-West Africa through the League of Nations to be administered by South Africa. From then on it is called The Mandate of South-West Africa.

1919–1939

South Africa administers South-West Africa like a fifth province. Several revolts of Nama and Ovambo take place during this time. South-West Africa received its own constitution in 1926.

1939–1945

World War II breaks out. German men are interned in South Africa or on their farms. Most of them returned only after the war ended.

1960

Unrest simmers against the Portuguese in adjacent Angola. South Africa begins to construct macadamized roads and an airport near Windhoek, and expands the harbor at Walvis Bay to ease the transportation of troops with an eye to keeping any opposition to its own rule over the indigenous peoples outside its own territory. SWAPO (South-West Africa's People's Organization) was founded in 1960. It begins to fight the Bush War from within the borders of Angola.

1966

South Africa rejects the International Court of Justice's decision to end its mandate over South-West Africa with the argument that the League of Nations terminated with WWII and that the United Nations was a new and different body that did not carry the legacy of the League.

1978

An attempt to establish the independence of South-West Africa is aborted.

1990

After a long and hard struggle, South-West Africa establishes its independence with its own constitution on March 21, 1990. Sam Nujoma, the leader of SWAPO, is its first president. Although the United Nations had already accepted the name Namibia for the country in 1968, it was only now commonly called the Republic of Namibia. In 1994 South Africa cedes its enclave of Walvis Bay to Namibia.

Appendix 2

Redecker Genealogy

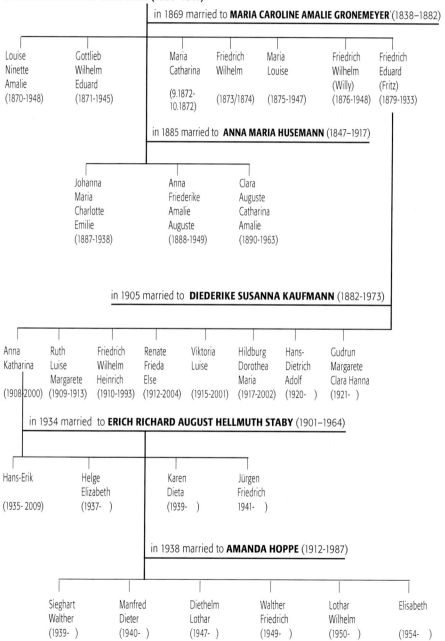

JOHANN WILHELM REDECKER (1836–1911)

in 1869 married to **MARIA CAROLINE AMALIE GRONEMEYER** (1838–1882)

| Louise Ninette Amalie (1870-1948) | Gottlieb Wilhelm Eduard (1871-1945) | Maria Catharina (9.1872-10.1872) | Friedrich Wilhelm (1873/1874) | Maria Louise (1875-1947) | Friedrich Wilhelm (Willy) (1876-1948) | Friedrich Eduard (Fritz) (1879-1933) |

in 1885 married to **ANNA MARIA HUSEMANN** (1847–1917)

| Johanna Maria Charlotte Emilie (1887-1938) | Anna Friederike Amalie Auguste (1888-1949) | Clara Auguste Catharina Amalie (1890-1963) |

in 1905 married to **DIEDERIKE SUSANNA KAUFMANN** (1882-1973)

| Anna Katharina (1908-2000) | Ruth Luise Margarete (1909-1913) | Friedrich Wilhelm Heinrich (1910-1993) | Renate Frieda Else (1912-2004) | Viktoria Luise (1915-2001) | Hildburg Dorothea Maria (1917-2002) | Hans-Dietrich Adolf (1920-) | Gudrun Margarete Clara Hanna (1921-) |

in 1934 married to **ERICH RICHARD AUGUST HELLMUTH STABY** (1901–1964)

| Hans-Erik (1935- 2009) | Helge Elizabeth (1937-) | Karen Dieta (1939-) | Jürgen Friedrich 1941-) |

in 1938 married to **AMANDA HOPPE** (1912-1987)

| Sieghart Walther (1939-) | Manfred Dieter (1940-) | Diethelm Lothar (1947-) | Walther Friedrich (1949-) | Lothar Wilhelm (1950-) | Elisabeth (1954-) |